D0561582

PRIVATIZING MALAYSIA
Rents, Rhetoric, Realities

PRIVATIZING MALAYSIA

Rents, Rhetoric, Realities

edited by

Jomo K.S.

Westview Press

BOULDER • SAN FRANCISCO • OXFORD

All rights reserved. No part of this publication may be reproduced or transmitted in any form or by any means, electronic or mechanical, including photocopy, recording, or any information storage and retrieval system, without permission in writing from the publisher.

Copyright © 1995 by Westview Press, Inc.

Published in 1995 in the United States of America by Westview Press, Inc., 5500 Central Avenue, Boulder, Colorado 80301, and in the United Kingdom by Westview Press, 36 Lonsdale Road, Summertown, Oxford OX2 7EW

Library of Congress Cataloging-in-Publication Data
Privatizing Malaysia : rents, rhetoric, and reality / edited by Jomo
    Kwame Sundaram.
        p.   cm. — (Transitions—Asia and the Pacific)
    Includes bibliographical references.
    ISBN 0-8133-8861-9
    1. Privatization—Malaysia.   I. Jomo K.S. (Jomo Kwame Sundaram)
    II. Series.
HD4300.6.P75   1995
338.9595—dc20

                                                                    94-9568
                                                                    CIP

Printed and bound in Malaysia

for "obstinate comics"
who stand up for the truth
in spite of the consequences

"The success of our privatization policy has been acknowledged by many and cited as a model for others. There still exists an obstinate band of comics who persists in their misguided view that privatization means mortgaging the interests of the *rakyat* (people). We will continue to pursue this proven and well tested policy."

Anwar Ibrahim
Malaysian Finance Minister
1994 Budget Speech, October 29, 1993

Acknowledgments

As with all collective enterprises, many people have contributed to this volume. I am grateful to the various authors for their cooperation and to James Currey of London for kindly allowing me to use the material by Adam and Cavendish originally published in *Adjusting Privatisation*.

Mark Selden, the series editor, as well as Susan McEachern and her colleagues at Westview Press have all been most helpful and encouraging. My friend and editor, Loke Chee Fong, and my colleague, Foo Ah Hiang, proved to be ever reliable. I am also grateful to Eugene Tang and Janakky for their assistance with preparing the index and glossary.

Many others, who remained unnamed, helped in a myriad other little ways. As usual, my children and my mother had to put up with my absences as I prepared this volume for publication. I am grateful to them all, but incriminate no one.

Jomo K.S.
September 1, 1994

Contents

Part Three: Sectors

Tables

Figures

Abbreviations

1MP	First Malaysia Plan 1966–70
2MP	Second Malaysia Plan 1971–75
3MP	Third Malaysia Plan 1976–80
4MP	Fourth Malaysia Plan 1981–85
5MP	Fifth Malaysia Plan 1986–90
6MP	Sixth Malaysia Plan 1991–95
ABIM	Angkatan Belia Islam Malaysia (Malaysian Muslim Youth Movement)
ADB	Asian Development Bank
ADL	Arthur D. Little consultancy
AIM	Aerospace Industries of Malaysia
AMMB	Arab Malaysian Merchant Bank
ASB	Amanah Saham Bumiputera
ASN	Amanah Saham Nasional
BCIC	Bumiputra commercial and industrial community
BIF	Bumiputera Investment Foundation
BN	Barisan Nasional (National Front)
B-O	build-operate
B-O-O	build-operate-own
B-O-T	build-operate-transfer
BP	British Petroleum
BSE	Bumiputra Stock Exchange
CAP	Consumers Association of Penang
CEB	Central Electrcity Board
CIC	Capital Issues Committee
CICU	Central Information Collection Unit
CIMA	Cement Industries of Malaysia Ltd
CMS	Cement Manufacturers Sarawak Berhad
CUEPACS	Congress of the Union of Employees in the Public and Civil Service
DAP	Democratic Action Party
DCA	Department of Civil Aviation

EON	Edaran Otomobil Nasional (National Automobile Distributor)
EPF	Employees Provident Fund
EPU	Economic Planning Unit (of the Prime Minister's Department)
ESM	Electronic Systems Malaysia
ESOS	employees' share option scheme
FACSMAB	Frequency Allocation Committee
FIC	Foreign Investment Committee
FIMA	Food Industries of Malaysia
FINAS	National Film Development Corporation
FOMCA	Federation of Consumers Associations in Malaysia
GDP	gross domestic product
GNP	gross national product
GOEs	government-owned enterprises
HHB	Hicom Holdings Berhad
HICOM	Heavy Industries Corporation of Malaysia
HSB	Hong Kong & Shanghai Bank
ICU	Implementation and Coordination Unit
IMF	International Monetary Fund
JPA	Jabatan Perkhidmatan Awam (Public Services Department)
JTM	Jabatan Telekom Malaysia (Telecommunications Department)
KCHB	Kedah Cement Holdings Berhad
KCT	Port Klang Container Terminal
KLSE	Kuala Lumpur Stock Exchange
KN	Kontena Nasional
KPA	Klang Port Authority
KPM	Klang Port Management
KTK	Konnas Terminal Klang Sdn Bhd
KTMB	Keretapi Tanah Melayu Berhad
LLN	Lembaga Letrik Negara (National Electricity Board)
LNG	liquified natural gas
LUTH	Lembaga Urusan dan Tabung Haji (Muslim Pilgrim Fund & Management Board)
LRT	Light Rail Transit
MARA	Majlis Amanah Rakyat
MAS	Malaysian Airline Systems
MBOs	management buy-outs
MESs	minimum efficient scale
MHA	Malaysian Highway Authority
MIC	Malaysian Indian Congress
MIDA	Malaysian Industrial Development Authority
MISC	Malaysian International Shipping Corporation
MITI	Ministry of International Trade & Industry
MoF Inc.	Ministry of Finance Incorporated

MRCB	Malaysian Resources Corporation Berhad
MSE	Malaysian Shipyard & Engineering Ltd
MTUC	Malaysian Trade Union Congress
NEP	New Economic Policy
NFPE	non-financial public enterprise
NICs	newly industrializing countries
NKVE	New Klang Valley Expressway
NSE	North-South Expressway
NST	*New Straits Times*
NSTP	New Straits Times Press Berhad
OBAs	off-budget agencies
OPEC	Organization of Petroleum Exporting Countries
OPP	Outline Perspective Plan, 1971–1990
OPP2	Second Outline Perspective Plan, 1991–2000
OSA	Official Secrets Act
P/E ratio	price/earnings ratio
PAP	Privatization Action Plan
PERNAS	Perbadanan Nasional Berhad
PETRONAS	Petroleum Nasional Sdn Bhd
PLUS	Projek Lebuhraya Utara-Selatan (North-South Highway Project)
PMB	Pos Malaysia Berhad
PMP	Privatization Master Plan
PNB	Permodalan Nasional Berhad
POAL	P&O Australia Ltd
PROTON	Perusahaan Otomobil Nasional (National Automobile Enterprise)
PSD	Postal Services Department
RAC	Railway Assets Corporation
RIDA	Rural Industrial Development Authority
RISDA	Rubber Industry Smallholders Development Authority
RMAF	Royal Malaysian Air Force
RTM	Radio Television Malaysia
RUM	Railwaymen's Union of Malaya
SCM	Sarawak Cement Manufacturers
SEDC	State Economic Development Corporations
SFI	Sabah Forest Industries
SGI	Sabah Gas Industries
SIA	Singapore International Airlines
SOE	state-owned enterprise
SRM	Survey Research Malaysia
STAR	Sistem Transit Aliran Ringan (Light Rail Transit System)
STMB	Sistem Televisyen Malaysia Berhad
TDC	Tourism Development Corporation
TNAAs	transnational advertising agencies

TNB	Tenaga Nasional Berhad
UDA	Urban Development Authority
UEM	United Engineers Malaysia
UHF	ultra high frequency
UMNO	United Malays National Organization
UMW	United Motor Works (Malaysia) Holdings
UPSAK	Unit Pengawasan Syarikat dan Agensi Kerajaan (Unit for Monitoring Government Agencies and Enterprisés)
VANS	Value-Added Network Services
VCR	video cassette recorder
VHF	very high frequency

Introduction

JOMO K. S.

The growth of the public sector since the 1930s has occurred in varied circumstances internationally. In the advanced industrial capitalist economies of Europe and, to a lesser extent, in North America, the growth of the public sector has been largely associated with the growth of the welfare state, especially under pressure from and the influence of social democratic movements and Keynesian economic ideas. However, in the Third World, the public sector has developed most under so-called "intermediate" regimes—often established by populist nationalist movements (e.g. Sukarno's Indonesia, Nasser's Egypt, and Nehru's India)—as well as statist capitalist governments, using state intervention to achieve rapid economic growth in favor of the ruling interests (e.g. Suharto's Indonesia, Marcos's Philippines and Malaysia under the NEP in Southeast Asia).

While different factors have contributed to the growth, nature and role of the public sector in these different contexts, there are also important similarities. This is especially true for public utilities and services, which sometimes involve natural monopolies not priced strictly according to profit-maximizing criteria. Important considerations of social welfare, political legitimacy and patronage have often been very influential in their development.

However, the current campaign for privatization internationally goes back to the beginning of the eighties, especially after the election of Margaret Thatcher in Britain in 1979 and Ronald Reagan to the United States presidency in 1980, the accompanying swing to conservative and right-wing economic thinking (e.g. monetarism and supply-side economics) in the West, and the promotion of privatization by powerful international agencies, such as the World Bank and the Asian Development Bank (1985), usually as part of a larger structural adjustment package favoring private, and often foreign, business interests.

Since then, there has been an accelerating pace of privatization in much of the world, reversing the variously inspired—Keynesian, social democratic, nationalist and socialist—expansions of the public sector in the post-war Golden Age period. While the rise of Thatcherism, Reaganism, supply-side economics and public choice theory in the context of stagflation, fiscal crisis and government failure have inspired and encouraged privatization and related initiatives in the developed industrial economies of the West, somewhat different political and other considerations have been more influential in the "developing" Third World economies with significant public sectors as well as the former socialist state economies.

Since the 1980s, privatization has been strongly recommended to most countries where key sectors have been dominated by public enterprises. In the early and mid-1980s, external price shocks led to a marked deterioration in macroeconomic performance globally, precipitating fiscal and debt crises. In this context, the loss-making public enterprises have been a particularly conspicuous drain on government resources, and privatization has been touted as the best answer to the problems of these public enterprises.

Nevertheless, privatization has proceeded unevenly since its inception. Of the 2,100 known cases of divestiture in developing countries between 1980 and 1991, over half (around 1,300) were in Mexico and Chile alone, leaving a low single digit average for the others (Kukers, Nellis & Shirley, 1992: 7). Hence, the wholesale approach—advocated by the *Privatization Masterplan* (*PMP*) (Malaysia, 1991a)—is the exception rather than the rule.

The ASEAN region is often said to be at the forefront of the privatization drive. While Malaysia appears to have been the pioneer in this region, other governments were not far behind. Singapore's Public Sector Divestment Committee has recommended that more successful government companies go public and be listed on the Singapore Stock Exchange, especially after it was sharply affected by the "splitting-off" of the Kuala Lumpur Stock Exchange (KLSE), its Siamese twin since its establishment in the early 1960s. Soon after her election in early 1986, President Corazon Aquino launched a five-year plan to sell off US$32 billion worth of Filipino state-owned enterprises. In 1987, Indonesian President Suharto established a special committee to study proposals to sell off such enterprises to reduce the government's financial deficit.

Malaysian Prime Minister Mahathir Mohamad's 1983 announcement of his government's intention to embark on a privatization policy represented a dramatic reversal of preceding Malaysian government policy although it was very much consistent with his own personal ideological and policy preferences as well as the then new wave of conservative market reforms beginning in the West with the election of the Thatcher Government in the United Kingdom in 1979 and the Reagan administration in the United States late the following year.

History

Colonial Malaya was prized as the economically most important colony in the British Empire for much of the first half of the twentieth century, with its export earnings (mainly from rubber and tin) in the crucial post-Second World War years exceeding those of all other British colonies and Britain itself. Colonial policy in Malaya was essentially conservative, but not foolhardy enough not to recognize the crucial need to develop utilities and other infrastructure so crucial to the profitable functioning of the colonial economy. Hence, public enterprises emerged during Malaya's colonial era to provide the public goods and services needed by British private enterprises to secure profits from their control of tin mining, plantation agriculture and international commerce.

Faced with a communist-led insurgency and the prospect of a debilitating stalemate or, worse still, defeat in its economically most lucrative colony after the Japanese Occupation during the Second World War, the colonial authorities sought to win "hearts and minds" from the early fifties after little success with its original strategy of reliance on repression from the late forties (Stubbs, 1989; Harper, 1991). In this context of social reform to complement repression, the British colonial authorities established new public enterprises oriented primarily towards rural development efforts to consolidate a Malay yeoman peasantry as a bulwark against a Chinese-led rural insurgency with some peripatetic efforts to encourage petty Malay business in the face of ubiquitous Chinese dominance of petty trade and industry.

The advent of an elected Malay-dominated post-colonial government saw a deepening of such efforts, by the ruling Alliance led by the United Malays National Organization (UMNO), mindful of its primarily Malay electoral base. Hence, after independence in August 1957, rural development efforts intensified, with some proliferation of new rural development agencies. The momentum to advance Malay business interests accelerated from the mid-sixties, especially after the convening of the first Bumiputera Economic Congress in 1965.

From the early sixties as well, the post-colonial government's import substituting industrialization policy required the establishment of some public enterprises to provide industrial financing and organize factory sites on industrial estates, but little more as the conservative Alliance government was concerned to ensure that it did not upset British and other foreign companies seeking to consolidate their market shares in the growing post-colonial market by relocating some plant and machinery, primarily for assembly and packaging, in the former colony.

From the mid-sixties, most Malaysian state governments also began setting up state economic development corporations (SEDCs) to enhance the flexibility of the state governments in undertaking initiatives of their own, particularly in exploiting their own natural resources and trying to ensure some spatial dispersal of new industries. The abolition of municipal elections—typically won by opposition parties since their advent in the fifties—from the mid-sixties may well have inadvertently pre-empted similar initiatives at the municipal level.

Making the transition to export-oriented industrialization in the late sixties with the exhaustion of import substitution, various federal and state government agencies provided much of the necessary infrastructure and other facilities to attract foreign manufacturers to relocate in and use Malaysia as their new export platform offering relatively cheap, docile and largely un-unionized labor.

The elections of May 1969 and the ensuing race riots and palace coup within the UMNO and hence government leadership, resulted in very significant regime changes, resulting in the tremendous expansion of state intervention and the public sector for the next dozen years until Mahathir's appointment as Malaysia's fourth Prime Minister in mid-1981. The new national leader, Razak, announced a New Economic Policy (NEP) committed to achieving national unity by reducing poverty and achieving inter-ethnic economic parity, especially between the politically dominant Malays and economically ubiquitous Chinese. Existing public enterprises were strengthened and new ones created to achieve these goals. Intensified rural development efforts continued to be directed mainly at the Malay peasantry. Greatly expanded educational efforts, particularly at the tertiary level, rapidly grew to expand and consolidate the Malay middle class. Malay employment in the modern sector grew rapidly, both in the public and private sectors, though not without some coercion in the latter case. And perhaps most importantly, in terms of what the NEP has come to mean in Malaysia, various "trust agencies" rapidly acquired tremendous corporate wealth, ostensibly on behalf of the predominantly Malay indigenous (Bumiputera) community.

The conservative fiscal policies of the early post-colonial era were abandoned in favor of growing deficit financing, primarily from domestic sources, mainly the forced savings of the Employees Provident Fund (EPF), set up as part of the labor reforms of the early fifties. The discovery and extraction of newly discovered petroleum reserves, as international oil prices rose from 1973, greatly increased the Malaysian government's degree of freedom in terms of spending and hence, public enterprise expansion, which extended to regional and spatial dispersal objectives as well. Malaysia's newfound status as a net petroleum exporter from the mid-seventies enabled it to continue to increase public spending until the end of the decade without any dramatic increase in foreign borrowing.

By the end of the decade, however, the decline of oil prices and the US-led tightening of liquidity induced a new international recession, which the Malaysian Government initially hoped to spend its way out of, with increased public spending and a public employment expansion policy financed with foreign borrowings, mainly from commercial sources. As the deep structural nature of the international recession became increasingly apparent, the government abruptly abandoned the counter-cyclical expansionary fiscal strategy by announcing an austerity campaign soon after improving its electoral position in the April 1982 general elections.

Nevertheless, however, the government continued to guarantee heavy foreign borrowings, mainly from Japan, to finance new, Prime Minister Mahathir's, heavy industrialization strategy, in the form of steel, cement, auto and motorcycle plants set up through public enterprises. Thus, Malaysia's foreign borrowings increased most dramatically in the first half of the eighties, after real interest rates increased as inflation dropped in the face of the deflationary tendencies associated with tightening international liquidity.

By 1985, the international recession adversely affected Malaysian export earnings from most commodities (especially palm oil, rubber, tin) and electronics. And in September that year, the major industrial economies agreed to a major international currency realignment, with the yen appreciating significantly against the US dollar. Malaysia's ringgit, which became increasingly tied to the US dollar after independence, and especially after the sterling devaluation of 1967, then depreciated against the US dollar, resulting in a virtual doubling of the value of the yen in ringgit terms, with a corresponding increase in the yen-denominated foreign borrowings. As a consequence, Malaysia experienced negative growth in 1985, for the first time since independence. With the collapse of the oil price in early 1986, the Malaysian authorities were under considerable pressure to respond with policy changes favored by the Bretton Woods institutions.

After quietly announcing the suspension of the NEP, the government basically discontinued its heavy industrialization program while consolidating and accelerating various economic liberalization measures, including several already announced by Mahathir in the early eighties, including privatization; in 1985, the Economic Planning Unit of the Prime Minister's Department announced its *Guidelines for Privatization*, spelling out the official rationale and broad guidelines for Malaysian privatization. Finance Minister Daim, appointed by Mahathir in 1984, is sometimes credited with responsibility for implementing these policy reversals, and it is interesting to reflect on his ability to pursue somewhat unpopular measures—including reversal of much of what the NEP had come to stand for—in the light of his relative insulation from political pressures, having been appointed to this powerful position without enjoying a personal political mandate from either the party or the population.

The subsequent sustained economic boom, led by export-oriented manufacturing, especially of industries relocating from Japan, Taiwan and other increasingly expensive economies of East Asia, has enabled the government to claim credit for it, also giving it the confidence to consolidate the economic development program with the expiry of the first Outline Perspective Plan (OPP) associated with the NEP for 1971–1990. In February 1991, Prime Minister Mahathir announced his Vision 2020 to achieve developed country status by the year 2020AD, on the basis of a liberal economic program including privatization. In the same month, the government issued its *Privatization Masterplan*, including a Privatization Action Plan.

Not surprisingly, Malaysia's privatization program was, at least initially, widely perceived as the antithesis of the NEP's expansion of the public sector despite official insistence that the program would contribute towards NEP objectives, referring mainly to the inter-ethnic redistributive efforts. After all, the NEP had come to be perceived increasingly in terms of Malay wealth accumulation, with 30 percent of total corporate wealth set as the target for 1990. The Malay share of corporate wealth seemed to be growing as scheduled—from 2.4 percent in 1969—during the first half of the seventies, but seemed to slow down thereafter, especially since 1983, when it reached 18 percent, and barely rose thereafter until the end of the decade. Perhaps more significantly, whereas the *Third Malaysia Plan, 1976-1980* envisaged that the Malay share would be held through government established trust agencies, on behalf of the entire community, the privatization program has actually accelerated private Malay accumulation, arguably at the expense of the community as a whole, and certainly its poorer members.

As suggested earlier, the advent of privatization in Malaysia did not occur in an international vacuum and was certainly encouraged by the changed ideological climate of the eighties, especially with the advent of governments of the new right in the Anglo-American world. While Prime Minister Mahathir was once believed to be hostile to such cultural influences, this is less true today, and possibly then as well, as suggested by the secret bilateral military treaty he signed— as Prime Minister and also Defence Minister—with the Reagan administration in the mid-eighties. Interestingly, the market conservative ideology of the new right accorded with views he had expressed in the mid-seventies—against the tide of prevailing Malay public opinion then.

Intellectually, the policies of the new right have been accompanied by new academic developments, generally supportive of privatization policies, ostensibly on the grounds of superior efficiency and growth. These include supply-side economics, public choice theory, property rights arguments and principal-agent considerations. There is also greater universal appreciation of the value of the market as an information economizer as well as greater attention to problems of government failure. All this and more have been extensively discussed, sometimes critically, in a growing literature on privatization, some—mainly the most relevant—of which is included in the bibliography to this volume.

Structure

However, as this book's examination of the Malaysian privatization experience suggests, the various theoretical gains ascribed to privatization have been severely compromised, and arguably undermined, by the Malaysian government's probably unique commitment to using privatization to achieve ethnic redistributive objectives. Several chapters in this volume examine the implications of the ethnic redistributive objective for privatization in Malaysia, including the trade-offs and compromises involved. Others examine the implications of the program for consumer and employee welfare as well as the public interest, variously perceived, defined and interpreted. Considered together, they suggest how privatization and its discourse has come to redefine issues of distribution and welfare, with all their attendant ideological and political implications.

"Privatizing Malaysia" is the first book-length examination of the privatization process in a developing country of the Third World. While primarily "political economic" in focus, the variety of perspectives contained in this volume provides a reasonably comprehensive survey of the privatization process in Malaysia in the first decade after the policy was announced. In this volume, Malaysia's privatization experience is critically reviewed, with a view to providing superior alternatives to improve overall economic efficiency, especially in the public sector, while protecting the public interest, broadly understood in terms of the national interest, consumer and worker interests, as well as other equity considerations. This volume therefore seeks to develop a more balanced perspective of the Malaysian privatization experience thus far, with a view to informing public sector reforms in the public interest.

The volume consists of eleven chapters and an extensive bibliography. After the Background and Overview chapters, the rest of the volume is divided into three parts with three chapters each. While the first part reviews general macro-policy issues involving Malaysian privatization, the second part examines more specific considerations and outcomes of the country's privatization experience, while the final part reviews the major economic and cultural implications of privatization on particular economic sectors and activities.

Adam and Cavendish's Background chapter outlines and introduces the context in which Malaysia's privatization policy was introduced in the mid-eighties. Besides providing a macroeconomic survey of developments culminating in the fiscal, debt and public sector crises of the mid-eighties, they also trace the development of the public sector from the colonial development of infrastructure and utilities to the modest post-colonial redistributive efforts in the fifties and sixties, the more ambitious, (mainly ethnic) redistributive efforts of the seventies, and the official promotion of heavy industries from the early eighties.

Jomo's general Overview then introduces and locates Malaysia's privatization experience in the global and national contexts of changing development policies. The official and other arguments for privatization are critically examined and a brief overview of Malaysia's privatization experience is provided in anticipation of the rest of the book and to contextualize the following chapters.

Rugayah Mohamed's survey of Malaysian public enterprises identifies the varying motivations for their establishment in different eras— the colonial period when the state undertook the provision of essential public goods especially infrastructure and utilities, the early post-colonial period of essentially *laissez faire* economic development with some modest efforts at promoting import-substituting industrialization and initial efforts at rural, regional and ethnic development dating from the late colonial period, and the more determined, primarily inter-ethnic "restructuring" and Malay peasant poverty reducing efforts associated with enhanced Malay political hegemony from the seventies. She also shows that public enterprise economic performance in Malaysia's manufacturing sector has not been poorer than that of their private counterparts, contrary to widespread assumptions and popular prejudice. She demonstrates that when compared on a matched pairs— or "like with like"—basis, public enterprises in the manufacturing sector have generally done as well as private enterprises. She concludes that market structural changes promoting competition are more likely—than privatization—to enhance efficiency.

Adam, Cavendish and Jomo then trace the evolution of declared Malaysian privatization policy, beginning with Prime Minister's original announcement in the early eighties, the *Guidelines* provided by the Economic Planning Unit (EPU) of the Prime Minister's Department in 1985, and the *Privatization Masterplan* drafted by British consultants, and issued by the EPU in February 1991. The unique element in Malaysia's declared privatization policy objectives is the commitment to ensure its consistency with the government's New Economic Policy (NEP) goals, particularly to achieve inter-ethnic economic parity among the different ethnic groups, especially between the politically dominant Malays and the economically ubiquitous Chinese.

Adam and Cavendish then review the evolution of Malaysia's early privatization experience in the 1980s. Their discussion locates the actual evolution of Malaysian privatization in the context of other policy influences, especially the inter-ethnic redistributive objectives of the NEP, and the politically dominant statist interests which dominate Malaysian economic policymaking. They also show how the predominance of the NEP's inter-ethnic redistributive objective has overwhelmed and possibly undermined the other ostensible aims of Malaysian privatization. They argue that Malaysia's privatization policy has severely compromised most of the policy's other declared objectives—raising efficiency and productivity, accelerating growth, reducing the government's financial and administrative burden, and trimming the public sector while strengthening the private sector.

The second part of the volume begins with Terence Gomez's examination of the most notable cases of management buy-outs associated with the Malaysian privatization experience in which two of the most profitable government-owned enterprises were taken over by close associates of the Prime Minister and the then Finance Minister, at heavily discounted prices and on very convenient terms. The circumstances of these privatizations are not particularly exceptional when compared to other privatizations of very profitable or potentially very lucrative government-owned enterprises to such "cronies" on very favorable terms. There was little pretence of transparency, competition or auction, with the choice of beneficiary justified solely in terms of a nebulous "first come, first served" principle, very liable to political abuse. He suggests that the apparent ethnic bias in Malaysia's privatization policy may well obscure a more important political bias in the selection of beneficiaries. This is particularly apparent in the withdrawal of the Government from public lotteries, with the main benefits accruing mainly to politically well-connected, non-Malay businessmen, and the continuing recent rise to prominence of a crop of previously not so well-known non-Malay businessmen such as Vincent Tan, Quek Leng Chan and Ananda Krishnan.

Two of the strongest and politically most attractive arguments in favor of privatization internationally as well as in Malaysia have been the expected gains from improved efficiency and consumer welfare as a consequence of privatization. Winnie Goh and Jomo argue that the evidence from Malaysia's experience does not point to any clear trend of improved efficiency which may be directly attributable to privatization *per se*, i.e. the "property rights" argument. The instances of greater efficiency coinciding with privatization are usually attributable to improved management and labor motivation, which can be achieved through public enterprise reform. By associating such efficiency gains with privatization, the rest of the public sector not subject to improved management is virtually condemned to remain in the moribund, inflexible and poorly motivated condition responsible for the enterprises' poor economic performance in the first place. There is also no unambiguous evidence of improved consumer welfare since improved services—which could have been achieved by means other than privatization—have generally been anticipated or accompanied by increased user costs, i.e. consumer charges. The much-touted privatization of the Kelang Container Terminal has actually involved a more complex story of modest gains simplistically attributed to privatization. In the case of Malaysian Airlines (MAS), most of the apparent improvements in welfare coinciding with the partial divestment of previously government held shares were captured by foreign consumers (passengers), probably due to lower ticket prices.

Kuppusamy's study of the impact of privatization on the employees of Tenaga Nasional (TEN) and the Malaysian Highway Authority (LLM) suggests that the Government has generally acted in such a way as to mollify the predominantly Malay employees already on its payroll, thus minimizing and pre-empting labor objections to the privatization policy. He shows that at least in the cases of privatized government monopolies, employees have generally been induced to support privatization by the prospect of improved remuneration and medium term employment guarantees for a labor force largely recruited before 1982, especially during the seventies, and frustrated by the prospect of limited upward mobility in a schooling credential-based employment structure and real wage erosion due to inflation since the last major wage increase in 1980. However, the study does not address the implications of these measures for the Malaysian labor market as a whole, which arguably has become more dualistic in nature as a consequence of growing labor flexibility, especially since the mid-1980s.

The third part of this volume begins with a review of privatization affecting infrastructure services in Malaysia by G. Naidu. Such privatization is mainly of two types, involving the partial or total divestment of the public authorities established to build and/or maintain existing infrastructural facilities (e.g. ports, airports, highways, bridges), and the assignment of the rights to build, operate and eventually transfer (B-O-T) to the government, and, more rarely, to build, operate and own (B-O-O) new physical infrastructural facilities, especially roads. While such privatization has undoubtedly reduced the economic burden of such provisions in the short term, previously borne exclusively by the government, it has also deprived the government of significant current and future revenue from their provision, especially as most of such infrastructural provision (except when motivated by "political" considerations) has been profitable to the government, albeit only in the medium to long term. The elimination of such revenue will significantly reduce the potential for cross-subsidization and is likely to exacerbate the government's fiscal position in the long run. This problem of short-termism has been compounded by the very generous and uncompetitive terms of privatization, usually to politically well-connected business interests. He also shows how easily privatization can and has been used for rent appropriation and how readily the declared objectives of the privatization policy lend themselves to abuse without necessarily enhancing consumer welfare or the public interest through the best means and in the most efficient manner possible. Naidu also argues that the Malaysian government had done a reasonably good job of providing infrastructure for economic growth as well as to reduce spatial disparities before the advent of the privatization program.

Laurel Kennedy then shows how the apparent public monopoly over telecommunications has been the subject of private "rent appropriation" by politically well-connected businessmen especially since the early eighties, and how such opportunities have been changed and somewhat enhanced by the corporatization and privatization of the Malaysian government's Telecoms Department. Her study provides an in-depth analysis of the intriguing political economy of privatization of the telecommunications industry, highlighting the considerable abuse which has undermined consumer and other public interests. What clearly emerges from her discussion is the impression that changes in Malaysian telecommunications development policy seem to have been primarily concerned with the welfare of politically well-connected businessmen, rather than the public, consumers or even employees. The Government's record in trying to "pick and nurse" winners, at high cost and with apparently little success, suggests that no industrial policy is, probably, preferable to bad policy.

The final chapter of this volume is significantly different from the preceding chapters. Rahmah Hashim addresses some socio-cultural consequences of the privatization of television programming with the licensing of a private, albeit ruling party-controlled television station in 1983 as well as production and advertising privatizatioh by the government broadcasting stations in response. Some cultural, ideological and moral consequences of the more commercialized nature of television programming on the fragile and vulnerable efforts to promote a national culture in an ethnically/culturally plural and divided developing country are highlighted. While apparently lucrative all round—for the government-owned television broadcasting authority, the reputedly politically well-connected concessionaire, the program suppliers and the advertisers—Rahmah Hashim's analysis of existing arrangements involving partial privatization of television programming of particular bands (time slots) raises important questions about the cultural implications and consequences of popular foreign or imitative television programming, well beyond her focus on Chinese language programming under a government ostensibly committed to promoting a national language (Malay) and culture (Malay-based). It also raises questions about levying television licence fees (ostensibly to pay for government broadcasting), while broadcasting paid commercial advertisements on government-owned television channels and restricting public access (especially by political and other dissidents) to these channels.

1

Background

CHRISTOPHER ADAM and WILLIAM CAVENDISH

Malaysia is a lower middle-income economy of approximately 19 million people, of whom 60 percent are indigenous (known as the Bumiputera), mainly Malay, and the remainder non-Malay (principally Chinese and Indian). Its GNP per capita in 1992 was RM7543 (US$2900). The two decades since 1970 have witnessed a period of significant growth in the Malaysian economy, in line with other emerging newly industrializing countries (NICs). However, during the mid-1980s, the economy experienced a severe recession, following a 17 percent deterioration in the terms of trade between 1981 and 1982. The current account deficit grew dramatically during the period, the public-sector deficit, which had averaged approximately 10 percent of GDP during the first New Economic Policy[1] (NEP) decade (1971–1980), reached 21.7 percent of GDP in 1982, and between 1984 and 1985, real growth fell from 8 percent to -1 percent. The subsequent recovery saw the economy returning to higher levels of activity, with real GDP growth rates at 5.3 percent for 1987–1989 and averaging over 8 percent during 1988–1993.

Gross domestic savings levels in Malaysia are particularly high, averaging approximately 29 percent of GNP during the 1970s and 1980s (Table 1.1), and exceeding 32 percent in 1992. However, much of this saving is contractual. In particular, the largest single savings institution, the Employees Provident Fund (EPF), accounts for approximately 20 percent of total employment income, while the investment trusts of the Permodalan Nasional Berhad (PNB) and the Islamic savings institutions attract a further large proportion of these savings.

As Table 1.1 indicates, the investment to GDP ratio has risen rapidly since Independence, and averages approximately 31 percent of GDP, having exceeded 40 percent in 1982-1983. Since the introduction of the NEP, the public-sector share of total investment has risen dramatically, reaching a peak during the early 1980s, when, for the only time since Independence, public-sector investment[2] accounted for 50 percent of total investment in the economy. The economic restructuring program, combined with the development of a more private sector-oriented

TABLE 1.1 Composition of Gross Domestic Product 1956–1992 (percentage)

	1956–60	1961–65	1966–70	1971–75	1976–80	1981–85	1986–90	1992
Real GDP growth	4.1	5.0	5.4	8.0	8.6	5.2	4.6	
Functional composition (% of GDP)								
Agriculture	40.2	31.5		27.7		20.8	21.1	16.3
Mining	6.3	9.0		4.6		10.5	10.6	8.6
Manufacture	8.2	10.4		16.4		19.7	24.1	28.9
Construction	3.0	4.5		3.8		4.8	3.2	4.0
Services	42.3	44.6		47.5		44.2	41.0	44.1
Economic classification (% of GDP)								
Consumption	79.2	80.5	80.3	77.7	69.5	72.5	69.0	61.4
Public	14.7	16.0	17.8	17.5	16.4	17.4	16.8	13.0
Private	64.5	64.5	62.5	60.2	53.1	55.1	52.2	48.4
Investment	12.6	18.9	16.7	24.4	27.4	36.3	27.5	35.9
Public	2.7	8.4	6.4	7.8	10.0	17.3	11.2	11.5
Private	9.9	10.5	10.3	16.6	17.4	19.0	16.3	24.4
Gross national savings (% of GDP)	16.6	17.8	18.3	20.8	30.0	27.5	31.3	30.8
Savings — investment (% of GDP)	4.0	-1.1	1.6	-3.6	2.6	-8.8	3.8	-3.3

Source: Bank Negara Malaysia.

development strategy, has seen public-sector investment drop back sharply since 1986.

Malaysia is a resource-rich economy, both in terms of oil and natural gas as well as non-mineral resources. Yet, despite this, its development since Independence in 1957 has been based on a broadening of its production and non-traditional export sectors. At Independence, the economy was dominated by the agricultural sector, which accounted for over 40 percent of GDP, 60 percent of formal sector employment, and almost 70 percent of export earnings. In particular, Malaysia was the world's largest producer of natural rubber and tin. Over time, however, though remaining a world leader in these two commodities, the country has successfully diversified activity across its broad resource base, and has seen the emergence of the petroleum industry and other manufacturing activity, which between them now dominate the economy. Real growth in the manufacturing sector averaged 10 percent per annum from Independence until the early 1980s, and although the sector's growth declined during the economic slowdown and recession from 1982 to 1986, recovery since 1986 has been rapid, with growth rates exceeding the pre-recession period.

Throughout the period from Independence until the late 1960s, the emphasis was on import substitution, but during the 1970s there was a shift towards labor-intensive and high-technology export-oriented production, to the extent that manufactured exports now account for over 50 percent of all exports. The 1980s saw even greater emphasis on the manufacturing sector, especially as Malaysia has developed an increasingly outward-looking stance, although there was some reorientation in the early 1980s towards the growing domestic market, especially in the capital-intensive and consumer durable sectors. The severity of the recession of the mid-1980s added extra stimulus to the need for even greater diversity in the economy, and has been followed by renewed measures aimed at greater liberalization of the domestic economy, the reduction of the role of the public sector in the economy, and the rejuvenation of foreign participation in the domestic economy.[3]

Structural Constraints and the New Economic Policy

One of the most pervasive problems of the economy, and one which has widespread implications for the privatization program as a whole, is the extent to which political structures create barriers to efficient intermediation of commercial risk. Consequently, domestic risk aversion is exacerbated, leading to low levels of investment in productive activities (relative to aggregate savings). Investment opportunities abound in Malaysia; there are skilled human resources, both industrial and managerial, and a sophisticated financial sector, capable of raising capital domestically and internationally. In addition, the economy is well served by transport and other communications systems. Despite this, however, and as a result of historical factors and the philosophy underpinning the New

Economic Policy, the economy, and the financial system in particular, function so as to divert risk capital away from private-sector investment towards non-productive, public-sector activities. Furthermore, even when funds are directed towards domestic investment, business licensing and employment practices create barriers to efficiency and competition in the private sector. At this stage it is necessary to establish the context for much of the analysis to follow by outlining the origins of the New Economic Policy, and its impact on the economy.

From Independence until 1970, the political economy of Malaysia was shaped by the so-called "Bargain of 1957". This was an agreement between Malay and non-Malay (i.e. Chinese and Indian) interest groups which allowed the latter a relatively free hand to pursue their commercial interests while the Malays retained political control, through which a degree of positive discrimination was exercised (mainly through public-sector employment policies). However, following race riots in Kuala Lumpur in May 1969, sparked off by growing resentment of Chinese domination of the economy, the predominantly Malay government moved quickly to develop an economic program of affirmative action towards the Bumiputeras. The New Economic Policy was the embodiment of this affirmative action program and was immediately integrated in the Second (1971–1975) and subsequent Malaysia Plans.[4] In doing so, it fundamentally altered the course of macro-economic policy-making for the next two decades. The NEP outlines the objectives of economic policy as "(i) the promotion of national unity and integration; (ii) the creation of employment opportunities; and (iii) the promotion of overall economic growth," noting that "the economic objective of national unity may be expressed as the improvement of economic balances between the races or the re-duction of racial economic disparities" (NEP quoted in Faaland *et al.*, 1990: 307).

Though the NEP embodied a broad range of socio-economic objectives such as employment, housing, education, and an exclusive civil service recruitment policy, the litmus-test was, and remains, the distribution of corporate asset owner-ship as the indicator of wealth distribution. In 1970, 62 percent of all corporate assets were owned by foreigners, 34 percent by non-Bumiputera Malaysians, and 4 percent by the Bumiputeras (PNB, 1990). The NEP consequently set target equity ownership levels of 30 percent foreigners, 40 percent other Malaysians, and 30 percent Bumiputeras to be reached by 1990. Aggressive programs were instituted in pursuit of this target, including the compulsory transfer of shares to the Bumiputeras and the creation of specialized financial institutions. By 1980 (half-way through the NEP period), the distribution of equity ownership had improved quite markedly, being foreign 43 percent, other Malaysians 45 percent, and Bumiputeras 12 percent (of which 7 percent was institutional), but was still a long way off the original NEP target. By 1985, it had reached foreign 25 percent, other Malaysians 57 percent, and Bumiputeras 18 percent (8 percent institutions).

Though corporate equity distribution was the central element of the NEP, the program was (and is) central to all other aspects of economic life in Malaysia. Most importantly, government policy towards the SOE sector during the 1970s, and, perhaps counter-intuitively, the push for privatization in the 1980s, has been driven by the needs of the NEP. The relationship between the NEP, the public sector, and the privatization program will be dealt with later in this volume.

The Outline Perspective Plan (OPP) of the NEP expired in 1990, and the debate surrounding post-1990 policy was intense. Aside from the equity distribution targets, evidence over the two decades of the NEP had been mixed. While real GDP growth had been impressive and the standard of living of the Bumiputeras as a whole had improved dramatically, the overall performance of the economy had not been outstanding by regional standards. It has been widely argued that growth was hampered by the NEP. When it was introduced, Malaysia ranked third only to Japan and Singapore among East Asian nations in terms of GDP per capita; by 1990, it had fallen behind South Korea, Taiwan and Hong Kong as well. Had growth not been constrained by the NEP, it is argued, the economic performance and welfare of the Bumiputeras would have been even more greatly enhanced. Moreover, it is argued, the NEP led to a serious degree of "cronyism,"[5] especially with regard to government contracting and licensing procedures. Preferential access to publicly funded business has reduced public-sector efficiency and raised concerns about the transparency of government policy-making and implementation.

The politics of the NEP aside, its predominant effect was to assign an extremely broad role for government intervention in the economy. It is, perhaps, this issue which most singularly characterizes the economic history of Malaysia under the NEP up to the mid-1980s, and, most certainly, which has shaped the privatization program. The NEP is an instrument of positive discrimination and, as such, its primary feature has been to attempt to shield the Bumiputeras from the ravages of commercial risk. This principle can be seen not only to operate in the acquisition of wealth-creating assets for the Bumiputeras, and the expansion of the public sector in the 1970s and early 1980s, but has been assimilated into the privatization program. As Vickers and Yarrow (1991) argue, "just as political agendas influence SOE behavior so do they also influence the conduct of privatization programs." This volume argues that this has been one of the overriding features of the Malaysian privatization program.

The SOE Sector: Origins, Structure, and Development

For an economy which is viewed as being fundamentally market-oriented, Malaysia's SOE sector has been surprisingly large. Indeed, it is among the largest in the world outside the centrally planned economies, with over 1,100 SOEs comprising both core utilities—transport, communications, water supply, energy, and finance—and also a large exposure in non-traditional sectors such as services, construction, and, particularly, manufacturing. The origins and development of the SOE sector in Malaysia are central to an understanding of the politics and structure of the current privatization program.

Within Malaysia itself, there are a number of different definitions of what constitutes an SOE, and frequently in official statistics, only the largest, wholly-owned SOEs are acknowledged. For our purposes, however, the term embraces the entire range of government equity holdings, both direct and indirect, whether it be a majority or minority interest. Since Malaysia is a federal state, this definition includes not only those SOEs in which equity is held directly by the central federal government, but also where equity participation is through either state governments or one of the many regional development authorities.[6]

Two measurement problems are encountered when assessing the size and scope of the SOE sector. First, in the national accounts, enterprises are not analyzed in terms of ownership; consequently there is no comprehensive measurement of the overall contribution of the sector to GDP. All measures reported in official statistics are thus only approximations. This is most noticeable with official statistics on the so-called 'consolidated' public-sector financial performance, in which the federal and state government financial position is consolidated with that of approximately 50 of the larger wholly-owned SOEs.[7] Second, the collection of detailed financial data on the SOE sector is a comparatively recent phenomenon in Malaysia. Following growing concern about the lack of a comprehensive database, the government contracted Permodalan Nasional Berhad to provide a financial data collection and monitoring system for the SOE sector. The unit, known as the Central Information Collection Unit (CICU), which began operations in 1985, provides an impressive array of data, allowing a reasonably comprehensive picture of the SOE sector in Malaysia to be built.

Origins of the SOE Sector

The *laissez-faire* implications of the "Bargain of 1957" were closely adhered to. During the period up to 1970, government intervention in commerce and industry was virtually non-existent and Malaysia maintained a minimal SOE sector covering the transport, energy, communications, utilities, and commodity marketing sectors. Following the Kuala Lumpur riots, it became widely accepted (among the ruling Bumiputeras) that economic discrimination was endemic and, if rapid economic advancement amongst the Bumiputeras was to be achieved, broader state intervention was required.

The 1970s therefore saw an unprecedented expansion in SOE participation in the commercial, industrial, and service sectors as well as in the emerging oil- and gas-based exploration sector. It was spearheaded by the federal government, but all the state economic development agencies also increased their equity participation. The expansion was so rapid that while the SOE sector was growing at a rate of over 100 enterprises per year by the mid-1970s, there was virtually no concomitant growth in the control or monitoring systems. Not only did this result in the creation of a huge class of companies whose managements were *de facto* acting independently of any effective shareholder control, but it also meant that the government, as shareholder of a significant proportion of the economy, remained ignorant of the extent of its assets and liabilities.[8] Only with the onset of economic crisis—in the form of recession in the early 1980s—was the government galvanized into action on the SOEs. With the appointment of Dr. Mahathir bin Mohamad as Prime Minister in 1981, the creation of new SOEs other than those for heavy industry came to a halt.

Size and Structure of the SOE Sector

Official estimates suggest that the output of the SOE sector accounts for around 25 percent of GDP (World Bank, 1989c: 58), while CICU records show that, as at the end of March 1990, there were 1,158 SOEs (78 percent of them operational), with a total paid-up capital of RM23.9 billion (Table 1.2). Of these companies, 396 (or 34 percent) were 100 percent government-owned; a further 429 (37 percent) majority owned; in the final 333 (30 percent), the government had only a minority equity stake. The government equity share in the sector accounted for 70.3 percent of the total, amounting to RM16.7 billion.

Malaysia's SOEs are broadly spread across all sectors, with finance, services, and manufacturing dominating in terms of simple number of enterprises, accounting for 12 percent, 27 percent, and 28 percent of all SOEs respectively. In terms of capitalization, a similar picture emerges, with the finance and manufacturing sectors accounting for approximately 60 percent of total capitalization. The sector is extremely concentrated: the largest 20 SOEs (less than 2 percent of the total) have a combined capitalization of RM5.2 billion (5 percent of GDP and almost 22 percent of total SOE capitalization) and a combined turnover of RM29 billion (57 percent of the estimated total turnover of the sector for 1988) (Table 1.3). The majority of the SOEs are small, however. Excluding the top 20 (whose average capitalization was RM260 million), average capitalization is only RM18 million (US$6.7 million at 1988 prices), and most enterprises operate in relatively competitive markets. Tables 1.4 through 1.6 classify the SOE sector between federal, state, and regional agencies, by capitalization, and by source of debt as at February 1990.

SOEs in Malaysia are held almost equally between the federal and the state governments, with only a few (4 percent) by the regional agencies. Their sectoral distribution (Table 1.7) indicates that state SOEs predominate in the primary sectors—agriculture, extractive industry, plantation agriculture, and logging—while the transport and finance sectors are dominated by federal SOEs. A further feature is the large number of state manufacturing and service SOEs, most of which were created as direct elements of the NEP, as an attempt to reduce regional income inequalities. Federal SOEs tend to be significantly larger than those held by state or regional agencies (both in terms of debt and equity capital), accounting in total for 78 percent of total equity capital and 79 percent of debt capital. State and regional SOEs are significantly smaller, and are much less likely

TABLE 1.2 SOE Distribution, 1990

Industry	Sector	Active[a]	Non-op[b]	Liq/Rec[c]	Shell[d]	Total	Government Ownership			Capital RMm.	Av Cap RMm.	Cap as % of Total	Frequency as % of Total
							100%	Maj.	Min.				
Agriculture	Forestry	19	5	0	1	25	6	5	14	58.77	2.35	0.25	2.16
	Liv/Fish	21	5	0	1	27	12	11	4	120.35	4.46	0.50	2.33
	Plantation	75	13	3	4	95	45	30	20	3,923.25	41.30	16.39	8.20
	TOTAL	115	23	3	6	147	63	46	38	4,102.37	27.91	17.14	12.69
Building & Construction	Building	25	2	4	1	32	10	16	6	72.91	2.28	0.30	2.76
	Mech. & Elec.	2	1	0	0	3	2	1	0	1.16	0.39	0.00	0.26
	Property Dev.	76	11	2	8	97	30	38	29	1,250.42	12.89	5.23	8.38
	TOTAL	103	14	6	9	132	42	55	35	1,324.49	10.03	5.53	11.40
Extractive	Mining	18	9	3	0	30	6	14	10	372.44	12.41	1.56	2.59
	Petroleum	4	0	0	0	4	0	4	0	150.75	37.69	0.63	0.35
	TOTAL	22	9	3	0	34	6	18	10	523.19	15.39	2.19	2.94
Finance	Comm Bank	9	0	0	0	9	0	7	2	3,209.01	356.56	13.41	0.78
	Dev. Bank	4	0	0	0	4	2	2	0	369.33	92.33	1.54	0.35
	Discount House	1	0	0	0	1	0	1	0	12.00	12.00	0.05	0.09
	Factoring	2	0	0	0	2	0	2	0	12.00	6.00	0.05	0.17
	Finance Co	8	0	0	0	8	0	4	4	182.23	22.78	0.76	0.69
	House Credit	2	0	0	0	2	1	0	1	176.42	88.21	0.74	0.17
	Insur. Co	12	0	0	0	12	1	6	5	186.51	15.54	0.78	1.04
	Invest. Co	62	12	2	2	78	30	25	23	4,270.91	54.76	17.85	6.74
	Invest. Trust	4	0	1	1	5	3	1	1	41.02	8.20	0.17	0.43
	Leasing	5	2	0	0	7	0	5	2	37.00	5.29	0.15	0.60
	Merchant Bank	5	0	0	0	5	0	3	2	86.25	17.25	0.36	0.43
	Unit Trust	1	0	0	0	1	0	1	0	32.00	32.00	0.13	0.09
	TOTAL	115	14	2	3	134	37	57	40	8,614.69	64.29	36.00	11.57
Manufacturing	Basic Metals	10	0	1	0	11	2	3	6	825.82	75.07	3.45	0.95
	Fabricated Metals	46	7	5	0	58	9	14	35	946.82	16.32	3.96	5.01
	Food, Bev. & Tob.	32	11	8	0	51	11	19	21	743.62	14.58	3.11	4.40
	Non-met minerals	37	6	3	1	47	14	14	19	598.28	12.73	2.50	4.06
	Paper & Printing	8	0	0	0	8	2	2	4	410.97	51.37	1.72	0.69
	Petro-Chemicals	61	5	5	0	71	10	26	35	1,646.88	23.20	6.88	6.13

TABLE 1.2 (continued)

Industry	Sector	Active[a]	Non-op[b]	Liq/Rec[c]	Shell[d]	Total	Government Ownership 100%	Government Ownership Maj.	Government Ownership Min.	Capital RMm.	Av Cap RMm.	Cap as % of Total	Frequency as % of Total
	Textiles	12	4	0	0	16	7	4	5	93.52	5.85	0.39	1.38
	Wood Products	40	9	2	6	57	37	11	9	241.82	4.24	1.01	4.92
	TOTAL	246	42	24	7	319	92	93	134	5,507.74	17.27	23.02	27.55
Services	Commod. Bkrs	1	0	0	0	1	0	0	1	0.25	0.25	0.00	0.09
	General Services	77	14	6	1	98	28	53	17	951.34	9.71	3.98	8.46
	Trading (Cons.)	29	7	3	0	39	14	12	13	120.38	3.09	0.50	3.37
	Trading (Inds.)	33	12	3	1	49	26	16	7	295.32	6.03	1.23	4.23
	Hotels	42	2	1	1	46	22	13	11	896.22	19.48	3.75	3.97
	Insur. Bkrs.	6	2	0	0	8	4	1	3	3.25	0.41	0.01	0.69
	Mgmt Services	56	7	2	1	66	37	21	8	366.81	5.56	1.53	5.70
	Money Bkrs.	2	0	0	0	2	0	0	2	0.37	0.18	0.00	0.17
	Restaurant	1	2	0	0	3	1	2	0	6.33	2.11	0.03	0.26
	Surveyors	2	0	0	0	2	0	1	1	0.23	0.12	0.00	0.17
	TOTAL	249	46	15	4	314	132	119	63	2,640.49	8.41	11.03	27.12
Transport	Airlines	4	0	1	0	5	0	2	3	470.60	94.12	1.97	-0.43
	Haulage	12	1	0	0	13	1	8	4	96.60	7.43	0.40	1.12
	Public Transport	28	1	0	1	30	12	16	2	67.74	2.26	0.28	2.59
	Shipping	9	2	1	8	20	4	12	4	575.90	28.79	2.41	1.73
	TOTAL	53	4	2	9	68	17	38	13	1,210.84	17.81	5.06	5.87
Other Ind	Others	0	3	0	6	9	6	3	0	6.70	0.74	0.03	0.78
	Public Utilities	0	1	0	0	1	1	0	0	0.00	0.00	0.03	0.86
	TOTAL	0	4	0	6	10	7	3	0	6.70	0.67	0.03	0.86
TOTALS		903	156	55	44	1,158	396	429	333	23,930.51	20.67	100.00	100.00

[a]Trading;
[b]Dormant or pre-operational;
[c]In liquidation or receivership;
[d]Shell companies—paid-up capital of RM2m. but no activity.
Source: PNB/CICU Database.

TABLE 1.3 Largest SOEs by Turnover

Company	Sector	Capital (RMm.)	Govt Equity (%)	Turn-over (RMm.)
1. PETRONAS Bhd	Petroleum	100	100	6,726
2. Malaysia Discount Bhd	Finance	12	100	5,150
3. Malaysia LNG Bhd	Petroleum	600	65	2,521
4. Malaysian Airline System Bhd	Airlines	350	60	1,895
5. Syarikat Telekom Malaysia Bhd	Telecom	500	100	1,699
6. Malaysia Intl Shipping Corp Bhd	Shipping	500	58	1,530
7. PETRONAS Dagangan Bhd	Petroleum	50	100	1,473
8. Perbadanan Kilang Bhd	Food Manuf	146	77	1,319
9. Bank Bumiputra Malaysia Bhd	Finance	1,376	100	1,209
10. Perbadanan Perusahaan Penapisan	Food Manuf	20	77	811
11. Permodalan Nasional Berhad (PNB)	Finance	100	100	805
12. Malaysian Rubber Development Corp Bhd	Rubber Manuf	125	100	758
13. Perbadanan Getah Felda	Petroleum	7	77	603
14. United Malayan Banking Corp Bhd	Finance	333	74	477
15. Perusahaan Otomobil Nasional (PROTON)	Vehicle Manuf	150	70	450
16. Sabah Gas Industries Bhd	Petroleum	372	100	442
17. Rakyat Berjaya Bhd	Forestry	1	100	422
18. Sabah Marketing Corporation Bhd	Services/Holding	15	100	364
19. PETRONAS Carigali Bhd	Petroleum	50	100	348
20. Perwira Habib Bank Malaysia Bhd	Finance	405	86	301
TOTAL		5,212		29,303
% of Total SOE		22		57

Source: PNB/CICU Database.

TABLE 1.4 SOEs by Paid-up Capital

	Number of Companies	Total Capital (RM mil.)	Govt Equity (RM mil.)	Govt Equity as % of Total Capital	Average Capital (RM mil.)
Federal	556	18,521	12,738	68.78	33.3
State	553	5,048	3,829	75.85	9.1
Regional	49	241	170	70.54	4.9
TOTAL	1,158	23,810	16,737	70.29	20.6

TABLE 1.5 SOEs by Size

	Number of Companies	Capital >RM20m.	Capital RM5–20m.	Capital RM1–5m.	Capital <RM1m
Federal	556	135	117	106	198
State	553	52	114	150	237
Regional	49	4	9	11	25
TOTAL	1,158	191	240	267	460

TABLE 1.6 SOEs by Source of Borrowing

	Number of Companies	Govt Loans	Foreign Loans	Domestic Loans	Total Loans	Debt/ Total Capital
Federal	556	21.38%	27.54%	51.08%	100.00%	184.89%
State	553	34.67%	24.28%	41.05%	100.00%	169.53%
Regional	49	41.35%	11.81%	46.84%	100.00%	98.34%
TOTAL	1,158	24.13%	26.81%	49.06%	100.00%	180.73%

TABLE 1.7 Distribution of SOEs by Sector

Sector	Federal	State	Regional	Total
Agriculture	5	19	3	27
Construction	8	26	1	35
Extractive	6	27	1	34
Finance	100	33	1	134
Manufacturing	153	155	14	32
Plantation	22	61	12	95
Property	44	53	1	98
Services	162	135	16	313
Logging	0	25	0	25
Transport	56	12	0	68
Others	0	7	0	7
TOTAL	556	553	49	1,158

to raise capital from sources other than the government. Whereas the average debt capitalization of federal SOEs was RM61 million from all sources, that for state SOEs was only RM15 million and for regional SOEs, less than RM5 million. The federal SOEs also had, on average, much larger exposure in the domestic and foreign financial markets (accounting for 51 percent and 27 percent of total debt respectively), while for state and regional SOEs the principal debt was to the government. The overall SOE debt–equity ratio of 180 percent was significantly higher than the average private-sector ratio (estimated to be approximately 100 percent),[9] although the implications of this are not clear since, while the government can (and does) extend cheap credit to SOEs, it is also a less demanding shareholder in terms of dividend requirements.

Performance of the SOE Sector

Aggregate performance figures for the SOE sector are determined to a significant degree by the performance of PETRONAS and its subsidiaries, which is closely tied to external conditions, and in particular the world oil market and the exchange-rate policy of the government. The 1980s were a period of considerable volatility for the world oil price, which fell from US$39 per barrel in 1981 to a low of US$14.8 per barrel in 1986 before improving again towards the end of the decade.

Using official data from the Ministry of Finance,[10] Table 1.8 shows that, despite relatively poor operating performance, the sector has undertaken extremely high levels of development expenditure. The generally weak performance is masked, however, at least in the early years of the decade, by high profits from PETRONAS and its subsidiaries (whose surplus alone (RM3.5 billion) reached 5 percent of GDP in 1982). The expansion of development expenditure during the Fourth Plan period, combined with the fiscal expansion from 1981 to 1984, was accompanied by a rapid expansion in development expenditure by the SOEs, which rose from 4.2 percent of GDP in 1981 to almost 10 percent in 1984.

This dramatic growth in the capital expenditure of the non-financial public enterprises reflected a general surge in public-sector capital expenditure, which for the three years 1981–1983 was consistently in excess of 25 percent of GDP, and which led to an unprecedented construction boom. The overall deficit of the sector rose concomitantly, touching 3.5 percent of GDP by 1984. Recession hit the sector hard, with revenues being depressed by low oil and other commodity prices as well as by a fall in Malaysia's export competitiveness. The bulk of the adjustment within the sector came with the contraction of development expenditure, from RM7.7 billion in 1984 to RM2.9 billion in 1987, leading to a modest overall surplus for the sector in 1987. More recently, however, reduced operating surpluses combined with increased development expenditure have again returned the sector to a situation of overall deficit.

TABLE 1.8 Non-financial Public Enterprise Performance (RM million)

	1981	1982	1983	1984	1985	1986	1987	1988	1989	1990
Operating Surplus	2,304	3,423	4,306	5,005	5,649	2,825	3,574	3,616	3,725	3,961
Capital Expenditure	2,419	4,006	6,127	7,762	6,186	3,850	2,885	3,730	4,464	4,900
Surplus/(Deficit)	(115)	(583)	(1,821)	(2,757)	(537)	(1,025)	689	(114)	(739)	(949)
As % of GDP										
Operating Surplus	4.00	5.47	6.16	6.29	7.28	3.94	4.48	3.98	3.70	3.66
Capital Expenditure	4.20	6.40	8.76	9.76	7.98	5.37	3.62	4.11	4.44	4.54
Surplus/(Deficit)	-0.20	-0.93	-2.60	-3.47	-0.69	-1.43	0.86	-0.13	-0.73	-0.88
Memorandum										
GDP (Mkt Prices)	57,613	62,579	69,941	79,550	77,547	71,729	79,711	90,806	100,650	107,948
Oil Price (US$/bl)	39.0	36.3	30.7	29.3	27.6	15.1	19.6	15.9	19.6	24.4

Source: Ministry of Finance, *Economic Report 1989/90*.

TABLE 1.9 SOE Financial Performance (RM million and as % of GDP)

	1980	1981	1982	1983	1984	1985	1986	1987	1988
Gross turnover	24,172	22,910	22,868	26,013	32,870	34,468	34,076	42,849	51,026
Operating profit	11,378	9,751	8,764	8,022	10,273	10478	9,133	8,738	11,277
Interest charges	536	697	912	1,218	1,673	1,643	2,099	2,820	3,103
Post-tax profit	7,368	5,285	4,465	3,208	5,096	4,731	3,553	3,217	5,096
Dividends	440	496	2,082	2,711	2,504	3,001	3,075	3,014	3,608
Gross fixed capital formation	0	3,612	4,642	5,784	5,407	2,713	2,233	8,093	1,620
Overall balance	6,928	1,177	(2,259)	(5,286)	(2,815)	(983)	(1,754)	(7,890)	(132)
External debt									
Debt to govt (o/s)	3,218	4,917	5,253	5,247	5,247	4,569	4,589	9,590	8,658
External debt (o/s)	4,483	5,964	7,345	8,672	8,578	10,031	9,744	9,542	9,669
Domestic debt (o/s)	2,560	2,904	3,536	3,317	3,698	4,085	4,623	4,397	4,147
TOTAL DEBT	10,261	13,785	16,135	17,235	17,523	18,685	18,956	23,529	22,504
SOE Performance as % of GDP	1980	1981	1982	1983	1984	1985	1986	1987	1988
Group turnover	45.3	39.8	36.5	37.4	41.3	44.4	47.9	54.5	56.2
Operating profit	21.3	16.9	14.0	11.5	12.9	13.5	12.8	11.1	12.4
Interest charges	1.0	1.2	1.5	1.8	2.1	2.1	2.9	3.6	3.4
Post-tax profit	13.8	9.2	7.1	4.6	6.4	6.1	5.0	4.1	5.6
Dividends	0.8	0.9	3.3	3.9	3.1	3.9	4.3	3.8	4.0
Gross fixed capital formation	0.0	6.3	7.4	8.3	6.8	3.5	3.1	10.3	1.8
Overall deficit	13.0	2.0	-3.6	-7.6	-3.5	-1.3	-2.5	-10.0	-0.1
External debt									
Debt to govt (o/s)	6.0	8.5	8.4	7.5	6.6	5.9	6.4	12.2	9.5
External debt (o/s)	8.4	10.4	11.7	12.5	10.8	12.9	13.7	12.1	10.7
Domestic debt (o/s)	4.8	5.0	5.7	4.8	4.6	5.3	6.5	5.6	4.6
TOTAL DEBT	19.2	23.9	25.8	24.8	22.0	24.1	26.6	29.9	24.8

Source: Permodalan Nasional Berhad Central Information Collection Unit.

Mindful of the narrowness of the Ministry of Finance database, however, we have attempted to create a broader picture of the SOE sector's aggregate financial performance, using the CICU's regular evaluations (Table 1.9).[11] The general pattern, in particular of the overall deficit, more or less reflects the picture of Table 1.8, although, importantly, Table 1.9 puts the scale of the sector as a whole into perspective, indicating SOE turnover accounting for between 40 percent and 50 percent of GDP, whilst the same pattern in operating profits and fixed capital formation emerges. Table 1.9 also shows a considerable rise in overall interest costs, which account for about 6 percent of turnover and 3.5 percent of GDP.

On the basis of these two tables, the SOE sector is, in aggregate, a net consumer of public resources and, were it not for the presence of the petroleum sector which was highly profitable during most of the late 1970s and 1980s, the financial burden would be sizeable. This general conclusion can be supported by detailed data from the CICU, which tracks the profitability of companies in the database (Table 1.10). Though there is a clear cyclical pattern, with the percentage of profitable SOEs falling sharply in 1985 and 1986, approximately 40–45 percent of all SOEs have been unprofitable throughout the 1980s. Of these, almost half (or 25 percent of all SOEs) had negative shareholders' funds[12]—a condition which would be unlikely to persist under private ownership.

TABLE 1.10 Summary of Profitable and Unprofitable SOEs (percentage)

	1980	1981	1982	1983	1984	1985	1986	1987	1988
Profitable[a]	61	60	54	58	58	52	52	53	60
Unprofitable	39	40	46	42	42	48	50	47	40

[a]Reporting net operating profit.
Source: CICU Report, February 1990.

TABLE 1.11 Relative Performance of SOEs, 1980–1988 (percentage)

	Sick[a]	Weak[b]	Satisfactory[c]	Good[d]
1980	12.53	26.24	10.88	50.35
1981	13.19	26.74	9.63	50.44
1982	15.25	29.15	9.86	45.74
1983	12.12	30.12	10.04	47.72
1984	14.02	26.98	11.80	47.20
1985	16.79	30.20	11.09	41.92
1986	18.95	29.54	13.31	38.20
1987	19.23	27.43	13.87	39.47
1988	16.67	24.15	14.42	44.76

[a]Companies with negative shareholders' funds.
[b]Loss-making companies with shareholders' funds <200% of paid-up capital.
[c]Shareholders' funds <100%, but currently profitable.
[d]Shareholders' funds >100% and profitable.

Finally in this section, Table 1.11 analyzes the relative performance of the SOEs over time according to general performance criteria based on enterprise profitability relative to capitalization. Although this table does not reflect the relative size of "sick", "weak", "satisfactory" and "good" companies, it does indicate the persistence of a very large number of unprofitable companies drawing on taxpayers' funds. Even at the height of the public-sector boom in 1981 and 1982, over 40 percent of all SOEs were either "sick" or "weak", which underlines one of the main criticisms of SOEs, namely that they are allowed to survive when commercial market conditions would have caused closure and reallocation of resources to more profitable activities.

Sectoral Performance

Despite the breadth of the SOE sector, three groups play a particularly important role in the sector as a whole. These are the petrochemicals, manufacturing, and finance sectors.

Petrochemicals

Malaysia is a medium-sized, non-OPEC oil exporter, producing high-grade crude oil, and liquefied natural gas (LNG). Approximately 80 percent of crude oil and condensates are exported, principally to Japan, Singapore and Korea, while 95 percent of LNG is exported to Japan. Petroleum exports (crude and LNG) accounted for approximately 22 percent of total Malaysian exports in 1989, a slight fall from the 27 percent share in 1984.

This sector is dominated by Petroleum Nasional Sdn Berhad (PETRONAS) and its subsidiaries. Under the Petroleum Development Act 1974, PETRONAS has full monopoly powers and privileges in the exploitation and development of on- and off-shore petroleum resources, which it manages through a system of up- and downstream licensing arrangements,[13] principally with foreign multinationals. A total of 22 upstream Production Sharing Contracts (PSC) are currently in force—mainly with Shell, Exxon, and BP.

PETRONAS is the single largest, and by far the most profitable, of the Malaysian SOEs, with a turnover in 1988 of RM6.7 billion and profits of RM3.8 billion. Moreover, the PETRONAS group as a whole (including Malaysia LNG Berhad) consists of 10 companies (4 of which are in the 20 largest SOEs) with a combined estimated annual turnover of RM12.6 billion, approximately 27 percent of total SOE sector turnover. PSCs and standardized international practices mean that, as well as being financially robust, PETRONAS is also an internally efficient domestic monopoly, which operates as a price-taker in international markets. Domestic financial performance is therefore determined principally by world market prices and, in particular, domestic exchange-rate management. PETRONAS has consequently remained outside the SOE reform ambit and, furthermore, in view of its strategic nature, it has not been considered in the privatization debate.

Manufacturing

Despite the paucity of hard data, survey and sample evidence suggests that manufacturing SOEs are, on the whole, less profitable and less efficient than their private-sector counterparts.[14] Poorer performance in the SOE sector is due principally to the standard catalogue of problems facing SOEs: poor project evaluation; pursuit of non-commercial objectives; weak, relatively passive management; and a persistent tendency to have weak capital structures. Evidence from the CICU on manufacturing SOEs suggests that SOE debt/equity ratios are consistently higher than those prevailing in the private sector.

Profitability in the manufacturing sector has been consistently and significantly lower in SOE operations. This low profitability, combined with high leverage brought about by erosion of the equity base and the accumulation of external debt (much of which was contracted to finance expansion during the early construction boom period of 1981–1982), has resulted in an extremely large number of unprofitable companies. Inappropriate capital structures are not the only problem, however, since, as the CICU notes, 87 percent of firms with negative net profits in 1989 also had negative operating profits, suggesting that the financial weakness in the sector is more fundamental than merely weak gearing.

Bumiputera Financial Institutions

State involvement in the financial sector in Malaysia is significant, more especially in terms of the specific functions undertaken by public-sector financial institutions rather than their actual share of the market. Whilst the vast majority of public-sector institutions operate relatively efficiently within a competitive environment, particular attention needs to be paid to the role of the Permodalan Nasional Berhad, which enjoys a unique position within the financial sector, and is central to the privatization process.

Early initiatives of the NEP in pursuit of equity participation targets involved direct compulsory share transfers to Bumiputera individuals and companies, the creation of the MARA unit trust and the Bumiputera Stock Exchange. However, in the face of persistent profit-taking on the part of recipients of equity (through the resale of equity to non-Bumiputeras), the government developed the concept of "ownership-in-trust" by establishing an investment trust dedicated to the Bumiputeras. This trust, the Yayasan Pelaburan Bumiputera (YPB), was established in January 1978, under a Board of Trustees chaired by the Prime Minister. In order to implement these objectives, YPB established the PNB in March 1978. PNB serves as the executive agency for YPB, evaluates, selects, and purchases shares in public and private-sector companies, and distributes selected shares to

Bumiputera individuals through the Amanah Saham Nasional (ASN) unit trust. The ASN was established by PNB in May 1979 as a subsidiary company to administer and market a unit trust scheme directed specifically towards equity participation amongst Bumiputera.

In January 1981, then Prime Minister, Hussein Onn, launched a "Scheme Transfer of Shares" held by government agencies to Bumiputera Individuals' through the PNB. This share transfer proceeds in two stages. First, shares in (profitable) SOEs are transferred to PNB at par value. Up to October 1986, the shares of 37 companies with a par value of RM1,300 million had been transferred to PNB, while data for March 1990 show that the equity of a total of 93 companies was by then held by PNB. The second stage involves the transfer of some of these shares to ASN, which then issues par-value units against the ASN share portfolio as a whole (which also includes other non-SOE equity). The relationship between ASN and PNB means that shares can be (and are) moved in and out of the ASN portfolio, since PNB directly manages the ASN portfolio, whilst ASN itself only manages a unit trust.

ASN is open only to Bumiputeras. Investments are denominated in RM1 units, with each unit holder allowed a maximum of RM49,900. Savings are mobilized through an extensive network of agencies, and take-up of units has been rapid and widespread: by 1982 there were over 1 million individual unit-holders, and by 1989, this had risen to 2.44 million (out of 12 million Bumiputeras), by which time the value of units outstanding was RM4.04 billion. It is now estimated that, in terms of unit holders, the ASN is one of the biggest unit trust schemes in the world. The popularity of the ASN owes much to the fact that it offers risk-free investment opportunities, whereby, in addition to enjoying generous tax exemptions on dividends and bonus shares (i.e. capital gains), all downside capital risk is effectively eliminated, since poor performing equities are removed from the unit by the PNB. Because of the attractiveness of the ASN, the fund almost reached saturation point in terms of membership. ASN was floated in early 1991, allowing the value of units to be directly market-determined. However, a second, 'lifeboat' fund, the Amanah Saham Bumiputera (ASB), has been created to fill ASN's role. The funding for ASB will again be from PNB companies, and it is expected that it will increasingly include shares from major privatization issues— most notably the STMB (TV3) and TNB issues.

These Bumiputera financial institutions currently play a major role in the economy, and this role is likely to expand as the privatization program proceeds. Their presence does, however, introduce distortions and anomalies into the capital markets. The most obvious distortion is the extent to which these institutions divert Bumiputera savings away from other (higher-risk) investment instruments through the cross-subsidization from other public resources. In addition, PNB's privileged access to all new issues[15] gives it a dominant role as shareholder, and it is a matter of debate whether this is beneficial to the efficient operation of the capital market. Thirdly, there is increasing concern among many of the SOEs that PNB has, through its CICU contract, a strategic advantage in acquiring commercial assets for its own portfolio at less than their market and/or social value. Finally, and perhaps most importantly in terms of the privatization program, there is concern that PNB's position as a major player in the capital market and as a key instrument of the NEP may lead to serious compromises in the management of privatization. Essentially, conflict arises when the argument for privatization on the grounds of improved efficiency through competition (i.e. the arguments being advanced for the privatization of telecommunications and electricity) conflict with the desire on the part of PNB to maintain the portfolio value through shareholding in enterprises earning monopoly profits.

Assessment of the SOE Sector

Only in the last few years has concern been raised about the overall performance of the SOE sector in Malaysia, in response to the realization that, as far as the NEP objectives are concerned, asset acquisition will engender changes in wealth distribution only if the value of these assets is maintained. Reflection over the first 20 years of the NEP seems to suggest that government intervention in the enterprise sector has, with a few exceptions when natural or other monopoly conditions prevailed, failed to maintain the value of assets appropriated for the Bumiputeras. Restoring the value of these assets (in terms of the income stream they generate) has thus become a priority.

One of the effects of the establishment of the CICU is that this fact has become obvious to government and the general public for the first time. The thrust of criticism has been directed more towards internal microeconomic weaknesses in the sector itself rather than the failure of the macroeconomic environment in which SOEs operate. Foremost among the concerns have been that, in many cases, management weaknesses exist, principally because of poor or non-existent shareholder discipline, arising from the fact that until the late 1980s, the government did not have even the most basic knowledge of the activities of the enterprises in which it was the major (or even sole) shareholder. Moreover, poorly designed incentive structures have created severe agency and accountability problems. These problems have been exacerbated by access to soft finances, leading to poor resource allocation decisions and frequent operational inflexibility.

The government's response to the need to enhance internal efficiency has been threefold: first, a marked change in the development expenditure program, with a switch away from using the SOE sector to implement development objectives; second, a direct attack on individual SOE enterprise performance; and, third, the privatization program itself.

The final three sections of this article attempt to marshal the available evidence on the issues of the private sector's ability to provide a conducive environment for competition and the realization of efficiency gains, the financial sector's capacity to mobilize savings for private-sector investment, and finally, the government's capacity to regulate private-sector monopolies effectively.

Private Sector Capacity

In general, the private sector in Malaysia is dynamic and relatively competitive. A liberal trade regime ensures that the domestic private sector is open to competition, even in the heavily regulated sectors such as petroleum. The development trajectory of the private sector has involved strong growth from the medium-scale enterprises serving both domestic and export markets. In addition, Malaysia has had an active policy towards foreign investment, and has been favorably placed to benefit from the growth of the other Asian NICs.

The private sector consists of three groups: the small enterprise sector, the medium- and large-scale domestic private sector, and the foreign private sector. Table 1.12 shows the size distribution in the manufacturing sector alone, which indicates the extent to which large firms dominate the sector. Firms with more than 200 employees account for 52 percent of total employment in manufacturing, 61 percent of total value-added, and 62.5 percent of fixed assets, while the small firm sector (i.e. employing fewer than 50 people) accounts for only 9 percent of sector value-added. In general, however, outside the import-substituting sector, industrial concentration is low, with most industrial sectors being relatively competitive. While this is in line with industrialization developments in other NICs, it is very different from the size distribution in many other countries, where there is a high level of industrial concentration, and is one important reason why, *ceteris paribus*, efficiency gains may be more likely to be forthcoming from privatization in the Malaysian context.

The small enterprise sector (which is dominated by Chinese-Malaysian firms) is constrained by economic structures elsewhere in the economy. Although, in general, the sector is efficient in production, it faces significant difficulties in creating linkages with the rest of the economy in the presence of domination by foreign and large-scale integrated operations and has consequently been in relative decline over recent years. The medium-scale, labor-intensive sector, on the other hand, is where Malaysia's comparative advantage in manufacturing currently seems to reside. Malaysia has progressively captured an increasing share of the manufacturing assembly market, and is a major assembler and exporter of electrical and electronic goods, measuring and scientific equipment, textiles, footwear, and clothing. Evidence suggests that these sectors are competitive (internationally) and, moreover, are not characterized by high levels of concentration and entry deterrence. In terms of privatization, it is noticeable that a large proportion of the SOEs covered by the UPSAK reforms and the Privatization Masterplan fall into this category. Again, this is in quite marked contrast to many other countries, where SOEs are often the dominant firm(s) in their sectors.

The relatively high degree of competition in the domestic economy is augmented by the effects of foreign competition. The average level of nominal tariff protection is relatively low in Malaysia compared to other countries in Southeast Asia and developing countries in general. Average nominal tariffs in

TABLE 1.12 Size and Structure of the Manufacturing Sector

Size by Employment	Total Employment ('000)			Number of Establishments (%)			Avg. Value of Output (RMm.)			Avg. Value of Assets (RMm.)		
	1978	1985	1991	1978	1985	1991	1978	1985	1991	1978	1985	1991
Below 50	–	78.5	81.6	66.3	64.0	50.5	12.6	9.5	5.5	11.7	7.8	5.3
50–99	–	69.6	103.3	16.3	17.0	19.7	13.6	10.3	8.2	14.2	8.8	7.2
100–199	–	87.2	152.7	8.7	11.1	15.2	18.5	17.0	13.7	17.8	14.8	13.8
200 and above	–	240.8	639.2	8.7	7.9	14.6	55.3	63.2	72.5	56.2	68.6	73.6

Source: Survey of Manufacturing Industries, Department of Statistics.

1985 were 14 percent compared to 23 percent for Indonesia, 22 percent for Korea, 28 percent for the Philippines, and 34 percent for Thailand (World Bank, 1989c). Tariff reform is currently under consideration, with the focus of attention being on the removal, in the first instance, of excessively distortionary effective protection rates. Combined with relatively free access and a non-distortionary exchange-control regime, competition within the Malaysian economy is thus not subject to extreme protectionism.

The Foreign Sector

In addition to competition through imports, foreign capital has historically played a major part in the Malaysian economy—indeed, to a significant degree, it was foreign participation which precipitated the NEP—and currently accounts for approximately 32 percent of total paid-up capital in the manufacturing sector (Ministry of Finance, 1989). A recent survey of foreign capital by the Malaysian Industrial Development Authority (MIDA), which serves as the central investment co-ordination office, suggests that the main growth sectors for foreign capital are petroleum, non-metallic mineral products, and electronics, accounting for 48 percent, 31 percent and 57 percent of the share capital in each subsector respectively. The bulk of foreign capital inflows originated in Taiwan, Japan, Singapore, and the USA. In terms of ownership, 60 percent of all approved investment since 1980 was in the form of joint ventures with Malaysian majority control. Up to 1986, only in about 10 percent of cases was there total foreign ownership, but following changes in 1986, which allow 100 percent foreign control when the company exports more than 80 percent of its products or when there are no suitable local partners, this share rose to 36 percent in 1988. A similar waiver was announced for foreign participation in privatization issues when no suitable Bumiputera buyer can be found (*Business Times*, 6 October 1990).

Subject to the constraints of the NEP, foreign participation is thus welcomed in Malaysia. Applications are considered by the Foreign Investment Committee (FIC), and are granted if: (i) the investment does not adversely affect control or ownership structures in the economy; (ii) it leads to benefits in terms of Bumiputera participation and employment; (iii) it has a positive effect on export earnings, diversification, and local resource use; and (iv) it does not have environmental or other strategic implications. These guidelines apply to any acquisition of Malaysian assets by foreign companies, any domestic acquisition which increases the foreign ownership share, and any joint venture or management contract which increases foreign control of the economy. This clearly covers privatization bids from foreign companies, although the FIC has granted a specific exemption to B-O-T contracts. Once FIC approval is granted, foreign investors face relatively light foreign-exchange restrictions. Free repatriation of capital and profits is permitted, and foreign-exchange accounts can be maintained in Malaysia. Furthermore, there are no foreign-exchange restrictions on non-resident portfolio investments.

Constraints to Competition in the Private Sector

Although measures of concentration and import penetration indicate that the private sector is relatively competitive, there are a number of constraints to its efficient functioning, most specifically, the system of industrial licensing managed by MIDA. Licenses are required for the import of capacity-enhancing (or labor-substituting) equipment and for the introduction of new products or processes. Licenses apply only to medium-scale companies and, despite substantial liberalization in recent years, have been identified as one of the main barriers to competition.

The licensing system is integral to the NEP, and a license is approved subject to the maintenance of NEP equity and employment criteria. Licenses are granted liberally and relatively quickly in cases where the Bumiputera participation criteria are met, and though the intention of the scheme does not seem to be to alter the supply process, the presence of the system is seen to impact on internal efficiency in a number of ways—other than in the most obvious sense of causing delays and increasing administrative costs. The general thrust of opposition to the scheme centres on the way in which the use of the licensing scheme to meet the goals of the NEP (Bumiputera equity participation and employment) creates efficiency loss by discriminating against projects able to exploit economies of scale and concentration through expansion. Similarly, the difficulty in finding Bumiputera investors prepared to supply sufficient capital to large-scale projects can lead to licenses not being issued, despite the fact that non-Bumiputera investors elsewhere may be prepared to absorb the commercial risk on the project. Finally, the licensing scheme acts as an additional barrier to entry for incumbent firms, denying contestability to markets, and permitting the continuation of monopolistic operations.

Conclusion

The evidence from the structure of the private sector seems to suggest that there is ample capacity within the sector to provide a competitive economic environment in which the efficiency gains from privatization are likely to emerge. The economy is relatively open to foreign competition and subject to low levels of protection. As a significant exporter of manufacturing goods—especially in the medium-scale assembly sector—economies of scale exist, yet barriers to entry are low. However, structural rigidities in the economy may preclude the attainment of higher levels of competition. Tight labor markets have led to an upward drift in real wages, and an erosion of unit labor competitiveness; the industrial licensing system reduces flexibility and permits an unwelcome degree of entry-deterrence in some sectors; and policy towards foreign participation is distorted by NEP considerations which may compromise the achievement of otherwise attainable levels of efficiency. Notwithstanding the above issues, however, the most fundamental problem facing the private sector is the low level of productive investment despite the high level of aggregate savings in the economy, which has been occasioned by the rigid interventionist nature of public sector savings institutions in the savings mobilization process. It is to this point that the discussion will now turn.

The Capital Market and Resource Mobilization
The Structure of the Capital Market

Malaysia has a large and well-developed equity market, regarded by many investors as one of the more dynamic emerging stock markets in the world (although it remains overshadowed by its NIC neighbors in Hong Kong, Taiwan, and Singapore).[16] It consists of two trading exchanges, the Kuala Lumpur Stock Exchange (KLSE) and the Bumiputera Stock Exchange (BSE), although the latter is virtually dormant.[17] The KLSE was established in 1973 following the dissolution of the Malaysian and Singapore Stock Exchange, and by the end of 1989, had an annual turnover in equities of RM18.5 billion (17 percent of GDP) and a market capitalization in excess of 150 percent of GDP (Table 1.13). The period has since the 1980s seen a significant upswing in activity on the market, especially through new issues (Table 1.14). There were 64 new issues (valued at RM4.4 billion) in 1984 alone, as the corporate sector shifted away from bank credit in response to the prevailing credit squeeze.

Secondary trade turnover has shown a similarly dramatic rise during the 1970s, with a peak of RM8 billion in 1981. Trading and market value fell back in the mid-1980s following the construction boom of 1982 and 1983, culminating in an emergency closure of the Exchange for three days in December 1985.[18] The market rallied in 1987, although it was not untouched by the 1987 worldwide stock market crash, when capitalization fell by approximately 36 percent in 14 days. The market remained intact, however, and since 1987, turnover has been buoyant. The KLSE is dominated by industrial shares (48 percent of total equity on the market), finance and property sector shares (approximately 15 percent each), with the remainder accounted for by commodity stocks (oil palm, tin, rubber). The major players on the market are nominee companies and other corporate bodies (including PNB) which hold almost 70 percent of total equity, although individuals still hold a relatively high proportion of stock (19 percent).

The KLSE is a relatively sophisticated market. It has 53 members, and in 1989, introduced a secondary trading board to encourage greater venture-capital participation. The market also deals in corporate bonds, and a secondary market in mortgage bonds has been developed by Cagamas, the national mortgage corporation. In addition, the Exchange has introduced a real-time computerized share price reporting system, and established research and surveillance systems to improve security.

Finally, one of the most significant features of the KLSE in recent years, and one which sets this market apart from many others, is the attraction of international portfolio investments. There are currently 49 country-funds investing in Malaysian stocks, including the IFC's Malaysia Fund Inc., which is listed on the New York

TABLE 1.13 Kuala Lumpur Stock Exchange, 1980–1992

	1980	1981	1982	1983	1984	1985	1986	1987	1988	1989	1990	1991	1992
Market Capitalization (RM billion)	27.5	34.3	32.3	53.3	47.1	39.4	39.2	46.1	63.1	107.5	131.7	161.3	246
Market Capitalization (US$ billion)	12.4	15.3	13.9	22.8	19.4	16.2	15.1	18.5	23.3	39.8	48.6	58.6	94.0
Capitalization as % of GDP	50.8	61.2	51.9	76.3	57.2	51.9	54.3	58.5	67.1	106.1	114.9	128.5	167.8
No. of Listed Companies	185	187	194	204	217	222	223	232	238	251	285[a]	324	369
Trading Value (RM million)	5,600	8,059	3,252	7,934	5,714	6,180	3,369	10,078	6,858	18,638	29,522	30,097	51,469
KLSE Composite Index	366.7	380.8	291.4	401.6	303.6	233.5	252.4	261.2	357.4	565.3	505.9	556	644

[a]The KLSE and the SES was split in 1990.
Source: IFC, Emerging Stock Markets Factbook.

TABLE 1.14 Malaysian Capital Markets: New Issues, 1961–1992

	1961–65	1966–70	1971–75	1976–80	1981–85	1986–87	1988	1989	1990	1991	1992
Ordinary Shares	124.9	276.2	291.9	618.9	5,470.9	1,579.4	2,931.2	2,508	8,649	4,392	9,181
Public Issues	107.5	115.3	101.1	77.4	929.1	343.1	169.0	1,316[b]	3,757	1,743	5,416
Private Placements	5.4	22.2	27.6	21.2	0.0	76.6	0.0	0.0	0.0	0.0	27
Rights Issues	12.0	138.7	163.2	387.3	3,234.8	937.2	668.0	1,145	4,419	2,158	3,438
Special Issues[a]	0.0	0.0	0.0	132.6	1,307.0	222.5	94.2	47	473	491	300
Bond Issues	0.0	0.0	0.0	20.0	0.0	325.0	1,909.0	2,143[c]	2,278[c]	1,841[c]	3,121[c]
Loan Stocks	14.5	9.0	57.3	0.0	579.0	70.0	36.3	0.0	0.0	0.0	0.0
MGS(net)	888.9	1,744.7	3,878.6	9,383.4	19,821.6	11,868.8	6,105.1	3,640	3,898	3,157	1,380
TOTAL	1,028.3	2,029.9	4,227.8	10,021.9	25,871.5	13,843.2	8,981.6	10,799	14,825	9,390	13,682

[a]Special share issues to Bumiputera institutions.
[b]Includes offers for sale.
[c]Net issues.
Source: Bank Negara Malaysia.

Stock Exchange with an initial capital of US$87 million. Such investment funds have, so far, been excluded from participation in the privatization program (as they have been from other primary issues), although the sale of equity in Telekom Malaysia includes a tranche (2.5 percent) reserved for foreign participation. This is to be effected through the sale of foreign-exchange bonds by the central bank which will be redeemable for Telekom Malaysia equity at an agreed rate, set 40 percent above the price at which Telekom Malaysia equity was sold on the domestic market.

Capital Market Regulation

Developments in the capital market have generally been shadowed by regular revision of regulatory structures for the industry. The over-arching regulatory framework is provided by the Securities Industry Act of 1973, and its successor of 1983. This Act provides legal authority to curb excessive speculation, insider trading, and other forms of share-rigging. It also includes provisions for licensing and regulation of dealers and for listing, and provides guidelines for the orderly functioning of the KLSE. In terms of listing and other matters, the 1973 Act provided for the Capital Issues Committee (CIC) to fulfill the role of overall market regulator. The 1983 revision to the Act, apart from updating a number of the technical provisions to reflect the changing technical environment of the financial sector, formalized the role of the CIC as principal market regulator. The CIC has its secretariat within the Ministry of Finance, and is responsible, *inter alia*, for price-setting for all new share issues (other than bonus issues), and the determination of listing requirements for the KLSE.[19]

The most controversial aspect of the CIC's activity lies in the issue of share pricing for new issues. The CIC is avowedly risk-averse in its pricing policy, and consequently, has a tendency to underprice new issues. It sets prices on the basis of pre-tax price/earnings (P/E) ratio guidelines. These cover a range from approximately 3.5 to 8.0 (the range for the financial sector is somewhat higher at 8-12). However, average market P/E ratios have been in the region of 30 (after the 1987 crash), and consequently, new share issues priced on the basis of CIC P/E guidelines tend to be heavily 'underpriced', oversubscribed, and return very high early trading premia on the secondary market.[20] Consistent underpricing is not a phenomenon exclusive to the KLSE, but a common feature of privatization sales by risk-averse governments. However, systematic underpricing can have other important public finance and social welfare implications, through an erosion of the public sector's net worth. This issue will be dealt with in later chapters.

Capital Market Absorptive Capacity

Estimates of the absorptive capacity of the capital market in any country are notoriously suspect, as they require an analysis not only of aggregate savings potential but also of the substitutability between savings instruments, on both a price and an institutional basis. Attempts have been made to assess the absorptive capacity of the equity market in anticipation of the Privatization Masterplan. The research attempting to assess the sustainable flow of new equity issues involves, in addition, an assessment of the structural limitations imposed on savings behavior, institutional restrictions in the economy, and, in particular, the role of the NEP-fostered institutions. A recent study has been conducted by the Arab-Malaysian Merchant Bank (AMMB), one of the merchant banks most closely associated with the privatization program in Malaysia.

As noted above, gross national savings in Malaysia are high—about 30 percent of GDP. However, a large proportion of this is accounted for by contractual savings, mainly channeled into government securities, the Employees Provident Fund alone accounting for approximately 25 percent of GDP. In addition, the presence of the PNB's ASN unit trust schemes means that Bumiputera household financial savings are currently being tapped extensively. On the other hand, the recent reduction in the overall budget deficit has reduced public expenditure substantially, and suggests that private-sector savings are increasingly being directed towards private-sector investment.

On the basis of this assessment of the levels of savings, the AMMB study concludes that there is excess demand in the capital market, that the market is supply-driven, and thus privatization will not crowd-out private investment. In 1989, net investment was RM2.4 billion (RM1.1 billion primary issues, RM1.3 billion rights, RM0.03 billion special Bumiputera issues), and it therefore estimates that the absorptive capacity is RM4 billion per year in the equity market at 1989 prices. AMMB stresses a number of provisos in this analysis, the main ones being that the institutional investors, and in particular the EPF, are becoming more active in equity trading, and that privatization issues become more affordable to small investors, through lower par value shares or smaller bundles.

One of the main problems with the AMMB study is that the figure of RM4 billion—cited as the annual absorptive capacity—has been determined, to a significant extent, by the high level of new issues in 1987. Furthermore, the main source of growth during that period was not in new issues *per se*, but rather in rights issues—i.e. the expansion of existing stocks. To extrapolate these volume measures forward abstracts from these price effects and, importantly, ignores the relative rate of return on other forms of investment. Table 1.15 compares the relative return from different instruments, and indicates clearly the volatility of direct risk-capital investment compared to government paper. Most striking, however, is the rate of return on PNB/ASN investments. As noted above, this high nominal rate/low-risk return can be maintained by PNB only if it can secure high-quality equity, can disintermediate risk away from the final equity holder, and can access monopoly rents.

On the basis of these comments, the AMMB estimate of absorptive capacity (for risk-capital investment) may seem on the high side. Even if it is reasonable, it remains low in comparison with the plans laid out in the Privatization Master-

TABLE 1.15 Nominal Rates of Return by Institution, 1981–1987 (%)

	1981	1982	1983	1984	1985	1986	1987
PNB/ASN	20.0	18.0	18.1	17.2	17.2	10.1	10.1
Employees Provident Fund	8.0	8.0	8.5	8.5	8.5	8.5	8.5
Commercial Bank Deposits	7.0	6.5	6.0	7.5	6.0	6.0	4.0
20-year Government Securities	–	–	–	8.6	8.6	8.6	7.6
KLSE Equity	13.9	-18.9	40.8	-19.3	-17.3	12.8	0.5
KLSE Equity (ex-dividend)	-4.6	-4.6	-3.0	-5.1	-5.5	-4.7	-4.7

Source: Treasury, *Economic Report*, PNB, EPF, and KLSE *Annual Reports*.

plan, especially in the proposals for the three large utilities, Telekom Malaysia, TNB and KTMB, which together could represent a public share issue of RM12–RM15 billion over a period of 2–3 years. If this is the case, then privatization issues may well crowd-out other private-sector issues, unless foreign capital and portfolio inflows are high. Moreover, as long as other capital-market instruments continue to pay relatively high rates, privatization equity will be taken up only if rates of return are kept high or, equivalently, issue prices are low. While the problems of underpricing have ready been discussed and are clear, maintaining dividend yields may have even more damaging effects on the privatization program. Many of the large SOEs planned for privatization are monopolistic, and dividends can be kept high for such companies only as long as monopoly pricing is maintained. If these monopoly profits are required to ensure that the capital market will absorb the issue, then the government immediately faces a conflict between the efficiency gains from greater competition and the continued transfer of wealth through the capital market. The evidence from the first phase of the privatization program would suggest that it has been the latter consideration which has predominated. However, efficiency considerations do figure in the debate, and it is to the regulation of enterprises in pursuit of efficiency gains that this discussion finally turns.

Regulation and Competition Policy

This last section discusses the regulation of private-sector commercial activities, and in particular the pricing decisions of privatized monopolies. Unfortunately, there is limited direct evidence on the government's thinking on, or capacity for, regulation prior to the privatization program. Regulation has generally been internalized within the government, with enabling legislation (for example, the Telecommunications Act, 1950) vesting all powers of control and regulation in a government department, while competition policy elsewhere in the economy has, not unsurprisingly, been overshadowed by the concerns of the NEP.

The Regulatory Tradition in Malaysia

Under the NEP, Malaysia is, in some aspects, a heavily regulated economy, and some evidence on the capacity for future market-based regulation of monopolies can be gleaned from the government's current regulation activity. However, this has generally been concerned with controlling market access in the case of the industrial sector, and with shaping asset-holding behavior in the case of the capital market. It is industrial regulation that will be considered here.

The approach to regulation in Malaysia is clarified in its *Rules and Regulations Regarding Acquisitions, Mergers and Take-Overs* which states that "the guidelines may be viewed as a means of restructuring the pattern of ownership and control of the corporate sector ... and to encourage those forms of private investment which contribute to the development of the country, consistent with the objectives of the NEP" (Ministry of Finance, 1989). This approach has resulted in a heavy emphasis on the form of corporate ownership, rather than on corporate performance *per se*, but whilst there is concern that the over-regulation of the economy—in pursuit of NEP objectives—has constrained growth and accentuated private-sector risk-aversion, the experience of recent decades suggests that regulation has been managed relatively judiciously. This is particularly so in the petroleum sector through the Petroleum Development Act, 1974, and in the financial sector through the Securities Industry Act, 1983, where the KLSE in particular and the capital market in general are regarded as accessible and well-managed markets.

It may also be noted that, outside the utilities and hydrocarbon sectors, the domestic economy is relatively competitive, and thus, the need for a re-evaluation of existing competition policy in the light of the privatization program is not as pressing. That there is a substantial capacity for regulation seems clear; whether the steps already taken point to the development of appropriate regulatory structures is less clear.

Notes

1. The New Economic Policy, introduced in 1970 in the aftermath of the post-election race riots of May 1969, was ostensibly intended to create the socio-economic conditions for national unity by reducing poverty and inter-ethnic differentials. However, it is generally seen as an ethnic-affirmative action program favoring the politically dominant Malays.

2. As discussed later, data on the public sector for periods earlier than 1985–1990 are sparse and many SOEs are not classified as public sector. These figures therefore tend to underestimate the true extent of public-sector activity.

3. One of the anomalies of this new program, which de-emphasizes the role of the state, is the stress put on the development of the Proton Saga car assembly plant as the jewel of the new industrial strategy. Proton was 70 percent government-owned through HICOM.

4. The New Economic Policy was issued by the Department of National Unity on 18 March 1970 as a directive to all government departments and agencies guiding their preparation of the Second Malaysia Plan.

5. Much of which has been picked up by the widespread business interests of the UMNO, the main Malaysian political party, and the majority member of the ruling coalition.

6. The holding agencies are organized under various Federal Ministries, the principal ones being the Ministry of Public Enterprises, the Prime Minister's Office, the Ministry of Primary Industries, and the Ministry of Regional Development. In addition, the Minister of Finance (Incorporated) holds equity directly in a small number of enterprises—in particular, those which have been partially privatized.

7. Although these 50 account for a major share of the sector on most economic criteria.

8. Zainal Aznam Yusof (1989) notes that "In the Malaysian story it seems fair to conclude that there was just not a very strong interest in arriving at an accurate estimate of the size of the public of private sector".

9. A value of 100 percent represents equal amounts of debt and equity capital in total long-term liabilities.

10. Which, as noted, captures financial data on only approximately 50 of the SOEs.

11. CICU data extend back to 1980, but cover only about 40 percent of the full SOE sample. Average enterprise performance indicators are applied to the full SOE sector (assumed to be 1,000 enterprises).

12. Where accumulated losses exceed paid-up capital.

13. Since 1981, downstream licensing has been the responsibility of the Ministry of Trade and Industry.

14. The World Bank (1989) finds average private-sector profit rates for manufacturing of approximately 6.6 percent and public-sector rates of only 1.9 percent over the 1981–1985 period.

15. In terms of the NEP, all new share issues on the KLSE must include a 30 percent tranche reserved for Bumiputera institutions.

16. The KLSE was the third largest of the IFC's 19 emerging equity markets worldwide by 1990.

17. The BSE was originally established as a share and unit trust company and became a functioning exchange in 1970. The BSE, which as its name suggests, quotes only Bumiputera-owned companies, is not covered by the Securities Industry Act, and is extremely small in comparison with the KLSE, trading in only eight companies, with a trading turnover of a little over RM150,000 in 1988. Attempts have been made to rejuvenate the Exchange, and, although the KLSE has made moves towards amalgamation, these have been rejected. It is consequently expected—within the financial community—that the BSE will gradually atrophy.

18. The Singapore exchange was also shut down at this time.

19. Main Board listing requires that a company has a 3–5 year profitable trading record, and a minimum capital of RM20 million. The Second Board, formally introduced in 1989, is geared to smaller, less mature companies, and therefore requires only a 2–3 year trading record, and a minimum capital of RM5 million. (up to a maximum of RM20 million). The Second Board is restricted to local companies, and listing fees are set at correspondingly lower rates than for the Main Board.

20. For example, the largest issue in 1989, by Southern Bank Berhad, was for 23.15 million shares at RM2.20 per share, raising RM50.93 million. Initial applications for the shares totalled RM1.27 billion, and at the end of the first five days of trade, the share was trading at RM4.50—a premium of 130 percent.

2

Overview

JOMO K. S.

The Malaysian government was among the first in the South to voluntarily climb on the privatization bandwagon, enthusiastically endorsed and promoted by the Bretton Woods institutions, particularly the World Bank. Less than two years after becoming Prime Minister in mid-1981, Mahathir Mohamad announced the Malaysian government's own commitment to privatization in 1983. Unlike the "Look East" policy and the "Malaysia Incorporated" concept—also associated with Mahathir's administration—which faded in significance by the mid-1980s, privatization achieved new vigor, especially after the appointment of Daim Zainuddin as Finance Minister in mid-1984 and the deepening economic crisis of 1985–86. To be sure, Mahathir's own commitment to private—rather than public—enterprise began much earlier, reflected in his *The Malay Dilemma* (1970) and especially his *Menghadapi Cabaran* (1976; published in English translation as *The Challenge* in the mid-1980s). His consistent commitment is all the more remarkable because of his two predecessors' commitment to public enterprise as the main vehicle for furthering national, and especially ethnic Malay communal business interests. Two years after Mahathir's first announcement in 1983, the Economic Planning Unit (EPU) of the Prime Minister's Department issued its *Guidelines on Privatization*, which remained the main official document on privatization until early 1991. In February 1991, the government published the *Privatization Masterplan* (*PMP*) document not long after the October 1990 general election, and just before announcing the rest of its post-New Economic Policy (NEP), or post-1990 economic policy. Hence, the *PMP* can be regarded as one of four major programmatic documents issued in 1991 outlining Malaysian economic development policy for the foreseeable future. Claiming success for its privatization program thus far, the *PMP* announced the government's intention to "expand and accelerate further the pace of privatization process" [*sic*].

From 1971, the Malay elite-dominated Malaysian government's New Economic Policy was officially committed to reducing poverty and inter-ethnic economic disparity, ostensibly to achieve national unity, understood primarily in terms of reduced inter-ethnic resentment. New statutory bodies, government corporations, government-owned or controlled publicly listed companies as well as government-owned or controlled private companies all became means to achieve government objectives, including—but not only—the NEP's corporate wealth redistribution target of increasing indigenous (Bumiputera) ownership share to 30 percent by 1990 from 2.4 percent in 1970. The NEP's Outline Perspective Plan for 1971–1990 also envisaged the creation of a Bumiputera commercial and industrial community (BCIC), while the Fourth Malaysia Plan for 1981–1985 expected Bumiputera "trust agencies" to account for 83 percent of Bumiputera share capital in 1990, i.e. only 17 percent—or 5.2 percent of total share capital—was to be held by Bumiputera individuals. By 1990, however, Bumiputera share capital[1] had risen to 20.3 percent of total share capital, with trust agencies accounting for 6.3 percent and individuals for 14.0 percent, i.e. 31 percent and 69 percent of the Bumiputera share respectively!

Generally, privatization has been defined in terms of the transfer of enterprise ownership from the public to the private sector. More generally, privatization—or denationalization—refers to changing the status of a business, service or industry from state, government or public to private ownership or control. The term sometimes also refers to the use of private contractors to provide services previously rendered by the public sector. Privatization can be strictly defined to include only cases of the sale of 100 percent or at least a majority share of a public enterprise, or its assets, to private shareholders. Full or complete privatization would therefore mean the complete transfer of ownership and control of a government enterprise or asset to the private sector. In Malaysia, such privatizations are not the norm, the most prominent cases involving the North-South Highway, Kumpulan Fima and Peremba.

In Malaysia therefore, the term "privatization" is often understood to include cases where less than half of the assets or shares of public enterprises are sold to private shareholders. In fact, privatization is usually understood to also include cases of partial divestiture where less than half of the assets or shares of public enterprises are sold to private shareholders, with the government retaining control through majority ownership. Before 1992, besides contracting-out, leasing and build-operate-transfer arrangements, privatization in Malaysia included nine official divestitures by the Economic Planning Unit and nine sales of relatively small enterprises by UPSAK, the Unit for Monitoring government Agencies and Enterprises, charged with reforming ailing public enterprises. Of the former, there have only been four full divestitures involving Sports Toto, Padang Terap Sugar Limited, the Security Printing Branch of the Government Printers and MAS, which was totally divested in early 1994. The other five—Kelang Container Terminal (KCT), Airod, Tradewinds, MISC, and Sarawak Cement Manufacturers—only involved partial divestiture with the government retaining control, even without majority ownership.

The definition of "privatization" in Malaysia is so broad that it includes cases where private enterprises are awarded licenses to participate in activities previously the exclusive preserve of the public sector, as in the case of television broadcasting from 1984. Contracting out of services, especially by municipal authorities, e.g. involving garbage disposal and parking, and private ownership or even contracted leasing of public properties, e.g. enabling the imposition of tolls on roads previously built by the Public Works Ministry or the Malaysian Highway Authority (Lembaga Lebuhraya Malaysia, or LLM), are also frequently equated with privatization.

In Malaysia, when a public enterprise, legally formed as a government department or statutory authority, is privatized, it necessarily first entails corporatization, or the formation of a limited company incorporated under the Companies Act, 1965. On the other hand, the privatization of a public enterprise which has been constituted as a limited company would merely entail a transfer in share ownership from the public to the private sector without any change in the legal form of the enterprise.

Trends

By the early 1980s, the generally lackluster performance of the Malaysian public sector, including many public enterprises, required a policy response. Various reasons have been advanced to explain the generally poor performance of public enterprises. In many instances, state-owned enterprises have been hampered by unclear or contradictory objectives. Similarly, performance criteria have been ambiguous. In Malaysia, the so-called "social"—usually ethnic redistributive, but sometimes also welfare—objectives were often invoked to circumvent profit, efficiency or other cost-effective criteria. Co-ordination problems have also been serious, especially with the different levels of government (federal, state, municipal, regional authorities, etc.) as well as inter-ministry and other intra-governmental rivalries. With the proliferation of such enterprises in Malaysia in the 1970s and early 1980s, many were assigned or developed similar, and often redundant, functions. Monitoring and evaluation of public enterprise performance was virtually non-existent until the mid-1980s, and continues to remain weak and superficial.

As the larger enterprises developed in size and clout, they often became less answerable to external monitoring, let alone supervision. The non-financial public enterprises (NFPEs)—previously known as the off-budget agencies (OBAs)—have proved especially problematic, especially as they were not subject to normal federal and state budgetary constraints. And even when public enterprises were subject to such constraints, the administrative and political circumstances often meant that they were only subject to "soft" budget constraints (Soenarno and Zainal 1985).

The key question here, however, should be whether such inefficiencies are necessarily characteristic of public ownership, and hence cannot be overcome except through privatization. If the record of Malaysian public enterprises is primarily due to the nature, interests and abilities of those in charge, rather than to the consequences of public ownership *per se*, then privatization in itself cannot and will not overcome the root problems. Also, while privatization may improve enterprise profitability for the private owners concerned, such changes may not necessarily benefit the public or consumers.

Since a significant portion of such activities are public monopolies, privatization will hand over such monopoly powers to private interests who are likely to use them to maximize profits. The privatization of public services tends to burden the people, especially if charges are raised for privatized services. Obviously, private interests are interested only in profitable or potentially profitable activities and enterprises. This may mean that the government will be left with unprofitable and less profitable activities—which, consequently, will worsen overall public-sector performance. Public sector inefficiencies and other problems need to be overcome, but privatization in Malaysia has primarily enriched the few with strong political connections to secure many of these profitable opportunities, while the public interest increasingly becomes sacrificed and vulnerable to the powers of private business interests. Some of the more well-known instances of such political patronage include the following:

The issue of the country's first and only private television broadcasting license in 1983 to Sistem Televisyen (Malaysia) Berhad (STMB/TV3), whose major shareholders then included the Fleet Group, UMNO's holding company, the UMNO-controlled Utusan newspaper publishing group, MIC's Maika Holdings, Daim Zainuddin himself, and the now bankrupt Syed Kechik group. Later, the then Daim-controlled New Straits Times group, previously held through Fleet and more recently by the Renong group, took control of the lucrative STMB/TV3 from the other main minority shareholders—before a management buy-out through the Malaysian Resources Corporation Berhad (MRCB) in early 1993—with not inconsiderable help from the Hong Leong group's Quek Leng Chan placed both STMB/TV3 and the NST group firmly in the camp of Finance Minister Anwar Ibrahim, which he effectively deployed to become UMNO Deputy President, Deputy Prime Minister, and clearly in line to succeed Mahathir as Prime Minister (Gomez, 1990, 1994).

In 1985, 70 percent of the potentially very lucrative Sports Toto was sold without any prior public announcement of its availability to the Vincent Tan-controlled B & B Enterprise Sdn Bhd (60 percent) and to Tunku Abdullah's Melewar Corporation (10 percent) at a very low price; while Vincent Tan was then reputedly very close to then newly-appointed Finance Minister Daim, Tunku Abdullah is well known to be a very close personal friend of Mahathir's for at least three decades (Gomez, 1990, 1994).

In September 1988, Big Sweep lottery operations were privatized to Pan Malaysian Sweeps Sdn Bhd, controlled by Ananda Krishnan, another close associate of Mahathir (*New Straits Times*, 16 February 1989). The license for the

Big Sweep lottery had been issued to the Selangor, Perak, and Penang Turf Clubs, which only sold lottery tickets to their members. Since Pan Malaysia Sweeps took over, tickets have been sold to the general public since February 1989. Big Sweep's more lucrative prizes adversely affected sales of the government Welfare Ministry's own Social Welfare Lottery, which was subsequently closed down by the government, ostensibly in line with its Islamization campaign.

In January 1989, the Totalizator Board of Malaysia, a statutory body which organized and regulated horse-racing totalizators since 1961, appointed Ananda Krishnan's Usaha Tegas Sdn Bhd to manage the Numbers Forecast Totalizator Operation (NFO), which had been managed by the turf clubs since 1988. The management of the NFO was undertaken by Usaha Tegas' wholly-owned subsidiary, Pan Malaysian Pools Sdn Bhd, incorporated in July 1988. The NFO operated two gaming activities—the "3-digit" operation, which commenced in 1961, and the "1+3" digit operation, introduced by Pan Malaysian Pools in September 1989 (*Malaysian Business*, 16 November 1991).

In 1987, the RM86 million Jalan Kuching/Jalan Kepong interchange project was contracted to a RM2 Bumiputera company, Seri Angkasa Sdn Bhd, set up by the family of Datuk Lim Ah Tam, and later 35 percent owned by Sri Alu Sdn Bhd, owned by Wahab Zainuddin, a brother of Daim, then the Finance Minister responsible for awarding such contracts, and Hassan Abas, who had worked with Daim in Peremba in the early 1980s. The entire project was sub-contracted to Mitsui Construction Co. from Japan and financed by a series of loans personally guaranteed by Wahab, Mohamed Amir Senawi, a nephew of Daim who became a director of Seri Angkasa, and their business associates. This lucrative "build-operate-transfer" (B-O-T) project enabled the Lim family to execute a reverse take-over of Kamunting Corporation, and eventually, the previously MCA-controlled Multi-Purpose Holdings, once the second largest company on the Kuala Lumpur Stock Exchange after the government-sponsored Permodalan Nasional Berhad (PNB) (see Jomo *et al.*, 1989; Gomez, 1992).

Also, in 1987, the government awarded the North-South Highway project on a similar B-O-T basis to United Engineers (Malaysia) Bhd (UEM), then an ailing public-listed company long suspended from trading on the Stock Exchange after an embarrassing construction (piling) scandal in Penang in the early 1980s, and with no previous experience in highway construction. UEM was by then majority-owned by an UMNO holding company, Hatibudi, on which the UMNO President, Deputy President, Secretary-General and Treasurer sat as trustees (*Asian Wall Street Journal*, 28 January 1988). The Prime Minister himself justified this privatization to an UMNO company on the grounds that the party needed funds to pay off the costs of building its massive new RM360 million party headquarters complex (*The Star*, 29 August 1987). After a public outcry, it was revealed, perhaps inadvertently, that UEM had not submitted the best offer in terms of cost to government (in terms of government-subsidized loans, government revenue guarantees, duration of the concession period, and government—including Malaysian Highway Authority—assets to be handed over) or to users (in terms of toll rates). Due to its inexperience and incapacity, UEM has been heavily dependent on its foreign partners—Mitsui and Co. (Japan), Taylor Woodrow International Ltd (UK), and Societe Francaise de Dragages et de Travaux Publics (France)— for which it pays a heavy price on terms undisclosed to the public, besides causing resentment among excluded sections of the Malaysian highway engineering community. UEM is also the beneficiary of several other privatized projects, including the Ministry of Health's pharmaceutical stores and services project and the lucrative second link to Singapore (see Jomo *et al.*, 1989; Gomez 1990, 1994).

UEM has also been the beneficiary of a number of other privatizations. In 1985, it was awarded the RM250 million contract to design the National Sports Complex near Kuala Lumpur (*Business Times*, 5 January 1987); UEM has also secured the RM400 million contract to build the National Sports Complex (*New Straits Times*, 20 May 1993). In 1987, UEM was awarded the RM47.5 million project management consultancy for the expansion of the gas processing plant and the export terminal in Terengganu under the Peninsular Gas Utilization (PGU) Phase II project (Lim Kit Siang, 1990). In February 1990, UEM secured a contract from the Penang State government to reclaim 392 hectares of foreshore land (*The Star*, 12 February 1990). In December 1990, UEM was given the project to construct the first phase of the RM1.671 billion second causeway between Malaysia and Singapore without any open bidding, ostensibly on a "first-come, first-served" basis (*New Straits Times*, 14 December 1990). In 1992, the Health Ministry announced that the government had hand-picked UEM to privatize the government's medical store, which handled around half a billion ringgit worth of pharmaceutical drugs annually (*The Star*, 10 January 1992).

In 1993, Indah Water Konsortium Sdn Bhd—a consortium of companies led by Vincent Tan's main listed vehicle, Berjaya Group Bhd, which has a controlling 20 percent stake—was awarded, without any tender process, the RM6 billion national sewerage project (*The Star*, 18 May 1993). However, it is generally believed that Berjaya and Indah are "fronting" for Northwest Water (M) Sdn Bhd, a subsidiary of the privatized British utilities company. The contract involves the privatization of "143 local water authorities throughout Malaysia to manage, operate and maintain the urban sewerage systems for 28 years" (*Malaysian Business*, 16 December 1993). "(C)omplaints of favoritism are underscored by Berjaya's relative lack of experience in public works. Although Berjaya is involved in small road-building projects in Malaysia, it has never built anything the size of the national sewerage project" (*Far Eastern Economic Review*, 1 April 1993).

In early 1994, the government announced the privatization of the RM15 billion Bakun hydroelectric dam project in Sarawak, which had previously been cancelled by the government in the late 1980s after protests by environmentalists and others doubting the technical and economic feasibility of the project. The contract was awarded, without tender, to Ekran Bhd, controlled by timber and construction tycoon, Ting Pek Khiing, a close associate of Prime Minister Mahathir, government Economic Adviser Daim and Sarawak Chief Minister Taib Mahmud (*Asian Wall Street Journal*, 2 February 1994). Other notable shareholders of Ekran include Robert Tan, a close associate of Daim, and Shuaib Lazim—closely associated with the Prime Minister—who had received and botched a privatized contract to develop a commercial center under Kuala Lumpur's Merdeka Square.

Shortly before the general elections in October 1990, it was suddenly announced that Food Industries of Malaysia Bhd (FIMA) and Peremba Bhd were being privatized through management buy-outs. The former went to Mohd. Razali Mohd. Rahman and Hassan Abas, both close associates of then Finance Minister Daim, while the latter went to Tan Sri Basir Ismail, reputedly very close to both Mahathir and, more recently, Daim as well.

Arguments

The Malaysian government summed up its five arguments for privatization in its *Guidelines on Privatization* (EPU, 1985). Firstly, it was supposed to reduce the "financial and administrative burden of the government," particularly in undertaking and maintaining services and infrastructure. Secondly, it was expected to "promote competition, improve efficiency and increase productivity" in the delivery of these services. Thirdly, privatization was expected to "stimulate private entrepreneurship and investment", and thus accelerate economic growth. Fourthly, it was expected to help reduce "the presence and size of the public sector, with its monopolistic tendencies and bureaucratic support." Fifthly, privatization was also expected to help achieve NEP objectives, "especially as Bumiputera entrepreneurship and presence have improved greatly since the early days of the NEP and they are therefore capable of taking up their share of the privatized services". To put it differently then, privatization was supposed to accelerate growth, improve efficiency and productivity, trim the public sector, reduce the government's financial and administrative role, and redistribute wealth to the Bumiputeras.

These arguments in favor of privatization have been refuted on the following grounds:

(a) The public sector can be more efficiently run, as has been demonstrated by some other public sectors, e.g. in Singapore (Rodan, 1989), Taiwan (Wade, 1990) and South Korea (Amsden, 1989). Also, privatization is not going to provide a miracle cure for all the problems (especially the inefficiencies) associated with the public sector, nor can private enterprise guarantee that the public interest is most effectively served by private interests taking over public-sector activities. Also, by diverting private-sector capital from productive new investments to buying over public-sector assets, economic growth would be retarded rather than encouraged.

(b) Greater public accountability and a more transparent public sector would ensure greater efficiency in achieving the public and national interest while limiting public-sector waste and borrowing.

(c) The government would be able to privatize only profitable or potentially profitable enterprises and activities because the private sector would be interested only in these.

(d) Privatization may postpone a fiscal crisis by temporarily reducing fiscal deficits, but it would not necessarily resolve it because the public-sector would lose income from the more profitable public-sector activities, and would be stuck with financing the unprofitable ones, which would undermine the potential for cross-subsidization within the public sector.

(e) Privatization tends to adversely affect the interests of the public-sector employees and the public, especially poorer consumers, which the public sector is more sensitive to.

(f) Privatization would give priority to profit maximization at the expense of social welfare and the public interest, except on the rare occasions when the former and the latter coincide; hence, for example, only profitable new services would be introduced, rather than services needed by the people, especially the poor and politically uninfluential.

(g) Privatization exercises in Malaysia may not even pretend to achieve their other alleged advantages and benefits by invoking NEP restructuring considerations, supposedly to increase Bumiputera wealth ownership and business opportunities. With increased Bumiputera competition, where prior collusion cannot be arranged, it seems that political influence and connections have become increasingly decisive.

(h) Public pressure to ensure equitable distribution of share ownership may inadvertently undermine pressures to improve corporate performance since each shareholder would then only have small equity stakes, and would therefore be unlikely to incur the high costs of monitoring management and corporate performance. However, if ownership is reconcentrated in the hands of state-owned or controlled enterprises—as seems to have been the case in Malaysia—then the exercise and transaction costs of privatization seem to be quite unnecessary.

Superficially, and according to several—usually ideologically set—criteria, privatization in Malaysia is making good progress, especially in terms of the government's own declared objectives. In terms of raising efficiency and productivity, it is generally agreed that the establishment of STMB/TV3 introduced some competition into the television broadcasting industry previously dominated by the government's two channels. After the privatization of the Kelang Container Terminal (KCT), average turn-around time per vessel fell from 11.7 to 8.9 hours while throughput rose from 244,120 TEUs (twenty-foot equivalent units) (1,113 ships) in 1985 to 273,335 TEUs (1,257 ships) in 1987. Since its corporatization in 1987, Telekom Malaysia has introduced several new services and improved existing services. Owing to its privatization, the Labuan Water Supply Project is said to have been completed ahead of schedule and at lower cost than suggested by the public-sector authorities (*New Straits Times*, 10 August 1989).

Privatization has also been credited with enhancing economic growth (Tan Chwee Huat 1991). Resources are said to have been released through efficiency gains for corporate expansion, although no evidence of this has been produced. Growth is also said to have been generated by allowing private entrepreneurship in sectors previously monopolized by the government. While this seems plausible, the examples of build-operate-transfer projects and licensed activities are less than convincing since they merely involve the private sector substituting for what the public sector would otherwise have undertaken at lower cost to users, as is clearly the case for the North-South Highway, for example (see Jomo *et al.*, 1989).

Privatization is also credited with having reduced the government's financial burden. According to the *PMP*, proceeds from the sale of government equity in privatized companies has generated RM1.18 billion, while the government is said to have saved more than RM8.2 billion in capital expenditure for infrastructural development through privatized B-O-T projects, and a further RM7.45 billion of the government's outstanding debt is said to have been transferred to the private sector (*New Straits Times*, 10 August 1989). With privatization, the government also now enjoys revenue from lease payments as well as corporate taxes. Moreover, with the availability of private loan financing arrangements from capital markets, demands on government finances have also been reduced. While these claims are valid, the apparently deliberate undervaluation of government assets—ostensibly to encourage and popularize the privatization policy—has greatly reduced the one-off revenues accruing from the sale of government assets as well as lease payments. One cannot and perhaps need not say much about corporate tax evasion. Also, it should be noted that corporate tax rates in Malaysia have been reduced across the board since the mid-1980s. But perhaps most importantly, this view ignores the important potential for cross-subsidization of socially desirable public works and other projects and programs with revenue from profitable ones. Privatization of the lucrative North-South Highway, for instance, means that toll revenues from it will not be available to subsidize the construction of rural roads and bridges since there is no mechanism established for the state to capture the rent from the former to subsidize the latter. The private capital market access argument ignores the fact that most of the non-financial public enterprises and even government development expenditure have been primarily financed from the private capital market, albeit with government-guaranteed loans in the former instance and government borrowings in the latter. On the contrary, it has been argued that the massive sale of government assets through privatization has resulted in considerable crowding-out of worthy investment options in favor of private acquisition of government stock, i.e. for the transfer, rather than the creation, of assets.

Privatization has undoubtedly deepened Malaysia's stock market very considerably. The public listing on the Kuala Lumpur Stock Exchange of the thirteen entities privatized by June 1992 raised market capitalization by RM201.09 billion, accounting for 28 percent of total capitalization and making the KLSE the largest stock market in Southeast Asia and the fourth largest in Asia (*Malaysian Business*, 16 August 1992; Investors Digest, November 1992). As of 25 February 1994, the 15 privatizations on the KLSE involved RM29.89 billion, or 22 percent of the KLSE's total market capitalization of RM117.33 billion (*New Straits Times*, 9 March 1994). However, it is moot whether the consequent deepening of the stock market is desirable in itself as the development of financial intermediation and instruments seems to have had a tendency of divorcing financial transactions from the real economy with all its casino-like consequences which contradict and threaten to undermine the equity financing objectives of stock market development. While privatization undoubtedly exerts heavy demands on private-sector financial resources to mobilize both debt and equity capital, it is not self-evident that deepening and broadening the Malaysian capital market are desirable in themselves. On the contrary, it has been suggested that with privatization, capital resources—which might otherwise have been invested into expanding productive capacity—have instead been diverted into acquiring or transferring existing public-sector assets.

In their detailed study of welfare improvements after partial divestiture, Jones and Fadil (1992c) claim efficiency gains of 53 percent in the case of KCT, 22 percent in the case of MAS, and 11 percent in the case of Sports Toto. In the case of KCT, the improvements came from (internal) management changes resulting in cost-efficiency gains. At MAS, (external) price competition and investment decisions have been credited with the improvements. Meanwhile, Sports Toto gained market share through improved marketing even before complete divestiture.

While the distribution of welfare consequences necessarily changes as a result of partial divestiture, firm behavior need not. Hence, partial divestiture may be merely cosmetic, e.g. to give the appearance of privatization without changing firm conduct. Advocates of partial divestiture claim, however, that the resulting mixed (public/private) enterprises ensure the best of both worlds, e.g. by introducing (private) pressures for greater efficiency while ensuring (public) accountability and interests. Critics emphasize that the result is the worst of both worlds, with the private pursuit of profits augmented by government privileges (regulation, licensing, credit, etc.).

Jones and Fadil (1992c) suggest that Malaysian partial divestiture emulates the recent Japanese trend, rather than British privatizations, which have tended to involve full divestiture. As with Singapore government ownership of mixed enterprises, recent Japanese partial divestitures—of telecommunications, the Japan National Railway, and the tobacco monopoly—have retained government control. They hint that such mixed enterprise is consistent with an ostensibly East Asian mode of intimate government involvement in business affairs, and is in line with Prime Minister Mahathir's "Look East" and "Malaysia Incorporated" policies.

The key question here is whether or not the ostensible efficiency and welfare gains from partial divestiture could have been achieved without such divestiture. For example, could such gains have been made through other means of ensuring greater autonomy, flexibility or managerial reform, such as through corporatization and commercialization? Jones and Fadil (1992c) admit that there is no necessary logical reason why this could not have been the case, but argue that this is irrelevant because they would not have been taken. The presence of private shareholders may also give the government the excuse it needs to do what it has wanted to do before, anyway. However, this does not negate the fact that the welfare gains they claim cannot be attributed to partial divestiture, or that there are policy alternatives to partial divestiture which have not been seriously considered by the authorities concerned. Their most compelling argument for partial divestiture is that the presence of private shareholders reduces the probability of reversal of efficiency-enhancing public enterprise reforms, e.g. with the change of government.

In most cases, supposed privatization has actually only involved partial divestment, with majority ownership, and hence ultimate control, still in the hands of the government, which remains the majority shareholder, as in the case of the Malaysian International Shipping Corporation (MISC). Even if the government share should decline to less than half, in preparing some enterprises for privatization, e.g. MAS and MISC, the government has created a "golden share", allowing it to retain control even with considerably diminished minority ownership.

In the case of MAS, in September 1985, a substantial minority (48 percent) of the company's shares was sold to the "private sector", of which the Brunei government held around 10 percent (*Malaysian Business*, 16 January 1994), raising only RM180 million from the sale of almost half the national airline. This, in itself, cannot be said to have led to any significant change in firm behavior which can be attributed to ownership divestment. A substantial amount of MAS stock was held by the central bank, Bank Negara Malaysia, giving the public sector as a whole continued majority ownership. Apparently, "the airline held weekly meetings with the government [at least] until [1990], even though it was privatized in 1985" (*Far Eastern Economic Review*, 20 December 1990). The government clearly continued to retain direct control over the company, first as the majority shareholder, and then as the single largest shareholder. Before 1993, MAS was in the black only because of the sale of some of its aircraft. For the financial year 1992/3, for example, although the airline had an operating loss of RM179.6 million, it was able to declare pre-tax profit of RM157.5 million due to revenue from aircraft sales worth RM337.1 million (*Malaysian Business*, 16 January 1994). After it became apparent that MAS could show a profit without having to sell any of its assets (*New Straits Times*, 28 February 1994), Malaysian Helicopter Services Berhad (MHS) acquired a 32 percent stake in MAS from Bank Negara for RM1.79 Billion, or RM8 per MAS share to be paid for "through an issue of 112 million new MHS shares of RM1 each at an issue price of RM16 a share"

(*Malaysian Business*, 16 January 1994). MHS—one fifth the size of MAS in terms of paid-up capital—is controlled by Tajuddin Ramli, a close associate of Economic Adviser to the government, Daim Zainuddin.

The government retains a 29 percent direct stake in MISC, 75 percent of Telekom Malaysia, 77 percent of Tenaga Nasional and 8 percent of Edaran Otomobil Nasional (EON), all of which still operate as virtual monopolies (*New Straits Times*, 8 February 1991; *Investors Digest*, November 1992). Such partial divestiture cannot really be considered privatization because the government's power to determine firm behavior is virtually unchanged, though, of course, firm behavior may change in response to the presence of minority owners, or to the presence of more minority owners than was previously the case.

Privatization has reduced the size of government bureaucracy in personnel terms as well. With corporatization and privatization, the number of public-sector personnel declined by at least 54,000 with their transfer to the private sector, according to the *Privatization Masterplan*. It has been argued, however, that the problems of public-sector personnel hiring, firing, promotion, and training remain, and possibly have been exacerbated with the New Remuneration Scheme (Sistem Saraan Baru or SSB) which took effect from early 1992. The perception and priority given to privatization, it has been argued, has contained and undermined much-needed public-sector reforms affecting personnel as in other areas.

It is believed that the predominance of Malays among public-sector employees, the presence of relatively large unions in the major public utilities earmarked for privatization, the virtual halt to public-sector employee recruitment since the post-election austerity drive from June 1982, and the virtual public- sector wage freeze since 1980 (despite considerable inflation, especially in the early 1980s) encouraged the government to ensure employment security for five years and better service terms and conditions as carrots to induce workers not to resist privatization.

Hence, though workers have the option of not joining the privatized entity, very few do so; the vast majority have yet another option of continuing with the government's scheme of service or accepting the new company's scheme, which the majority tend to pick. The impact of privatization on public-sector employees is studied by Kuppusamy in this volume, though it would also be interesting to look at the impact of privatization in consolidating labor market dualism between a primary labor market in the public sector and large private—including privatized— enterprises, and a secondary market of casualized, contract, female, immigrant, unskilled and less skilled or credentialed workers (see Siti Rohani, 1993).

While most affected public-sector employees used to feel threatened by privatization, many other Malaysians fed up with the waste, inefficiency, and corruption usually associated with the public sector have been indifferent to, if not supportive of, the policy. Many Malaysians also associate the growth of the public sector with increased state intervention and the ascendancy of Malay hegemony under the New Economic Policy (NEP), and see privatization as a desirable policy change that would reverse these trends, which have apparently discouraged private investment, and thus slowed down growth. Some others identify state intervention with socialism and support privatization as a measure to restore capitalist hegemony. While statist capitalism (Jomo, 1986) is not socialism, undermining the public sector, especially public services, by privatization has important adverse welfare implications for the people, especially public-sector employees, consumers, and the poor.

The government has had to legislate many changes to existing laws to facilitate privatization. However, the primary concern has been with overcoming legal obstacles to privatization. Little attention has gone to ensuring greater competition or public or consumer accountability, which are matters of considerable concern since many of the privatized entities remain virtual monopolies. Since the Malaysian government tacitly, and sometimes explicitly acknowledges that there is not much scope for increasing competition with natural monopolies, it promises an appropriate regulatory framework to protect consumer interests, particularly in terms of price, quality and availability of services, as well as "commercial freedom" for private monopolies. Implicit in this formulation is the acknowledgment that such regulation does not yet exist, and, if introduced, is unlikely to threaten enterprise autonomy.

Deregulation and other efforts to encourage competition are well behind those of privatization. While there has been a great deal of rhetoric about deregulation accompanying privatization, such efforts have been quite limited and mainly oriented to inducing foreign investments. And in many instances, especially with public utilities, the government has retained effective control despite changes in ownership. With corporatization and privatization of such utilities and services, the government has retained special rights through maintaining a "golden share", which basically guarantees it control over the privatized enterprise, ostensibly to enable it to exercise veto powers over decisions deemed to be of strategic and public significance. Such control suggests that there is only limited loosening of public-sector control through privatization. Privatization in itself involves only the transfer of property rights, and in many instances in Malaysia (e.g. the privatization of major public utilities and management buy-outs), management personnel have not even been significantly changed.

Improvements in management generally reflect management initiatives encouraged by increased enterprise and administrative autonomy as well as new incentive systems, i.e. changes which do not require privatization as a prerequisite, but can alternatively be achieved by greater decentralization, devolution, or administrative authority—long advocated by trade unions (e.g. see Mustapha Johan & Shamsulbahriah, 1987) and others in the public sector, which became increasingly centralized in the early 1980s with the Cabinet Committee Report on new salary structures for the public sector, chaired by then Deputy Prime Minister Mahathir, and the later centralization of authority over the public sector, in the Prime Minister's Department under Mahathir, especially through the strengthening of the Public Services Department (JPA). Also, the so-called Non-Financial Public Enterprises or Off-Budget Agencies were less subject to the Treasury's budgetary discipline, especially after then Finance Minister, Tengku Razaleigh Hamzah, challenged Mahathir's preferred candidate (Musa Hitam) for the ruling party's deputy leadership, and traditionally, the deputy prime ministership as well.

If one accepts the view that it is competition and enterprise reorganization— rather than mere changes in ownership status—which are likely to induce greater enterprise efficiency, then it becomes difficult to conclude that economic efficiency has been improved because of privatization in Malaysia. Some of the often exaggerated efficiency gains have been brought about by greater employee and managerial motivation with new incentive systems and greater scope for managerial initiatives with administrative autonomy, i.e. enterprise reform.

Privatization is also supposed to free market forces and encourage competition in the economy generally, especially in the sectors concerned. However, this is negated by the fact that potential beneficiaries have a common interest in getting the public sector to privatize services, which can be far more important. Not surprisingly, with the limited experience of privatization thus far, there is already widespread concern about and even evidence of:

— the existence of formal and informal collusion, e.g. cartel-like agreements.
— possible patterns in bidding for contracts, suggesting collusion among bidders.
— some companies enjoying special influence and privileged information, and thus are consistently able to bid successfully for profitable opportunities from privatization.

While privatization undoubtedly reduces the role of the public sector in the economy, it is not clear whether this should be an end in itself or merely the means to an end. If the former, then the policy is essentially either intended to aggrandize its politically influential beneficiaries, or clearly ideological in inspiration, or else meant to please the ideologically motivated governments and powerful international economic institutions (such as the World Bank and the Asian Development Bank) the Malaysian government seeks to find favor with. There is evidence that all three factors may be operative in the Malaysian case.

Advocates of privatization in Malaysia also claim that it will reduce the government's financial and administrative burden. While there undoubtedly are one-off revenues for the government from the sale of public assets, it is not self-evident that the retention of such assets would not have been in the government's and the public's medium- and long-term interest for a variety of reasons mentioned above. Perhaps most importantly, the considerable evidence of heavy discounting in asset prices for sale or lease suggests otherwise. Also, the sale of the government's most valuable assets, while it is obliged to retain those less profitable activities and assets of little interest to the profit-seeking private sector, contributes to the self-fulfilling prophecy of the unprofitability of public-sector economic activities. The diminution of the public sector also reduces the scope for government intervention, e.g. for equity reasons or in support of industrial policy.

The Malaysian government's claim that privatization contributes to growth is vague and even spurious. After the announcement of the policy in 1983, Malaysia went through a deep recession in 1985-1986, before experiencing rapid export-oriented manufacturing-led growth since the late 1980s. Although the mid-1980s recession was exacerbated by the deflationary consequences of public spending cuts, which can be analytically distinguished from privatization *per se*, there is also no clear evidence that privatization in particular has significantly contributed to recent economic growth. No claim has yet been made that privatization is a necessary and indispensable ingredient for the broader economic liberalization measures of the mid-1980s which probably induced the foreign investment increase associated with the recent boom. On the contrary, however, it may be argued that private acquisition of public assets has probably diverted potential investment funds, while it is now generally agreed that the stock market—undoubtedly expanded by privatization—has not been important for corporate financing of the dynamic foreign-dominated manufacturing sector.

Some other adverse consequences of privatization to be considered include:

— increased "costs" to the public of reduced, inferior or costlier services, e.g. the unit charge for local telephone calls was increased by 30 percent just before Telekom Malaysia was incorporated.
— the implications of two sets of services, i.e. one for those who can afford privatized services and the other for those who cannot, and hence have to continue to rely on public services, e.g. medical services and education.
— the effects of minimal investments by private contractors concerned with short-term profits.
— increased costs of living and poorer services and utilities especially in remote and rural areas—due to "economic costing" of services, e.g. telephone, water supply and electricity.
— reduced jobs, overtime work, and real wages for employees of privatized concerns.
— the deflationary consequences of fewer jobs or lower wages, or both.

In terms of the government's own stated objectives for the policy, it appears that privatization in Malaysia has probably been most successful in contributing to the government's NEP objective, particularly Bumiputera wealth acquisition. One might even argue that the prioritization of this objective has probably seriously undermined achievement of the other stated aims of its privatization policy. However, it is unclear how the creation and distribution of substantial economic rents through ethnically-biased privatization has been in the national interest, whether this is understood in developmentalist or equity terms. There is now official acknowledgment that most of these rents have not been efficiently deployed through productive investments to accelerate industrialization significantly or to consolidate genuine Bumiputera entrepreneurship. Instead, much has been wasted on rent-seeking costs associated with political involvement in business, while the very source of such rents and the limited abilities of those who control them has contributed to their deployment in real property, construction, finance and other investments with a short-term time horizon, thus adversely affecting investment priorities and activities generally in an economy officially committed to sustained manufacturing-led growth. The foregoing analysis also implies that privatization is unlikely to enhance the NEP's other equity objectives (inter-ethnic parity in occupational and employment distribution, and poverty reduction), and may instead undermine public welfare as a result of the strengthening of private monopolistic interests.

In many cases of privatization in Malaysia, it is popularly believed that there are strong influences from private interests who try to determine what is to be privatized, in what manner and to whom. For example, Sapura Holdings commissioned a consultancy report by Arthur D. Little of Boston entitled "The Advantages and Feasibility of Privatizing Jabatan Telekom Malaysia" in 1983 for the attention of the Malaysian government; with the benefit of hindsight, it is generally acknowledged that Sapura is undoubtedly the main beneficiary of the privatization of telecommunications in Malaysia (Kennedy, 1991).

Often, privatization in Malaysia has not even involved the formalities of an open tender system, as sanctioned by the official "first come, first served" policy by which the government justified awarding privatization opportunities to those who have supposedly first proposed the privatization of a government property or activity. Instead, many beneficiaries are believed to have been chosen on the basis of political and personal connections.

For example, in 1986, it was announced that RM1.4 billion worth of water supply projects involving 174 schemes had been awarded to Antah Biwater without open tender. Though hailed as the nation's first privatized water supply project, it does not seem to involve significantly more than awarding all such construction contracts to a foreign company and—its politically well-connected local partner with no previous relevant experience—as the government will remain responsible for the operation and maintenance of the schemes. Antah Biwater— which is 51 percent owned by the Negeri Sembilan royal family's Antah Holdings Bhd and 49 percent owned by the British water supply and treatment group, Biwater Ltd—had in fact secured a turnkey contract with a British government financing arrangement thrown in as part of an aid for trade project (ATP). Most of the design and engineering work has been and will be handled by Biwater— since Antah has no relevant engineering experience—at the expense of Malaysian engineers and consultants who have long handled such projects.

In December 1986, the Malaysian parliament passed amendments to the Official Secrets Act (OSA) which extended the definition of official secrets to include, among other things, government tender documents (even after completion of the tender exercise) and any other documents or material which ministers and public officials may arbitrarily deem secret or confidential. The classification of a document or other material as an official secret cannot be challenged in any court of law, while the amendments impose a mandatory minimum one year jail sentence for any OSA offence. Such legislation, accompanying the privatization drive, further limits the already limited scope for meaningful governmental transparency and public accountability.

In the increasingly authoritarian and centralized Malaysian polity, with public accountability and governmental transparency considerably diminished deliberately by those in power, the strengthening of private business interests, especially of those who are politically well connected, is very likely to transform, and even increase, rather than eliminate the opportunities for rent appropriation. Ironically, the remaining democratic features of the system in such a context may well serve to sustain rent-seeking behavior and costs. This is not intended to legitimize further authoritarianism to reduce such waste. Rather, it serves to emphasize that enhanced public accountability, governmental transparency and other democratic safeguards are crucial for reducing rents—which can be productively deployed—and, more importantly, rent-seeking behavior in the context of privatization.

Malaysia's experience thus far suggests that the government-revenue-generating, government-deficit-reducing, private-sector-control-increasing and capital-market-deepening official objectives of Malaysian privatization have largely been subordinated to the ostensibly Malay-wealth-enhancing objective through rent redeployment, particularly to the politically well-connected. The privatization policy's multifarious objectives undoubtedly require various trade-offs, but the apparently consistent bias suggests serious abuse for the purposes of political patronage and personal aggrandizement at the expense of the other objectives of privatization, ostensibly in the national interest.

There should instead be a comprehensive critical review of the public sector, including the statutory bodies and other public enterprises, with a view to reform to enhance efficiency, cost-effectiveness as well as dynamic, equitable, balanced, and sustainable national economic development. After all, many public enterprises were set up precisely because the private sector was said to be unable or unwilling to provide the services or produce the goods concerned. Such arguments may still be relevant in some cases, no longer relevant in other cases, and perhaps never even true or relevant in yet other cases. And regardless of the validity of the rationale for their establishment in the first place, many public enterprises have turned out to be problematic—often inefficient, frequently even failing to achieve their own original declared objectives or abused by those who control them for their own ends, and draining scarce public resources due to their "soft budget constraints" and the very inertia of their existence.

But privatization is certainly not the universal panacea to the myriad problems of the public sector it is often touted to be. Privatization may be no more of a solution to the problems of public enterprises than the public enterprises have been a solution to the problems they were set up to overcome. In many instances, the problem of public enterprise is not a problem of ownership *per se*, but rather due to the absence of explicit, feasible or achievable objectives, or even to the existence of too many, often contradictory goals. In other cases, the absence of managerial and organizational systems (e.g. flexibility, autonomy) and cultures supportive of and encouraging fulfillment of these goals and objectives may be the key problem. Privatization may facilitate the achievement of such organizational goals or objectives with the changes it may bring about in train, but this does not necessarily mean that the fact of privatization is responsible for the improvements concerned. In such cases, managerial and organizational reforms may well achieve the same objectives and goals, or even do better, at reduced cost to the state or consumer interests than the privatization option; in other cases, privatization may well be the superior option. However, the better option cannot be determined *a priori*, but should instead be the outcome of careful study of the roots of an organization's malaise.

Such a critical review with a view towards reform should consider the variety of modes of privatization, marketization and other reform measures as options in dealing with the public sector as it has evolved in Malaysia. With such an approach, privatization becomes one among several options available to the government for dealing with the undoubted malaise of the Malaysian public sector. This flexible approach seems superior to the current narrow and dogmatic approach which apparently views privatization as the only—and presumably best—solution to a complex variety of problems faced by the Malaysian public sector.

The existing approach also tends to neglect the persistent problems faced by the rest of the public sector not targeted for privatization, which may in fact require more urgent attention. Ironically, their problems are probably the most serious—and hence in greater need of remedy—which may explain the lack of private-sector interest in privatizing them. Furthermore, if privatization succeeds in selling off the sector's most profitable enterprises and activities, the public sector will be left with uneconomic, unprofitable, and unattractive enterprises and activities, thus only confirming prejudices and charges of public-sector incompetence and inefficiency, besides worsening the public-sector deficit with the reduction of possibilities for cross-subsidization.

Unfortunately, however, there does not seem to have been any significant progress in checking the various problems which have emerged from the privatization process thus far and in avoiding them in future privatizations. The entire privatization process itself seems to be beyond accountability, and the lack of transparency hampers the few who might feel inclined to blow the whistle. The significant increases in consumer prices for privatized or soon-to-be privatized utilities, services and infrastructure have been reluctantly accepted by consumers without much public dissent, except in the case of the Cheras tolls just before the 1990 general election. The staggered nature of such price increases as well as of the privatizations themselves renders mass protest against privatization most unlikely. Nevertheless, however, when the cumulative effects of these privatizations are finally realized at the public level, it is quite possible that the political consequences may undermine the mandate to rule of those responsible.

In contrast to privatization, which essentially involves only property rights, the broader concept of marketization—sometimes termed "commercialization", or sometimes even more ambiguously, "economic liberalization"—is understood not only to entail denationalization, but also market liberalization, involving greater competition. Privatization is then expected to be accompanied by the relaxation or abolition of monopolistic practices, including statutory monopoly powers, such as those usually conferred on and enjoyed by public utilities. Privatized entities are thus expected to find themselves in competitive markets or environments.

Competition generally encourages more efficient behavior among private— as well as public—entities or companies, in order to achieve both productive and allocative efficiencies. Enhanced efficiency is therefore conceived of as the result of the interaction between private ownership and the competitive environment. Hence, a privatization exercise which merely involves selling a portion, even a majority, of the shares of a public enterprise to the public, but is not accompanied by greater exposure to market forces, may not bring about desired efficiency improvements. Conversely, efficiency gains may be achieved through other changes, e.g. management reforms, without any changes in ownership. Even improvements in capital resource allocation may be achieved by eliminating soft budget constraints typically identified with, but not a necessary characteristic of, public sectors—and strengthening management accountability, e.g. through greater organizational transparency.

In the case of Malaysia, therefore, desired improvements in efficiency may not be achieved through privatization, since there has been little evidence of increased competition associated with privatization. Some of the selected enterprises already privatized or expected to be privatized are natural monopolies. Thus, if privatization merely involves transforming a public monopoly into a private monopoly, consumer welfare may well be adversely affected. In such circumstances, even greater enterprise efficiency may not necessarily enhance consumer welfare, but only the monopoly profits accruing to the privatized enterprise.

To evaluate the impact of privatization on the economic performance of an enterprise is not easy. In the case of Malaysia, there is some uneven evidence suggesting improvements in various aspects of some firm performances following privatization. The problem here is that such improved performance may be wrongly attributed to changes in ownership *per se*, without any conclusive evidence of such causation. Efficiency gains, for instance, may well be due to other changes coinciding with, but not caused by, the change in ownership considered to be privatization.

Note

1. However, it should also be pointed out that various criticisms have been made about official share distribution data. Besides the valuation problem raised by using nominal or par values—which, it is claimed, especially underestimates the market value of Bumiputera corporate wealth—and underestimation owing to the use of nominee companies, the Malaysian government has not explained how share capital owned directly by the government and other bodies—such as Bank Negara Malaysia (the central bank) or the Employees Provident Fund—is categorized.

PART ONE

Macropolicy Perspectives

3

Public Enterprises

RUGAYAH MOHAMED

By 1957, the year of independence, there were already 29 public enterprises in Peninsular Malaysia. In the next twelve years up to 1969, 54 more public enterprises were established, and in the following four years (1969–1972), 67 new public enterprises were set up. Between 1972 and the early 1980s, the establishment of public enterprises gained greater momentum as such enterprises proliferated in Malaysia. The historical evidence of a rapidly growing public sector raises the question of why public enterprises grew so much and proliferated in the country.

With the First (1956–1960) and Second (1961–1965) Five-Year Development Plans and the First Malaysia Plan (1966–1970), the government's strategy of development was to undertake rural development directly, to develop the infrastructure of the economy, and generally to leave the development of commerce and industry to private enterprise. This development strategy was increasingly considered unacceptable by many, especially among Malays, from the mid-1960s, and particularly after the suspension of parliament from May 1969 in the aftermath of the post-election racial riots.

Extensive use of public enterprises to overcome various socio-economic problems attributed to market failure and inequity suddenly became the new orthodoxy. Public enterprise was recommended as the vehicle for industrialization (Wheelwright, 1965: 110) to ensure manufacturing growth was evenly distributed across ethnic lines. Wheelwright argued that the Malayan Government's commitment to private free enterprise had rendered it hesitant to initiate public enterprises for this purpose. He pointed out that this need not be an obstacle, as public enterprises can, after pioneering industrial development, be sold off to private enterprise (Wheelwright, 1965: 113).

With increasing pressure from the Malay public for greater efforts to overcome ethnic economic imbalances in the Second Economic Congress of the Indigenous People in September 1968, the general election of May 1969 and the shift in power within the ruling UMNO after that, the Government expanded the public sector. This became expressed government policy through the New Economic Policy, enunciated in 1971 and incorporated into the Second Malaysia Plan (1971–1975).

Besides their traditional role in providing public utilities and infrastructure, the expansion of public enterprises in Malaysia since the 1970s has mainly been aimed at addressing ethnic economic imbalances. Public enterprises have been explicitly used for the purpose of redistributing asset ownership and employment in favor of Malaysian indigenous citizens. This policy was adopted when "less direct methods of state intervention" apparently failed to produce the desired results (Mallon, 1982).

The 1970s saw an accelerated increase in the public sector role in the economy, but the continued importance of the private sector was still stressed. At this time, the government-in-business strategy, involving the government as owner of business enterprises, was adopted (see Malaysia, 1971; 1976). The role of public enterprises became more pronounced after the launching of the Second Malaysia Plan (1971–1975) and the New Economic Policy (NEP) with an Outline Perspective Plan for 1971–1990. Their increasing importance was due to their envisaged role in reducing the inter-racial economic differences in the country. It was thought that the NEP's ownership and employment redistribution targets could not be attained if exclusive reliance was placed on the private sector, including the then minuscule Malay-owned private businesses. In the name of the NEP, the public sector ventured into commercial and industrial enterprises.

The "government-in-business" strategy was implemented through government participation in the establishment of enterprises, and was manifested in three main forms: first, by establishing new companies with the government as sole owner; second, by setting up joint-venture companies with private entrepreneurs as part-owners; and third, by buying a proportion of publicly-traded shares of existing companies.

With its commitment to the NEP objectives, the Government became directly involved in many economic activities, with equity participation ranging all the way up to 100 percent seeking to establish industrial activities in selected new areas, often involving long gestation periods before profits could be reaped. The advantages accruing from greater spatial dispersal of industries were not attractive enough for private enterprises. Such private-sector aversion prompted the government to play a more active role in the establishment and operation of such industrial enterprises. Right up to the mid-1980s, the Government continued to invest in various new economic activities. However, in the early 1980s, it prioritized investing in capital-intensive heavy industries.

Under the NEP, there was a rapid growth of public-sector employment during the 1970s and early 1980s. As shown in Table 3.1, the total number of employees in the public sector grew by an average of 5.5 percent in the 1970–1975 period. Initially, the growth of public-sector employment in 1970 and 1971 was primarily due to the absorption of previously temporary staff into permanent positions

TABLE 3.1 Public Sector Employment in Malaysia, 1970–1991 ('000)

Year	Total employment	Government employment	Govt. % of total employment	% Change in govt. emplymt.
1970	3340	398	11.9	
1971	3467	420	12.1	5.5
1972	3599	443	12.3	5.5
1973	3735	467	12.5	5.4
1974	3877	493	12.7	5.6
1975	4020	520	12.9	5.5
1976	4177	577	13.8	11.0
1977	4340	582	13.4	0.9
1978	4486	596	13.3	2.4
1979	4700	622	13.2	4.4
1980	4817	692	14.4	11.3
1981	5031	757	15.0	9.4
1982	5165	765	14.8	1.1
1983	5429	804	14.8	5.1
1984	5565	811	14.6	0.9
1985	5625	820	14.6	1.1
1986	5907	829	14.5	1.1
1987	5881	836	14.2	0.8
1988	6088	844	13.9	1.0
1989	6351	847	13.3	0.4
1990	6603	850	12.9	0.4
1991	6840	854	12.5	0.5

Sources: Treasury, *Economic Report* (various years); Ismail Salleh and Osman Rani (1991).

(Ismail Salleh and Osman Rani, 1991). During 1975–1980, public-sector employment increased further by an average of 6 percent per year. Public-sector employment increased to a high of 11 percent in 1976 due to the implementation of the Harun Commission Report, which recommended that all employees of statutory bodies and local governments be included in the public sector on a permanent basis. As a per-centage of total employment, public-sector employment grew from 12 percent in the early 1970s to a peak of 15 percent in 1981, after the employment-creating "Operasi Isi Penuh" (Fill Vacancies Operation) as part of the counter-cyclical expansionary fiscal strategy of the early 1980s, before declining to 12.5 percent by 1991.

TABLE 3.2 Number of Public-Sector Enterprises

Industry	1960	1965	1970	1975	1980	1985	1992
Agriculture	4	5	10	38	83	127	146
Building and Construction	2	9	9	33	65	121	121
Extractive Industries	0	1	3	6	25	30	32
Finance	3	9	17	50	78	116	137
Manufacturing	5	11	40	132	212	289	315
Services	3	6	13	76	148	258	321
Transport	5	13	17	27	45	63	68
Others	0	0	0	0	0	6	9
TOTAL	22	54	109	362	656	1,014	1,149

Sources: Ismail Salleh and Osman Rani (1961); *Economic Report, 1992/1993*.

By 1979, the Government had shares in 557 companies. All but ten were private limited companies, i.e. their shares were not traded on the Stock Exchange. Table 3.2 shows that the biggest number of public enterprises was found in the manufacturing and services sectors.

The government's financial allocation for such investments has been large. For instance, in the 1966–1970 period, total development expenditure allocated to all public enterprises amounted to RM1.4 billion, or about 32 percent of the total development expenditure allocation. This increased to RM3.9 billion, or about 40 percent of the allocation, during the 1971–1975 period. Additional revenue from newly found oil and inflation in the 1976–1980 period raised development allocations to RM12 billion, or 48 percent of the allocation. In the 1981–1985 period, the allocations more than doubled to RM27.7 billion, or about 56 percent of the total development budget (Supian, 1987: 121).

During the prolonged global recession of the early 1980s, the decline in commodity prices resulted in Malaysia's terms of trade deteriorating by about 17 percent, causing sizeable deficits in the current account of the balance of payments. With interest rates rising globally, continued foreign borrowings would have been an increasingly expensive way to sustain the growing public investments. Total investments reached a substantial 36 percent of GNP between 1981 and 1985, with public investments accounting for almost half, or about 17.5 percent (see Table 3.3). High operating costs resulted in substantial deficits in the government budget (rising from RM120 million in 1981 to RM3.5 billion in 1987). Gross national savings, however, were only 28.0 percent of GNP in 1991. As a result, foreign borrowings grew rapidly, and by 1986, the country's external debt was

TABLE 3.3 GNP Shares (in current prices), 1970–1991 (percentages)

Year	Consumption			Investment		
	Public	Private	Total	Public	Private	Total
1970	16.4	61.6	78.0	5.7	12.0	17.7
1971	17.9	64.5	82.4	6.8	13.4	20.2
1972	20.4	61.4	81.8	9.6	13.0	22.6
1973	16.2	57.1	73.3	7.0	16.4	23.4
1974	16.1	58.4	74.5	7.5	19.0	26.5
1975	18.2	60.6	78.8	9.8	16.2	26.0
1976	15.9	54.5	70.4	9.3	13.7	23.0
1977	17.3	54.1	71.4	9.9	14.1	24.0
1978	16.8	54.1	70.9	9.4	16.5	25.9
1979	14.6	50.5	65.1	9.3	18.3	27.6
1980	17.1	52.4	69.5	12.1	20.2	32.3
1981	18.7	55.0	73.7	16.7	20.6	37.3
1982	19.2	55.7	74.9	19.1	19.0	38.1
1983	16.8	55.6	72.4	20.5	17.9	38.4
1984	15.8	53.4	69.2	16.2	18.0	34.2
1985	16.5	56.0	72.5	15.1	17.1	32.2
1986	18.2	54.6	72.8	12.9	15.3	28.2
1987	16.4	50.5	66.9	9.7	14.7	24.4
1988	15.2	52.3	67.5	9.3	16.3	25.6
1989	14.8	55.4	70.2	11.6	19.8	31.4
1990	14.2	56.6	70.8	12.1	22.1	34.2
1991	15.0	57.7	72.7	12.7	24.4	37.1

Sources: Malaysia, Ministry of Finance, *Economic Report* (various years) and *Sixth Malaysia Plan, 1991–95.*

RM50.7 billion, equivalent to 76 percent of GNP, of which the public debt component (including government-guaranteed borrowings) accounted for 86 percent (Jomo, 1990). However, by 1991, external debt had fallen to RM43.8 billion. Although the government switched from an expansionary to a contractionary public spending policy in mid-1982, recovery prospects were clouded by the failure of projected increases in private-sector investment to materialize. In 1986 and 1987, private investments rose to RM7.2 billion and RM8.2 billion respectively, compared to the average of RM12 million per annum over 1981–1985 (*Bank Negara Annual Report, 1988*).

The financing of public enterprises came largely from the Federal Treasury,[1] sometimes channelled through public agencies such as the Majlis Amanah Rakyat (MARA), the Urban Development Authority (UDA) and the thirteen state economic development corporations (SEDCs). These funds were, in turn, given to the companies in the form of grants, loans, or as payment for their shares. Loans from abroad also helped to finance some larger public enterprises, especially in the early 1980s. For instance, RM7,105 million in foreign loans guaranteed by the Federal Government were made to the non-financial public enterprises (NFPEs) by the end of 1984 (Ariff and Semudram, 1987: 34–5). Another important source of funding has been the Malaysian public, who have deposited their money in a variety of government-controlled or sponsored financial institutions, including the Muslim Pilgrim Fund and Management Board (LUTH), the Employees Provident Fund (EPF), and the Bumiputera Investment Foundation.

Formerly known as off-budget agencies (OBAs), NFPEs are now so classified because their budgets are not reflected in the budgets of the Federal and State Governments. Therefore, their activities lie beyond the normal scope for control and monitoring by the Government. Some of these agencies have become self-financing, but the majority still depend on the Federal Government for equity and loans, both domestic and external, guaranteed by the Government.

No less than 20 ministries and departments are involved in controlling and coordinating public enterprises. However, the responsibility for overall coordination of policies, resources, allocation, as well as monitoring and evaluation of performance, lies with four central agencies. These are the Federal Treasury, which deals with budget and loan approval, the Economic Planning Unit (EPU), which is responsible for government allocations and project approval, the Public Services Department, which is concerned with personnel management, and the Implementation Co-ordination Unit (ICU), whose function is to monitor and evaluate the performance of public enterprises in the country.[2]

The Public to Private Sector Policy Reversal

With the fiscal and debt crises of the mid-1980s, pressure mounted for a review and reversal of earlier public-sector expansion. Huge losses incurred by some of the public enterprises and worsening fiscal and debt conditions, especially in the mid-1980s, became too burdensome for the government's finances. With policy changes in the mid-1980s, the overall public sector deficit of 24 percent of GNP in 1982 and 1983 shrank to about 12 percent in 1985 (Salleh, 1987: 6). In the 1980–1985 period, public enterprises accounted for about 64.3 percent of the public-sector deficit (Nair and Fillipides, 1988: Table 2.2). During the 1982–1984 period, investment grew by 39 percent per annum, and by 1984, NFPEs accounted for half of all public investment (World Bank, 1989: 6–8). The NFPEs, in particular, had a deficit of 1.2 percent of GNP during 1976–80, reaching a peak of 3.4 percent in 1984; but in 1985, it fell to 1.2 percent (World Bank, 1989), and by 1987, they registered a surplus of 1.1 percent (Bank Negara, *Annual Report, 1988*).

The huge public-sector deficits of the late 1970s and early 1980s have been explained by the fact that the public enterprises were then relatively new; some NFPEs involved projects which require long gestation periods before economic returns could be realized. However, the public sector was also beset by other problems, including inefficiency, soft budget constraints, incompetence, and multiple (and contradictory) objectives.

The multiplicity of objectives that public enterprises have to fulfill (e.g. re-distribution of economic resources and employment generation, among other socio-economic and political objectives) evidently constrained their performance. Some public enterprises found it almost impossible to fulfill some of the objectives assigned to them, and had to change some of their original objectives in order to show better results. One example was the Rural Industrial Development Authority (RIDA), whose original objective was to develop industries in rural areas. Instead, 50 percent of its funds went to the construction of amenities and infrastructure, such as roads, bridges and water systems, and to providing loans to small producers (Raja Mohd. Affandi, 1975: 55–6).

The poor performance of many public enterprises brought forth strong criticisms. Public enterprises have become popularly associated with waste, inefficiency, and corruption. It is claimed that public enterprises in Malaysia not only increased the public debt, but also that their inefficiency and accumulated losses led to wastage of investment resources, which increased the government's fiscal burden and slowed down economic growth (Kamal and Zainal Aznam, 1989: 22–3; Supian, 1988: 120–3).

Lack of co-ordination and accountability in Malaysian public enterprises has also been evident. For instance, out of a total of about 900 public enterprises, the Ministry of Public Enterprises only reported annual returns for 269 enterprises in 1984, which recorded an accumulated loss of RM137.3 million (Supian, 1988). Their rapid growth has also involved an unhealthy escalation of self-aggrandizing and inefficient state intervention and the "ascendancy of Malay political and economic hegemony under the NEP", which has created a rentier Bumiputera political cum business elite (Jomo, 1990: 213). Calls have been made for policy changes to curb or reverse such abuses.

In response to calls to cut down public-sector involvement, the Government began to cut down public-sector employment and the size of budget deficits. A variety of other new policies consistent with the 1980s trend towards economic liberalization have been introduced, including divesting government shares, corporatization of public service or utility enterprises, letting the private sector undertake major new ventures and allowing higher user charges for corporatized or privatized public services (Mohd Noor *et al.*, 1984). To improve relations between the public and the private sectors, the "Malaysia Incorporated" concept had also been introduced in 1983. This apparent reversal of policies associated with the NEP was also in response to mounting complaints by the business community, including foreign investors who found it hard to comply with NEP conditions imposed by the Government (Ariff and Semudram, 1987: 31–2). Another important factor is that NEP inter-ethnic economic redistribution generally benefited the Bumiputera middle and upper income groups rather than the Bumiputera poor. It was anticipated that further pursuit of NEP policies would widen the gap between lower-income Bumiputeras and their well-to-do counterparts (Syed Husin, 1985).[3]

By the end of 1986, there were at least 736 public enterprises in Malaysia.[4] Of these, 380 enterprises were federal agencies and 356 were state government-established level enterprises. These public enterprises operated across a broad range of activities, but mainly in manufacturing, services, construction and agriculture. In the manufacturing sector, public enterprises concentrated mainly in food, chemicals, iron and steel, petroleum, cement, transport equipment and wood-based industries.[5] The greatest contribution of value added by publicly owned enterprises was for the manufacture of industrial gases (85.0 percent of total value added in 1985). Government enterprises also dominate the manufacturing sub-sectors of petroleum (63 percent), tires and tubes (63 percent), sugar (56 percent), hydraulic cement (45 percent), food products (45 percent), vegetable and animal oils (33 percent), palm oil (33 percent) and palm kernel oil (31 percent).[6] By 1989, there were more than a thousand public enterprises in Malaysia.

Privatization

Criticisms against public enterprises climaxed during the early 1980s when privatization, spearheaded by the US and British governments then, became fashionable. Malaysia, too, was not left far behind in this global privatization drive.

Privatization in Malaysia was officially inaugurated in March 1983. The pronouncement of the "Malaysia Incorporated" concept on 25 February 1983 is widely seen as a prelude to Malaysia's privatization program. The "Malaysia Incorporated" concept was a strategy to accelerate industrial development through co-operation and collaboration between the government and the private business sector. The nurturing of a closer alliance between the government and the private sector was aimed at intensifying national economic growth through expansion of the private sector, which was identified as the main generator of future economic growth.

From 1983, a number of public-sector activities were privatized, with more earmarked for privatization, including the health and medical services, transport, storage and communication, construction, agriculture, and public utilities. Public enterprises in the manufacturing sector, however, were only targeted by the government for privatization from the late 1980s. Ten years after the first official announcement of Malaysia's privatization policy, about 64 public enterprises have been privatized, while eight others have been corporatized in preparation for privatization (see Table 3.4).

TABLE 3.4 Methods of Privatization

Method	1983	1984	1985	1986	1987	1988	1989	1990	1991	1992	1993	Total
Sale of Equity	–	–	1	–	–	–	1	2	9	8	–	21
Public Listing	–	–	1	1	–	1	1	3	3	–	–	10
Leasing	–	–	1	–	–	–	–	1	–	–	–	2
Management Contract	–	–	–	1	3	1	–	–	–	–	–	5
Sale of Assets & Leasing	–	–	–	1	–	–	–	1	–	–	–	2
Sale of Assets	–	–	–	–	–	–	–	3	1	3	–	7
Management Buy-out	–	–	–	–	–	–	–	2	–	–	–	2
Corporatization & Listing	–	–	–	–	–	–	–	1	–	1	–	2
Build, Operate, Transfer (B-O-T)	1	–	1	–	2	2	2	1	1	–	–	10
Build, Operate, Owned (B-O-O)	1	–	–	–	–	–	–	–	–	–	–	1
Build, Operate (B-O)	–	–	–	–	–	–	–	–	–	–	2	2
Corporatization	–	–	–	–	–	–	–	–	1	4	3	8
TOTAL	2	–	4	3	5	4	4	14	15	16	5	72

Source: Economic Planning Unit.

Besides bringing in revenue for the government from the sale of stock (Table 3.5 shows the amount of revenue earned from some privatized projects), privatization has also deepened the Malaysian capital market. All the 15 privatized companies listed in the Kuala Lumpur Stock Exchange (KLSE) thus far have made promising progress in securing higher profits as well as expanding market capitalization. The combined market capitalization of MAS and MISC (listed in the KLSE in 1985 and 1987 respectively) increased from RM1.93 billion at issue price to about RM8.3 billion in September 1992. The market capitalization of Telekom Malaysia, which was listed on the KLSE in 1990, rose from RM9.85

TABLE 3.5 Revenue from Sale of Some Privatized Government Assets

Project (Names of companies translated into English)	Amount (RM million)
Sports Toto Ltd	113.00
Malaysian International Shipping Corporation Ltd (MISC)	1,329.14
Malaysian Airline System (MAS)	1,327.70
Tradewinds (M) Ltd	11.00
Port Kelang Container Terminal (KCT)	56.00
Padang Terap Sugar Ltd	51.10
Fima Holdings Ltd	190.00
National Automobile Distributor Ltd (EON)	38.70
PERNAS International Hotels and Properties Ltd	20.34
Peremba Limited	170.65
Security Printing Branch, Government Printers	5.00
Telecommunications Department (Telekom Malaysia)	525.00
Desaru Tourist Resort	70.88
Holiday Villages Pte Ltd	10.50
Cement Industries of Malaysia Limited Ltd (CIMA)	11.00
Malaysian Shipyard and Engineering Ltd (MSE)	227.00
Kuala Penanti Quarry, Penang	5.10
Kuala Dipang Quarry, Perak	5.77
Sungai Long Quarry, Selangor	5.56
Langkawi Island Resort Pte Ltd	47.00
Motel Desa Pte Ltd	3.30
Tanjung Jara Beach Hotel Pte Ltd	12.00
National Automobile Enterprise Ltd (PROTON)	199.50
Malacca Port	1.20
Port Kelang	361.00
TOTAL	4,797.34

Source: Economic Planning Unit.

TABLE 3.6 Market Capitalization of Privatized Projects (as at 19.2.1993)

Projects	(RM million)
MISC	4,987.5
KCT	875.0
Tradewinds	365.4
TNB	25,950.0
Telekom Malaysia	25,537.4
Cement Manufacturing Sarawak Berhad (CMS)	94.1
EON	2,486.6
CIMA	612.1
Kedah Cement Sdn. Bhd	911.4
Proton	4,000.0
Pernas International Hotel (PIHP)	504.5
TV3	373.4
Sports Toto (Berjaya Leisure)	876.8
Far East Holding (FE Hldg)	121.0
TOTAL	71,195.2
%	28.9

Source: Economic Planning Unit (EPU); *Investors Digest*, February 1993.

billion based on the offer price to RM26.3 billion by September 1992, an increase of 167 percent. Table 3.6 lists the market capitalization of all privatized companies listed on the KLSE. Tenaga Nasional Berhad (TNB), which is the largest privatized entity, induced a market capitalization of RM13.5 billion at the offer price, but was valued by the market at RM26.3 billion at the time of listing on 28 May 1992. By mid-February 1993, about 29 percent of total market capitalization in the KLSE came from privatized projects.[7]

It is difficult to assess the extent of foreign control due to privatization because most of the initial stock issues (with the exception of TNB) were not offered to foreign investors. Hence, foreign investors can only purchase the privatized companies' shares after the initial issue. In the case of TNB's public offer, 60 million out of 685 million shares were offered to foreign and local investors through open tenders.

In more developed economies, the stock market may discipline inefficiently managed private firms. A take-over will enable the new owners to improve management and reap the potential profits derived therefrom. Such take-overs will be profitable because the company's shares will be valued lower due to lower profits owing to managerial inefficiency. The prerequisite for this check-and-balance-system, however, is a perfectly functioning capital market. Even well-developed financial markets may not serve this function effectively. Hence, the privatization objective of achieving greater managerial efficiency is less likely to be realized in a smaller, less well-developed capital market such as Malaysia's.

The probability that privatized government monopolies will remain private monopolies, at least for a number of years to come, also poses a challenge to the allocative efficiency objective. Allocative efficiency is achieved when existing resources are distributed to produce what society demands most within the constraints of resource costs. The argument that the profit motive itself will increase efficiency ignores the possibility that profits can be raised by exploiting monopoly power and raising prices rather than by reducing costs. The allocative inefficiency of a private monopoly (even a regulated one) can thus easily outweigh the gains in economic efficiency stimulated by the profit motive.

Two important circumstances which cause allocative inefficiency are when increasing returns to scale exist in the production of particular commodities or the provision of certain services (e.g. electricity distribution) and when negative externalities, such as congestion, predominate (e.g. urban transport). In the first case, the resulting "natural monopoly" can induce profit-maximizing consumer prices to be set above marginal cost. In the second case, the marginal social benefit from mass transport utilization exceeds the marginal private benefit since the resulting reduction in congestion benefits all commuters.

Advocates of economic liberalization expect privatization to be accompanied by changes in market structure. Private enterprises are said to promote efficiency if there is market competition, i.e. when there exists a sufficient number of firms not in collusion selling closely substitutable products. Another ingredient for a competitive market structure is the relaxation of entry barriers to potential entrants into the market.

Public enterprises usually have to fulfill several government objectives. In the process of privatizing these enterprises, it is important to examine the extent to which these objectives are transferred to the privatized entities. If the objectives of the government are not identical with the objectives of the privatized entity, then "principal-agent" problems might emerge. Ideally, privatization presupposes that the government's interests are compatible with the privatized firm's objective, principally profit maximization. Hence, other government objectives, such as allocative, distributional, and stabilizing requirements, may be irrelevant to the privatized firm, and would have to be pursued by other means, such as taxation and subsidies.

Privatization may also undermine the redistributive and welfare objectives of certain public enterprises and related government policies. Privatization may not be able to fulfill certain social and economic responsibilities previously assigned to state enterprises. The privatization of Tenaga Nasional and Syarikat Telekom Malaysia Berhad (STMB) has involved the establishment of specific regulatory bodies, such as Bekalan Tenaga Elektrik and Jabatan Telekom, which are supposed to monitor services, including prices, to protect the interests of the government and the public, especially consumers. Evidence of considerable user price increases prior to corporatization and privatization suggests that these safeguards do not inspire much public confidence. There are other areas of concern. For example, there are great doubts as to how the poor can receive good health and education services if users are increasingly expected to bear the full costs of such services.

Performance of Public and Private Enterprises

Public enterprises are usually expected to pursue social objectives which may be as diverse as income redistribution, employment creation, price stability, infrastructure provision, industrial development and economic growth. In addition, they are often expected to rectify market "failures," and at times, even to overcome "'failure" in the rest of the public sector. While it is true that many Malaysian public enterprises have incurred financial losses, such evaluation is based only on the profitability criterion. Since public enterprises are assigned socio-economic objectives, judging their performance solely by achievement with respect to profitability can be misleading. Committed to other objectives, public enterprises are expected to deviate from profit-maximization and cost-minimization objectives to a greater extent than their privately owned counterparts.

There have been many claims on the allegedly inherent inferiority of public compared to private enterprises and the beneficial impact of privatization. A study (Rugayah Mohamed, 1992) found that not all public manufacturing enterprises in Malaysia are inherently more inefficient than their private counterparts when compared on a like-with-like basis. The ownership factor (public or private) does not seem to fully explain observed differences in productivity performance between public and private enterprises in the 31 industries compared on a 5-digit classification basis in the sample study. Estimations of public and private firms' production functions of the Cobb-Douglas and the Constant-Elasticity of Substitution forms were carried out to compare total factor productivity levels between the two enterprise types. From the study findings (Table 3.7), one is not able to conclude that public enterprises in the Malaysian manufacturing sector are inherently less efficient in productivity performance than their private counterparts.

The favorable achievement of public-sector firms in quite a number of industries is indeed surprising. The performance of public-sector firms engaged in food manufacturing was found to be as promising as private-sector firms in terms of productive efficiency, though not overwhelmingly so. However, in terms of productivity growth, the public-sector firms appeared to be more encouraging. In heavier industries, such as shipbuilding and repairs as well as motor vehicle assembly, publicly owned firms had considerably better performances, though not without governmental preferential treatment, including protection. Such activities involve huge capital investment and likely economies of scale. Similarly, for the

TABLE 3.7 Relative Productive Efficiency of Public and Private Firms in
31 Manufacturing Industries Using Cobb-Douglas and CÉS Production Functions

Industry		C-D	CES
Classification	Code		
Dairy Product (n.e.c.)	31129	1.70[a]	0.17[a]
Pineapple Canning	31131	-0.70	-1.30
Fruit Canning & Preserving (n.e.c.)	31139	16.16[b]	12.97[b]
Fish Canning & Preserving (n.e.c.)	31140	-30.42[b]	-46.45[b]
Palm Oil	31152	1.89	1.34[b]
Palm Kernel Oil	31153	1.44[a]	1.51[b]
Vegetable & Animal Oils (n.e.c.)	31159	-1.31[b]	–
Sugar Factory	31180	-6.28	143.23[b]
Cocoa, Chocolate & Sugar Confectionery	31190	21.98[b]	-3.69[b]
Food Products (n.e.c.)	31219	9.14[b]	9.14[b]
Natural Fibre Weaving	32111	26.93[b]	30.64[b]
Dyeing, Bleaching & Printing	32112	0.54[b]	0.53[b]
Tanneries & Leather	32310	5.80[b]	10.73[b]
Sawmills	33111	-8.01[b]	-5.94[a]
Plywood	33112	-1.30	-12.78
Planning Mills	33113	20.56[a]	0.99[a]
Prefabricated Wooden Houses	33114	-1.67[a]	-0.47
Furniture & Fixtures	33200	0.47	1.80
Containers, Boxes & Paperboard	34120	-165.41	0.41
Industrial Gases	35111	1.82[b]	1.88[b]
Chemical Products (n.e.c.)	35290	11.76[b]	5.56
Petroleum	35300	1.61[a]	-8.91
Tire & Tubes	35510	76.88	-0.34
Rubber Products (n.e.c.)	35599	1.30[b]	1.29[b]
Plastic Products (n.e.c.)	35600	0.28	0.29
Structural Clay	36910	-8.63[b]	-1.34[b]
Hydraulic Cement	36921	2.44	-3.07
Primary Iron & Steel	37101	-2.99[b]	2.08
Shipbuilding & Repairing	38410	1.02[b]	0.91[a]
Motor Vehicle Bodies	38431	0.84[b]	0.91[b]
Assembly of Motor Vehicle	38432	-4.63	-3.22

[a]significant at 90 percent confidence level.
[b]significant at 95 percent confidence level.
n.e.c. not elsewhere classified.

manufacture of chemical products, an industry with considerable capital requirements, the government sector firms also had higher levels of technical efficiency, despite poor growth performance.

These findings also strengthen the claim that differences in relative efficiency between public and private firms are industry-specific. Of special interest is the suggestion that the characteristics of the markets or industries in which these firms operate, strongly influence their relative performance. Non-competitive behavior in the form of barriers to entry associated with high capital intensity in some industries, scale efficiency in others, and advantages gained by greater substitutability between factors of production as well as growth apparently play important roles in determining the performance of public manufacturing enterprises in Malaysia *vis-à-vis* their private counterparts. Thus, the question of whether public or private firms perform more efficiently seems to involve a broad range of issues which encompass the structural features unique to the industries or the markets in which the firms operate.

An extension of the above study (Rugayah Mohamed, 1993) examined the structure of the markets in which the public and private firms operate to see whether competition plays a role in influencing firm performances. The characteristics of a market or industry which affect the level of competition among firms include the number and size distribution of sellers (measured using various concentration ratios, the most discriminating one being the Herfindahl-Hirschman index (Hf)), which reflect the extent of monopoly or oligopoly. This is, in turn, affected by the existence or absence of barriers to entry such as minimum efficient scale (MES), advertising intensity (ADV), competition from exports (XPA), competition from imports (IC), capital intensity (K/O) and growth (GR).[8] Table 3.8 shows the market structure features of the three categories of industries where: 1) public firms are found to be more efficient, 2) private firms are found to be more efficient, and 3) neither public nor private firms are conclusively superior in performance (inconclusive outcome). It appears, on average, that the structural features of the markets differed among the three categories. The mean concentration index Hf appears to be relatively higher for industries in which public firms have achieved better performance. The same is observed for other market-structure variables such as scale efficiency, advertising, and export and import intensities. The capital intensity and growth rate variables, however, reveal higher values for industries in which relative performance is indeterminate between the two enterprise types.

In industries for which superiority of performance is inconclusive between public and private sector firms, the level of concentration is found to be relatively low, which may perhaps indicate that public and private firms could perform equally favorably in a more competitive environment. When the correlation coefficients between differences in performance and market variables are examined (Table 3.9), it is observed that differences in performance between the two enterprise types are found to be generally correlated with concentration, minimum efficient scale and industrial growth. These observations strengthen the presump-

TABLE 3.8 Mean Values of Market Structure Variables in Three Industry Groups by Ownership and Relative Efficiency

Market Variables	More Efficient Firm Group		
	Public'	Private	Inconclusive
Herfindhal Index (HF)	0.243	0.188	0.158
Minimum Efficient Scale (MES)	0.268	0.217	0.191
Advertising (ADV)	0.013	0.011	0.003
Exports (XPA)	1.066	0.685	0.391
Imports (IC)	0.810	0.753	0.405
Capital-output ratio (K/O)	0.419	0.429	0.612
Growth (GR)	0.062	0.189	0.297

TABLE 3.9 Correlation Coefficients between Differences in Performance and Market Structure Variables

HF	MES	GR	K/O	ADV	IC	XPA
0.297*	-0.274[a]	0.348[a]	-0.235	0.047	-0.010	-0.197

[a]significant at 90 percent level.

tion that differential performances between public and private firms are related to market structure. As such, attributing differential performance merely to ownership structure becomes suspect.

Concluding Remarks

Public enterprises have been the main instruments of direct government involvement in the economy since Independence, and especially during the Second, Third, and Fourth Malaysia Plan periods (1971–1985). In the period 1978–1983, there was a conspicuous increase in government involvement in the development of the manufacturing industry. This proliferation of public enterprises was deemed necessary to propel economic development and industrialization consistent with the employment-creating and ethnic-redistributive NEP objectives of eradicating poverty and restructuring society. From 1983, and especially after 1985, Malaysia's development strategy shifted to the privatization of selected public enterprises.

Privatization in Malaysia seems to have primarily involved the transformation of public monopolies into private monopolies, without any significant change in market structure. With this being the case, one wonders to what extent Malaysian privatization can achieve its usual objectives including those officially identified by the government. If the objective of the Malaysian privatization policy is to improve the efficiency of enterprises, transferring ownership rights alone will not be able to improve the performance of the enterprises.

The objective of improving enterprise efficiency has two possible consequences. One is to encourage a competitive market structure, while the other is to examine and rectify the weaknesses observed in enterprise management.

In offering a market structure more conducive to the improvement of enterprise performance, competition policies—such as removal of entry and exit barriers through regulatory reforms—should be considered and implemented. Regulatory policies—such as entry policies, exit policies, and pricing policies—should be reformed. Entry into markets can be improved through licensing liberalization by reducing restrictions on the issuance of licenses; investment incentives (e.g. tax relief) can be reduced by cutting down the extended periods for which fiscal incentives are awarded; and more equitable procurement systems developed whereby government bids are fully publicized in the media (thus improving transparency). Exit policies should include financial restructuring, which could facilitate the closure of firms with huge outstanding loans, as well as greater labor flexibility to adjust the volume and nature of the workforce and its labor. To help retrenched workers, for example, the government should fund better job information retrieval systems and retraining programs linked to specific employment opportunities and skill requirements. In uncompetitive markets, the removal of barriers to mobility and competition, including substantial reductions in trade barriers, should accompany price decontrol (Frischtak *et al.*, 1990: 12–14).

Non-competitive practices, such as collusive actions (e.g. price fixing) and monopolistic tendencies can be mitigated by implementing anti-trust policies. As a further safeguard against the increasing dominance of large firms in highly concentrated industries, the government could also systematically monitor the level of market concentration in these industries to suppress anti-competitive activities. As yet, unfortunately, there is no implementation of such policies in Malaysia, although awareness of the problem seems to be growing. Greater competition may also stimulate industrial restructuring as firms strive for innovations and expansion into new markets. Public as well as private firms that face competition should therefore allocate and use resources more efficiently.

In so far as the weaknesses of public firms are concerned, policy-makers should implement reforms to restructure their management and institutional set-up. Managers as well as workers should be better motivated to accomplish their duties. Whatever the form of ownership may be, public or private, by rewarding honesty and deterring unethical business, as well as promoting a genuine reward system based on merit, the question of public or private property rights to ensure efficiency becomes less significant. For instance, with public ownership, the benefits of greater public accountability, coupled with a good reward system based on merit, may lessen "shirking" and motivate workers to maintain and improve efficiency. At the directorial and managerial level, there should be an effective machinery by which directors and managers are appropriately penalized for any deviations or mismanagement of enterprise operations. Since the directorships of several public enterprises have been dominated by politicians and serving as well as retired senior civil servants or businessmen with strong political loyalties, efforts to improve enterprise performance must be accompanied by the recruitment of a new breed of more efficient directors and managers.

The lackluster performance of many of the less successful public enterprises can be improved by exposing them to greater competition. This entails giving public enterprises sufficient financial autonomy, and holding managers accountable by ensuring that they pay an adequate return on capital in much the same way as private firms do. Public enterprise reform also calls for stricter financial discipline, e.g. by eliminating subsidies and concessions. Publicly owned firms should not be given preferential treatment by other government institutions, such as the privilege of "captive markets" (purchasing privileges contracted between government firms and government departments or agencies) and easier access to credit, business contracts and licenses. This would create an environment requiring public enterprises to fend for themselves. There should be reforms in the financial system to put public and private enterprises on an equal and competitive footing. Excessive political interference in operational matters should also be reduced by making explicit the boundaries between the roles and responsibilities of the government, the board of directors, and the management of the enterprises. Greater autonomy and exposure to competitive markets should create a stronger sense of responsibility and greater commitment among public enterprises to cut waste and improve performance. Another item on the agenda for public enterprise reform is to make social goals explicit and to clarify their costs, which must also be weighed against their ostensible benefits, in order to develop more cost-efficient ways to meet their objectives.

Notes

1. Net financial flows from government to public enterprises came to 3.26 percent of GDP in 1981, but fell to 2.74 percent in 1985 (Nair and Fillipides, 1988: Table 2.4).

2. However, this does not apply to enterprises incorporated under the Companies Act, 1965, which behave autonomously in such matters.

3. However, it should be noted that the NEP also made commendable achievements. During the NEP period some of its important goals were achieved. Average rural household incomes improved as well as income distribution between classes and races. The incidence of poverty has been reduced from 49.3 percent in 1970 to 17.3 percent in 1987 and 15.0 percent in 1990 (Malaysia, 1991). Bumiputera poverty fell from about 46 percent in 1976 to about 24 percent in 1987, while Chinese poverty fell from about 17 percent to 10 percent over the same period (Kamal and Zainal Aznam, 1989: 34–5).

4. Statistics from the Central Information Collection Unit (CICU) of the National Equity Corporation or Permodalan Nasional Berhad (PNB).

5. Information gathered from CICU.

6. Data from the Statistics Department.

7. EPU Privatization Unit.

8. Other market variables such as vertical integration and direct foreign investment were also included in the study, but were found to be not statistically significant for the 31 industries under study.

4

Policy

JOMO K.S., CHRISTOPHER ADAM and WILLIAM CAVENDISH

The earliest references to privatization in Malaysia are found in discussions in 1983 of what was known as "Malaysia Incorporated," Prime Minister Mahathir's concept of the country as a corporate entity in which the government provided the enabling environment in terms of infrastructure, deregulation and liberalization, and overall macroeconomic management, but where the private sector assumed the role as the main engine of growth (see also the *Fifth Malaysia Plan, 1986–1990*).[1] Central to "Malaysia Inc." was an extremely ambitious program of privatization. The specific stimulus for the nature and style of the privatization policy seems to have come from the UK, and many of the decisions and methods have mirrored contemporaneous moves in the UK program.

Two years after Malaysia's privatization policy was first announced in 1983, the Privatization Section of the powerful Economic Planning Unit (EPU) in the Prime Minister's Department issued its *Guidelines on Privatization*, which outlined policy aims, modes of privatization, and means for implementation. Since then, various laws have been reformed to facilitate the incorporation of government departments and agencies as public limited companies and to facilitate privatization more generally.

The Malaysian government summed up its argument for privatization as follows in its *Guidelines on Privatization* (EPU, 1985):

> "Privatization has a number of objectives. First, it is aimed at relieving the financial and administrative burden of the government in undertaking and maintaining a vast and constantly expanding network of services and investments in infrastructure. Second, privatization is expected to promote competition, improve efficiency and increase the productivity of the services. Third, privatization, by stimulating private entrepreneurship and investment, is expected to accelerate the rate of growth of the economy. Fourth, privatization is expected to assist in reducing the presence and size of the public sector, with its monopolistic tendencies and bureaucratic support, in the economy. Fifth, privatization is also expected to contribute towards meeting the objectives of the New Economic Policy (NEP), especially as Bumiputera entrepreneurship and presence have improved greatly since the early days of the NEP and they are therefore capable of taking up their share of the privatized services."

The emergence of the policy reflected two concerns. The first was growing disillusionment with the performance of the SOE sector. Though this was less prevalent during the public-sector boom of 1981 and 1982, it became particularly important more recently, and has progressed to the fore since the recession in 1985–1986.

The second force behind the emergence of the policy was the reassessment of the role of the NEP. At first glance, privatization may seem a peculiar *volte-face*, in which the Government has swung from public-sector asset acquisition to an emphasis on private ownership as the key to pursuing Bumiputera asset ownership. However, a closer examination of the concept of public and private ownership in the Malaysian context reveals consistency in the policy. The motivating factor behind the rapid growth of the SOE sector in Malaysia stems almost exclusively from the issue of distribution. Successive governments have remained ideologically neutral on wider issues of collective state control versus private control (outside the sphere of essential services), with the only relevant division being Bumiputera and non-Bumiputera. Consequently, the process of asset acquisition by a Bumiputera government was viewed more as an off-budget activity directed to meeting the private objectives of its constituency. The implicit ideology remained one in which the Government acted as trustee for Bumiputera institutions, through the YPB and its associated institutions, the PNB and ASN. Against this background, the apparent change in attitude towards the concept of asset ownership seems less perverse: the desire for ownership to reach the 30 percent target has stimulated a need for not only a greater supply of asset stock to the Bumiputera, but also to ensure that asset values are maintained through the promotion of a higher overall level of growth and profit within the economy. As will be noted in this volume, the eventual methods of asset sale employed have tended to emphasize the close link between the objectives of the NEP and the privatization program.

Defining Privatization

In Malaysia, public, including official, discussion of privatization has included reference to the following types of phenomena:

(a) sale or divestment of state concerns. The public service concerned usually has to first be incorporated legally as a public limited company to facilitate such a sale, e.g. the establishment of Syarikat Telekom Malaysia Berhad on 1 January 1987 to take over the activities of the Telecoms Department (Jabatan Telekom) or the incorporation of Tenaga Nasional Berhad, taking over the National Electricity Board (Lembaga Letrik Negara).

(b) public issue or sale of a minority or even a majority of shares in a state-owned public company, e.g. Malaysian Airlines System (MAS) in 1985 and the Malaysian International Shipping Corporation (MISC) in 1987.

(c) placement of shares with institutional investors, e.g. the sale of about 5 percent of MAS stock to the Brunei government in 1986.

(d) sale or lease of physical assets, e.g. the lease of the Lady Templer Hospital to Rampai Muda in 1984.

(e) joint public-private-sector ventures, e.g. the establishment of Perbadanan Otomobil Nasional (Proton) in 1983, with 70 percent held by HICOM, the Heavy Industries Corporation of Malaysia, and 15 percent each by two Mitsubishi companies, the Mitsubishi Corporation and the Mitsubishi Motor Corporation (see Jomo, 1985).

(f) schemes to draw private financing into construction projects, e.g. North Port Kelang toll road bypass, the Jalan Kuching toll flyover and the North–South Highway as well as the low-cost housing scheme 'privatized' since the mid-1980s.

(g) "contracting out" public services previously provided within the public sector, e.g. the contracting out of various local government authorities' activities, such as parking services and garbage disposal, Telecoms' RM2.5 billion telecommunications development projects (Kennedy, 1991), and Port Kelang's container terminal services.

(h) allowing private competition where the public sector previously enjoyed a monopoly, e.g. the launching of a third television channel (TV3) in 1984 owned by Sistem Televisyen Malaysia Berhad, now controlled by the New Straits Press Berhad, and controlled in turn by the UMNO-owned Fleet Group, and now by the UMNO-controlled Renong Bhd.

However, the *Guidelines on Privatization* (1985) employs a relatively standard definition of privatization, encompassing principally asset sales, including partial sales. Nevertheless, it also includes leasing, management contracting and contracting-out of services or other activities, including the increasingly popular Build-Operate-Transfer (B-O-T) schemes for large capital investment.[2]

Privatization policy in Malaysia consists of two main, currently independent, elements. The first is the mainstream reform process co-ordinated by the Economic Planning Unit (EPU) of the Prime Minister's Department, and is the program which is promoted (and widely acknowledged) as the sole privatization program. The EPU program has included all the major asset sales and the corporatization of SOEs for future sale, has co-ordinated the deregulation, licensing and B-O-T aspects of the program, and in addition has developed the *Privatization Masterplan*.

Privatization also appeared as an important element of the work of the Unit Pengawasan Syarikat and Agensi Kerajaan (UPSAK) or the Unit for Monitoring Government Agencies and Enterprises. UPSAK, which was created in 1987 following a report by the Auditor-General highlighting the parlous state of the SOEs, is principally responsible for SOE reform measures. It is an advisory unit and is charged with advising the Finance Division of the Treasury on reform and restructuring of (mainly smaller) SOEs. In addition, it provides small-scale consultancy services to many of the SOEs with a view to stimulating self-funded restructuring, some of which may involve privatization.[3]

EPU Privatization Policy Framework

The Guidelines

The centerpiece of privatization in Malaysia was the Economic Planning Unit's *Guidelines on Privatization*. Issued in 1985, these establish the government's privatization objectives, identify key sectors for privatization, and outline the administrative structures to be employed. They cite five objectives to be pursued through privatization: (i) reduction of the financial and administrative burden of government; (ii) promotion of competition and increased productivity of SOEs; (iii) stimulation of private entrepreneurship, investment and growth; (iv) reduction in the role of the state; and (v) promotion of the objectives of the NEP through increasing the supply of private equity.

Typically, privatization programs involve a selection by the government of enterprises for privatization, most frequently within a well-defined framework of targeted and proscribed sectors. Sequencing is determined by the government and the program is managed on a tender or public sale basis. In a departure from this method, the Malaysian government initially adopted an "invitation" approach. All private-sector initiatives were welcomed, with no sectors or activities being explicitly ruled out,[4] and with the enticement that consideration would be given on a "first-come, first-served" basis. Approval of submissions was to be based on a number of criteria, principally that privatization proposals were profitable and viable; that any social objectives being previously carried out by SOEs be continued; that employees were "not disadvantaged" by privatization; and that the cost–benefit analysis directly addressed the needs of the NEP. Bumiputera participation thus emerges as a central element of the privatization process. There is a clear preference for private Bumiputera participation, but as the *Guidelines* state (p. 8, para 33): "priority will need to be given to private Bumiputera interests. Depending on circumstances, however, the government will also consider allowing trust agencies, or other government companies [*sic*], to participate initially in the ownership of the privatized enterprises." Similarly, foreign and non-Bumiputera participation is allowed, but subject to strict ownership conditions in accordance with the NEP (Malaysian ownership must be 70 percent of the total, of which 30 percent must be Bumiputera).

Administrative Structures

Following the publication of the *Guidelines*, the institutional arrangements for managing the privatization program were established.[5] The main advisory body, reporting directly to the Cabinet, is the Privatization (Main) Committee under the chairmanship of the Director-General of the EPU and consisting of the Secretaries-General from the main ministries (Finance, Energy, Communications, and the Implementation and Co-ordination Unit). The executive body below the Main Committee is the Privatization Secretariat, established within the EPU, and consisting of between 10 and 15 staff. Private-sector submissions received by the EPU are initially sent to the relevant technical committees, after which successful applications are reviewed by the Main Committee and sponsors are called to give evidence prior to final recommendation being sent to the Cabinet. Successful privatization proposals are then co-ordinated by the EPU, at which point external assistance is traditionally employed, generally from among the numerous institutions in the Kuala Lumpur financial sector.

In addition to the "invited" submissions, the Secretariat also initiates, plans, and manages the large-scale privatization projects which have emerged directly from government policy initiatives (for example, the telecommunications, electricity, and proposed railways sales). To date, this aspect of identification and selection has been extremely *ad hoc*, relying more on personal whim and precedent from other countries than on structured proposals.

Assessment of Privatization Structures

The approach to the planning of privatization adopted in Malaysia has met with a mixed response. While international observers have welcomed the clear structures, in particular the publication of a concise and accessible set of guidelines setting out the government's own objectives and implementation strategies, there is severe criticism about the policy structures from within the country.

The most pervasive criticism is that the "first-come, first-served" approach—which was initially promoted as a way of accelerating the process of privatization and also a mechanism whereby the private sector had an incentive to submit projects—lacks transparency and has had the effect of perpetuating the "cronyism" which has pervaded the NEP era (see *Malaysian Business*, 1 December 1987). The problem came to a head over the awarding of a B-O-T contract for the prestigious North–South Highway, a RM1.6 billion road project through Peninsular Malaysia linking Thailand with Singapore, to United Engineers, a company with a poor record and limited experience with road construction, but in which the government party, UMNO, held a significant equity stake.

The second main concern arising out of the lack of transparency in the policy is the opportunity this extends to the significant bureaucratic élite opposed to privatization. Opposition is grounded principally in a concern to maintain rent-seeking capacities and is apparent not only among officials of the federal government but, perhaps more vigorously, within the state governments, where privatization is seen as synonymous with increased centralization of economic power in the hands of a Kuala Lumpur elite (see *Malaysian Business*, 1–15 September 1989).

Third, there was a perception on the part of the private sector that opposition to privatization came from the highest levels within the civil service, and not merely from those directly affected by the loss of rent-seeking opportunities. In particular, the view is widely held that it was only the personal commitment of Mahathir which maintained the early momentum of the program. The Prime Minister took personal charge of the "Malaysia Inc." program and the privatization process, and his personal interventions have shaped a number of the larger initiatives. It is strongly believed that, without Mahathir, privatization in Malaysia would peter out.[6] The widespread uncertainty about the government's broader political commitment to privatization has meant that enticements and other reputation costs emerged as a constant feature of the program during the 1980s.

To a significant extent, the force of these criticisms has been acknowledged, and prompted the development of the Privatization Masterplan (PMP), which is seen as an attempt both to re-establish the momentum of privatization (there were no large-scale asset sales from the time of the sale of MISC in 1987 until the STMB sale in late 1990) and to address the criticisms of "cronyism" and lack of transparency by strengthening the "government initiative" aspect of the policy relative to the "invitation" element. Concern that the bureaucracy still retained strong incentives to sabotage the policy was, however, inferred by some observers from the long delays in bringing the PMP to the Cabinet.

Ad Hoc Policy

During the first seven years, privatization policy proceeded on an *ad hoc* basis. Candidates emerged through the first-come, first-served basis, with little apparent guidance from EPU (although the decision to pursue the privatization of the larger utilities was determined within the government). Conscious of this problem, the government commissioned a "Privatization Masterplan" (PMP) for Malaysia. Commissioned in 1985, it was undertaken jointly by J. Schroder Wagg of London and Arab-Malaysian Merchant Bank. It identified approximately 424 enterprises, with a market capitalization of RM15 billion to RM20 billion, for privatization over a period of 5 years.

The essence of the PMP, which remained under embargo until early 1991, was to replace the previous approach to privatization with a coherent and integrated program covering the entire spectrum of the SOE sector, and bringing together the currently separate operations of the EPU (which is under the Prime Minister's Office) and UPSAK (under the Ministry of Finance). The draft PMP established not only the enterprises to be identified for privatization, but also outlined a possible sequencing: 246 were found to be privatizable, 69 within two years, 107 within two to five years, and the remainder beyond five years. In addition to the identification of candidates for privatization, the draft PMP was reported to have assessed the issues of savings mobilization (the program required mobilization of up to RM4 billion per annum over the five-year program) and of regulation of the monopolies.

The first phase of privatization in Malaysia established the program in the centre of macroeconomic policy-making, and particularly as a complement rather than a challenge to the NEP. The progress until 1990 was relatively slight, with the impact being threefold. First, in the view of many observers, the main effect of the privatization program had been to put the brake on SOE expansion and creation, and make explicit the debate over the appropriate role of the state in the economy. Second, the program had used as a component of the "Malaysia Incorporated" push to enhance and rejuvenate the NEP prior to its renegotiation. Thirdly, however, it may also be argued that the first years were used by the Government to establish its credibility, mainly with the Bumiputeras, to outline the principles which would be followed in future privatizations, and to acquire the technical expertise for the large-scale program heralded by the Masterplan.

Having firmly established the program and, possibly, having signalled the government's commitment to the policy, conditions were set for a major second-phase program under the auspices of the PMP. Implementation of Masterplan proposals would involve an unprecedented shift of resources from the public to the private sector over a short space of time. While, at one level, this raises the issue of government capacity to manage this transfer, the more important debate focuses on the structural constraints which may impinge on the program. To date, the program has not "challenged" the absorptive capacity of the Malaysian economy.

Regulation of the Utilities

As with most privatization programs, the issue of post-privatization regulation received limited attention until quite late in the privatization program. Most noticeable is the fact that, though the *Guidelines on Privatization* do not address the issue, the Privatization Masterplan did include proposals for a single unifying regulatory structure for all privatized enterprises (the Privatization Act). Events on the ground have preceded it, however, and there already exists a separate regulatory structure in the Telecommunications Act of 1989. This is very similar to the 1984 UK Telecommunications Act, and follows a number of regulation and competition structures employed in the UK. STM will retain a monopoly on the provision and leasing of lines, but competition will be allowed in the supply and installation of "value-added networks," such as public telephone kiosks, facsimile equipment, dedicated computer lines, cellphones, and, significantly, the laying of fiber-optic cables. Price regulation for STM itself will be implemented by the Director-General of Telecommunications, and the Act specifies the use of the RPI–X formula for price-setting, introduced in the UK for British Telecom.[7]

A number of issues present themselves with this form of regulation for the telecommunications industry in Malaysia. The first is the absence of timely and clear thinking on the structure and capacity of regulatory agencies for private-sector monopolies (despite the fact that STM is now operating as a corporate entity). Though Jabatan Telekom Malaysia (JTM) has existed as a regulatory body since 1987, the industry has operated since without any formal regulatory structure. Even at present, there is a lack of clarity surrounding the exact structure of regulation as a whole in Malaysia. Whilst the drafting of the regulatory Act for the telecommunications industry implicitly envisaged a structure of related but independent regulatory bodies (the UK case), the draft Privatization Masterplan, on the other hand, proposes a uniform regulatory framework covering regulation of all utilities. It seems that, even if a decision is made to pursue the unified regulatory structure proposed by the PMP, a significant time-lag may be expected before an operable structure is established.

Secondly, there is a perception that, in following the UK model, the government may well have underestimated the resource costs required to manage price regulation, not least in terms of the informational asymmetry between STM and its regulator, the Director-General of Telecommunications. Finally, concern has been raised about the degree of competition in the private-sector supply of equipment and other services. Casual evidence suggests that, though this end of the telecommunications market is not naturally monopolistic, entry-deterrence behavior is prevalent, and concern has been expressed about the capacity, or willingness, of JTM to avoid capture of this end of the market.

Privatization Masterplan

In early February 1991, the Malaysian government finally published the *Privatization Masterplan* (*PMP*) document, just before announcing the rest of its post-NEP (or post-1990) policy, in the form of Prime Minister Mahathir Mohamad's "Vision 2020" speech later the same month, as well as the *Second Outline Perspective Plan, 1991-2000* and the *Sixth Malaysia Plan, 1991-1995* documents announced in mid-1991. Hence, the PMP can be regarded as one of four major programmatic documents issued in 1991 outlining Malaysian economic development policy in the foreseeable future.

In response to criticisms of the arbitrary and *ad hoc* nature of privatizations in the early years after the Malaysian government's initial announcement of its privatization policy in 1983 and recognizing some of the problems and constraints associated with the absence of a more comprehensive and systematic privatization program or plan, around 1987, the Malaysian government decided to commission the preparation of a privatization master plan. It was also accepted that such a plan would facilitate and accelerate the privatization process besides ensuring better outcomes. In brief, the plan was intended to more clearly define the objectives, guidelines and very policy of privatization, develop an overall strategy, with a more consistent approach and criteria for privatization, and prepare an action plan consistent with the above to facilitate and expedite privatization. According to Ismail (1991), the plan consultants were assigned to incorporate the following into the preparation of the plan:

a)   review existing privatization policies and objectives, and recommend changes
b)   appraise existing privatization guidelines and recommend appropriate changes

c) identify viable candidates for privatization, and prioritize them
d) assess the privatization administrative machinery, and recommend improvements to the organizational structure and decision-making process, and
e) prepare an action plan with a 10-year timescale, indicating how the recommendations should be implemented.

According to Ismail, the study identified the following six requirements for an expanded, accelerated, and more effective privatization program, relating to the overall policy framework and actual program implementation:

1) incorporating privatization as part of a wider process of economic reform
2) aligning privatization strategies with national objectives
3) improving implementation machinery
4) ensuring careful management of staff sensitivities
5) improving the relevant legal framework
6) providing support mechanisms for the program.

Claiming success for its privatization program thus far, the *PMP* announced the government's intention to "expand and accelerate further the pace of privatization process" [*sic*]. The main features of the Malaysian Government's *PMP* are summarized below. Implementation of the *PMP*, particularly its "Privatization Action Plan" (PAP), is also to be evaluated two years after the Plan's announcement, which coincides with the Plan's own short-term period for implementation, although the findings of this evaluation have not been made public at the time of writing (May 1993).

The *PMP* outlined six recommendations for an accelerated and expanded privatization program:

— privatization should be part of a broader, more comprehensive process of economic liberalization reform;
— privatization strategies have to be more carefully tailored to meet national objectives;
— the machinery for policy implementation has to be improved;
— personnel sensitivities should be carefully handled;
— appropriate reforms to be the legal framework are still needed;
— official and public support for the program need to be further enhanced.

Modes

The PMP considers four main modes of implementing privatization, namely:

— sale of assets or equity
— lease of assets
— management contract
— "build-operate-transfer" (B-O-T) or "build-operate" (B-O) new infrastructure.

However, the document also cites other examples of privatization which have nothing to do with any of these, e.g. the so-called privatization of TV3 through issue of a license for a private television broadcasting company, and contracting-out services.

The *PMP* also mentions broad alternative methods, considerations, and criteria for the valuation of assets for sale or lease—net tangible assets (NTAs), price-earning (PE) ratios, and discounted cash flows (DCF)—emphasizing that only the last two take account of potential earnings, which the *PMP* favors. However, there is no evidence that any of these methods have been strictly adhered to in determining the actual price (or lease rate) of privatized government assets. On the contrary, very substantial discounts (in the case of sales) and premiums (in the case of privatized infrastructural projects) seem to have been the norm, with the proportion apparently not unrelated to the political influence of the beneficiary.

Until early 1993, the Capital Issues Committee (CIC) was responsible for setting prices of new shares. Before 1992, the CIC seemed to have a record of fairly consistently underpricing new share issues, especially in relation to trading prices on the first day of issue and also within the first three months after issue. Such underpricing has deprived the government and the public sector of considerable revenue from the sale of shares (see Ismail 1991, and Goh and Jomo's chapter in this volume). It has been claimed that the CIC's pricing practices are based on previous price–equity ratio considerations being kept within a range of 3.5 to 8.0. But since this range is not reflective of share prices in the market as a whole, the new share issues of privatized government enterprises have been greatly underpriced. As Adam and Cavendish as well as Goh and Jomo show in their chapters, even after three months of secondary trading, the premia over the issue prices were fairly close to those prevailing when trading commenced.

Since the *PMP* acknowledges that there is not much scope for increasing competition with natural monopolies, it promises an appropriate regulatory framework to protect consumer interests, particularly in terms of price, quality, and availability of services, as well as "commercial freedom" for private monopolies. Implicit in this formulation is the acknowledgment that such regulation does not yet exist, and, if introduced, is unlikely to threaten enterprise autonomy. The proposed regulatory framework does not seem to have materialized despite continued progress on privatization of public utilities and other enterprises which might be deemed natural monopolies. Perhaps more alarmingly, there has been little public discussion in the officially controlled mass media about what form and when such regulation may come about, except for some occasional rhetorical assurances that the government will always ensure that public interest will be protected after privatization.

The *PMP* reiterates the government's intention to advance Bumiputera corporate participation through ethnically preferential privatization. This is expected to include collaboration between Bumiputera institutional investors and others as well as management buy-outs (MBOs) and employee share ownership plans

(ESOPs). The *PMP* also promises an institutional mechanism to ensure sustained Bumiputera participation after privatization although it remains unclear what this is or will be.

Anticipating public objections, the PMP recommends allowing foreign investments in privatized entities where:

— foreign expertise is needed and local expertise is not available;
— foreign participation is crucial for export market access and promotion;
— international linkages and exposure are required by the business;
— the supply of local capital is not sufficient to buy up the shares offered.

The *PMP* also recommends that foreign investments should not exceed 25 percent in such cases, presuming that this will ensure that national interests can thus be adequately protected. The document seems oblivious to the various problems faced by majority Malaysian interests in other joint ventures, where foreign shareholders are effectively dominant despite having only a minority stake.

An interesting innovation proposed by the *PMP* is the establishment of a special fund to finance related expenses such as feasibility studies, preparing candidates for privatization, and disbursing compensation related to privatization. Again, it is unclear to what extent this has materialized.

To motivate staff, the *PMP* recommends employee share ownership as well as other incentives. However, it acknowledges that such schemes have not benefited poorer employees very much, while loyalty and commitment to the company has been undermined by the subsequent sale of shares. To overcome these problems, the *PMP* recommends Employee Share Ownership Plans for future privatizations involving the establishment of a trust to hold shares for employees who will only be able to sell them when they retire or resign. This recommendation does not seem to have been implemented with the subsequent preferential sale of shares to employees in corporatized public enterprises such as Telekom Malaysia.

The *PMP* also recommends management as well as management cum employee buy-outs, i.e. MBOs and MEBOs, though there have not been any such sales since the *PMP* was announced; the two major MBOs involving previously state-owned enterprises occurred in late 1990, just before the October 1990 general election (see Gomez, 1991).

Action Plan

The *PMP* also proposes a Privatization Action Plan (PAP) consisting of a two-year "rolling plan" reviewed at the end of each year, identifying the targets for privatization and for preparation for eventual privatization in the following years.

According to the *PMP*, 434 government-owned entities (GOEs) were studied by private consultants to determine the desirability and suitability of their privatization. The consultants identified 246 as privatizable within the first year of the program, with 69 privatizable within two years, 107 in two to five years, and the remaining 70 projects after five years. However, the Government has deemed some of these 246 not suitable for privatization on various grounds. As of March 1993, i.e. more than two years after the announcement of the *PMP* in February 1991, only a few of the 315 targeted by the *PMP* for privatization within the first two years had actually been privatized. There has been no public explanation for this delay in implementation of the PAP. Nevertheless, according to press reports, the Prime Minister has obliquely hinted at opposition to such privatization without being very specific, which probably suggests dissent from influential elements within the public sector as well as possibly from ruling party (UMNO) politicians, civil servants or public enterprise managers, or even a combination of them. The *PMP* also claims to be considering others not covered by the study for possible privatization. Such government-initiated privatizations are supposed to be subject to competitive bidding.

However, according to the *PMP*, the Government is still prepared to consider private sector-initiated privatization if it is convinced that no other private sector party can privatize a particular project, as in the following circumstances:

— the proposer offers a unique cost-effective solution to an economic problem or potential savings to the government;
— the proposer has unique possession of certain technical know-how or patent rights essential to the proposal;
— the privatization would not be viable on its own as its viability is dependent on another component possessed by the proposer.

Although still open to abuse, if strictly interpreted, these criteria represent a significant departure from the earlier "first come, first served" policy, which has still not been unequivocally rejected.

The *PMP* claims to be influenced by both feasibility and desirability criteria in determining priorities for privatization. Feasibility is, in turn, said to be determined by both ease of privatization and attractiveness to the private sector, whereas desirability seems to be defined by the government's perception of private sector superiority. Using a 2 x 2 matrix, the *PMP* distinguishes four categories:

— *immediate privatization* candidates will be the main focus in the early years of the PAP as they rank highly on the feasibility and desirability criteria;
— *priority restructuring* candidates are deemed to require preparation (e.g. restructuring) for privatization despite the government's desire to privatize them;
— *back burner* candidates are deemed feasible for privatization, though the benefits of privatization are considered to be less than self-evident;
— the *consider future* candidates rank poorly on both feasibility and desirability criteria.

The PAP distinguishes six different categories of candidates for privatization requiring different treatment, namely:

— "flagships"—comprising GOEs of national importance, in terms of size and complexity, thus meriting special treatment (such as JTM and LLN)—are to be privatized over several years, usually one annually;
— "easily privatizable government majority-owned companies," especially in manufacturing and agricultural production, are most likely to be given priority for privatization;
— "restructuring candidates" mainly refer to unprofitable companies needing financial and operational restructuring; however, the government prefers to minimize pre-privatization restructuring, which usually involves financial aspects;
— "services" previously protected from commercial competition are to be deregulated and privatized in the consumer interest;
– listed and minority shareholdings are to be given low priority since the private sector is already quite involved;
– "new projects"—usually involving infrastructural development—are to be privatized on a B-O-T basis.

To facilitate implementation, the PAP distinguishes those ready for privatization from those requiring preparation, e.g. most flagships. The preparation required may include:

— commercialization (e.g. raising user charges, commercial accounting and commercial performance criteria);
— legal corporatization.

Other changes at this stage before actual divestment may include:

— replacing bureaucratic administration with profit-oriented management;
— replacing centralized production-oriented decision-making with market-driven consumer preferences;
— introducing clear financial and operational performance criteria and commercial accounting.

The main divestment options considered by the *PMP* include:

— public flotation
— private sale
— management buy-out
— employee share ownership plan

As of the end of 1990, according to the *PMP*, 37 privatizations had taken place since the announcement of the policy, of which 27 involved private interests taking over existing government entities, while the other 10 involved the construction of new infrastructure. The government had also approved another 18 privatizations, of which 7 are new infrastructure projects. This did not include government divestments since 1981 to transfer government equity to Bumi-puteras, involving some 30 companies transferred to Permodalan Nasional Berhad and another 120 or so to private Bumiputera interests—which remain to be systematically documented. Also, minor privatizations—such as contracting out of services (such as security, cleaning, and laundry)—are not included.

Of the 27 privatizations, 17 involved ownership divestment by sale of equity or assets to the public, or by way of private placement and management buy-out; 2 involved leasing arrangements, 5 involved management contracts, and 2 more a combination of sale and lease; also the Lembaga Letrik Negara (LLN, or National Electricity Board) was corporatized as Tenaga Nasional Berhad (National Power Ltd.) as a step towards privatization. Of the 10 new infrastructure projects, eight involved "build–operate–transfer" (to government after some time), or B-O-T arrangements, while the other two involved "build–operate" (for perpetuity), or B-O arrangements.

The advocates of privatization in Malaysia have not been honest in presenting a full and balanced record of what has happened with privatization. Instead, anecdotal claims have been selectively advanced to imply that the Malaysian experience has been an unqualified success, as in the *PMP*. The existence of mistakes or negative consequences and implications is not even acknowledged in order to avoid their recurrence. While the policy-makers or those in charge presumably know better, the *PMP*'s failure to consider them publicly bears ominous implications about how the policy has been formulated, adopted, and implemented. While the *PMP* undoubtedly represents an advance, at least on paper, over some of the most blatant abuses of early Malaysian privatization policy, especially the "first come, first served" policy, it offers little ground for comfort about the future of privatization in Malaysia, especially in the light of what has taken place and seems likely to occur in the foreseeable future.

Claims

While the *PMP* admits that "it is still too early to make an assessment of the effectiveness of the privatization program", it nonetheless claims several major achievements, including:

- efficiency gains:

    The *PMP* cites four examples:

    — reduction of average vessel turnaround time at the Kelang port container terminal from 11.7 hours to 8.9 hours two years after privatization;
    — improvements in television broadcasting with greater competition after the licensing of a private third television channel, TV3;
    — improved telecommunication services since the corporatization of STMB in 1987;
    — completion of the Labuan water supply project ahead of schedule.

- stimulus to growth:

The *PMP* claims privatization has stimulated economic growth by providing greater opportunities to (and thus motivating) the private sector, generating multiplier effects (e.g. TV3's stimulus to the domestic film-making and advertising industries), compensating for the decline in public expenditure and encouraging private entrepreneurship.

- reducing governmental responsibilities:

The *PMP* claims a significant reduction in the government's administrative and financial burden due to privatization, citing the reduction of the public-sector workforce by 54,000, of whom 29,000 were Telecoms employees. One-off proceeds from the sale of Government properties came to RM1.18 billion, while recurrent revenues are expected from taxation and leases (e.g. Kelang Container Terminal); meanwhile, the government's tax burden has been reduced as privatized companies take over loan refinancing. The *PMP* also claims that privatizing new infrastructure projects has saved the government RM8.2 billion, while other capital spending (development expenditure) commitments have been significantly reduced.

- redistribution:

Since most privatizations have involved at least 30 percent Bumiputera participation, the policy is said to have furthered the NEP's inter-ethnic wealth redistribution objectives. The *PMP* also claims that privatization has enabled the government to spend more on poverty alleviation although there is no real evidence of this.

Despite the *PMP*'s claim that privatization is "premised on the superiority of market over administrative directives in governing economic activity to achieve efficiency" and that the "government's intervention in the economy will be minimal", actual deregulation efforts are well behind those of privatization.

Despite the publication of the *PMP* in February 1991 and the earlier (1985) publication of the official *Guidelines*, Malaysia's privatization policy remains unclear. Although the *PMP* contained a Privatization Action Plan (PAP), its apparent irrelevance in determining the progress of privatization in the following two years, for which it identified hundreds of state-owned enterprises to be privatized during this period, suggests that the PAP can hardly be taken seriously as a guide for what is likely to be done. In the absence of any clear program of action which is likely to be implemented, one can only expect the actual policy on privatization to be somewhat arbitrarily determined and implemented except where public information is crucial to the success of a particular privatization exercise, e.g. in the case of the sale of shares to the public through placement on the stock market.

A privatization master plan should instead emerge from a critical review of the public sector as a whole in relation to various growth, efficiency, and equity developmental objectives. In such a review, the variety of privatization measures as well as other public-sector reform measures should be considered as some among various options for reforming the public sector. Where particular modes of privatization are recognized and recommended as the most suitable and desirable measures in particular circumstances, clear objectives and guidelines have to be established. Hence, although it took so long for the *PMP* to be prepared and approved by the authorities, it fails to address, let alone satisfactorily resolve many other matters crucial for acceptance of the government's privatization policy, including the following:

* The *PMP* seems oblivious to the variety of problems facing the public sector, and anxious to accelerate privatization as an end in itself, instead of regarding privatization as an option, or rather options, among many, for addressing problems of the public sector in relation to national development objectives.
* While the *PMP* recommends privatization for hundreds of economic enterprises and activities currently handled by the public sector, it fails to address the conceptually prior question as to why privatization is superior to other options in various different circumstances, but only deals with whether something can be privatized, the answer to which is almost invariably "yes".
* The *PMP* recommends different modes of privatization for different types of activities, sectors, and organizations. It says this is the way to privatize something, but does not really tell us why we should privatize it in the first place, though it does suggest why a particular mode is considered superior to other modes of privatization in particular circumstances.
* The *PMP* seems to insufficiently recognize, let alone address the difficulties, problems, and adverse consequences of privatization, e.g. rent-seeking and capture, private-sector capacity, implications of foreign control.
* Even the most basic economic welfare trade-off issues, e.g. involving efficiency and equity, are not seriously addressed by the *PMP*, both generally for the economy as a whole, and particularly, in considering the implications of a particular privatization.
* Similarly, crucial macro-economic implications—e.g. for savings, investments, capital market, capital flows, public-sector revenues and expenditure, employment, inflation—are not addressed by the *PMP*, despite the magnitude of the privatizations recommended by the document.

  Even issues involved in privatization are inadequately addressed in the *PMP*, including measures required to achieve the five official objectives of privatization, namely government bureaucracy and expenditure reduction, public-sector contraction, competition and efficiency enhancement, growth stimulation, and Bumiputera entrepreneurship advancement. It is virtually silent on crucial questions of accountability and transparency. In other words, the *PMP* fails even to address the concerns of those who favor privatization but are unhappy about how privatization has proceeded in Malaysia thus far, e.g. over the loss of potential government revenue due to share underpricing.
* Post-privatization concerns are also inadequately addressed by the *PMP*, which has very little to say about monitoring the performance and conduct

of privatization as well as privatized activities and enterprises, consumer protection and protecting the "national interest," however defined, in an economy with a much reduced public sector and a considerably enhanced private sector. While taking for granted that "government failure" requires privatization as the best, if not the only possible response, it has little to say about market failure, even though many of the major candidates for privatization are public monopolies. The *PMP* does not seem to have much to say about marketization or competition enhancement, seemingly subscribing to the implicit equation of privatization with marketization, and ignoring the impact and implications of privatization thus far, or at least until the end of 1990.

To put it bluntly, the *PMP* is a disappointment on many scores. This disappointment is all the greater because of the time (almost four years from the government's announcement that the Plan was being prepared) and expense (reportedly several million ringgit paid to a British consultancy) apparently required to prepare it. It is, of course, quite possible that much was excised from the consultant's report before official release, but there is little to suggest that there were significant revisions between the unofficial previews available from mid-1989 (e.g. see Sheriff. 1990) and the final document released in early 1991, although some interesting differences exist. Hence, it may not necessarily be a bad thing that it does not appear that the *PMP*'s PAP does not seem to have been implemented in the two years after the document's release.

Notes

1. The Plan was based on policies aimed at reviving private domestic investment following the slump in the period since 1985, and these have been relatively successful. Private investment fell by 8 percent in 1985 and by a further 16 percent in 1986, but has grown very strongly since then (5 percent in 1987, 20 percent in 1988, and 27 percent in 1989).

2. A Build-Operate-Transfer (B-O-T) contract involves government agreeing with the private sector on (usually) the construction of a public or infrastructural asset. Instead of standard contracting or turn-key arrangements, the project is private sector-financed with the private sector recouping outlay over a fixed period through tolls or other fees; the assets eventually revert to the public sector asset stock after a given period.

3. From discussions with officials, the impression is gleaned that divestiture and closure through the UPSAK structure are seen as elements in the broader SOE reform brief. There is little sense of the politics of privatization emerging in this program.

4. Although the *Guidelines* do make clear that issues of strategic significance to the country will be taken into consideration in considering the applications.

5. Only one major privatization was completed before the *Guidelines* were published—the Klang Port Authority container terminal. Most of the administrative arrangements subsequently adopted were a formalization of procedures adopted for the KCT sale.

6. *Malaysian Business* (1–15 September 1989, p. 15) noted: "Pro-privatization groups are said to have held their breaths when a heart attack seized Mahathir early this year, as concerned for the program as for the Prime Minister's health. Privatization proposals froze and meetings at the EPU stalled. The momentum has since picked up in tandem with the PM's recovery."

7. In terms of the UK telecommunications industry, the first 5-year license for BT embodied an allowable annual price increase for an index of BT's services equal to the rate of inflation (RPI) less 3 percent (X). This simply means that the company is committed to a 3 percent per annum efficiency gain in order to maintain real unit-cost increases constant. See Vickers and Yarrow (1988).

5

Early Privatizations

CHRISTOPHER ADAM and WILLIAM CAVENDISH

Malaysia has frequently been portrayed as one of the standard-bearers of privatization amongst developing countries. As early as 1985, the *Euromoney* business magazine claimed that "outside the UK, Malaysia's program of selling off huge chunks of the public estate is probably the most extensive of its kind in the world."[1] However, throughout the 1980s at least, this reputation was unwarranted. Though the program has had a high profile and has involved a considerable volume of resources, its net impact on the relative balance of the public and private sectors has been minimal. It has been more closely linked with other government policy objectives than with the basic economic objectives assigned to privatization. This is somewhat ironic since Malaysia has a strong economic base on which privatization can thrive. It is a large economy, has a sophisticated capital market, and a thriving private sector. However, much of the potential of the economy, including the effects of the privatization program, has been constrained by government intervention, in the main through the structures and consequences of the New Economic Policy (NEP), the ethnically-oriented affirmative action program which has shaped the conduct of economic policy in Malaysia since the early 1970s.

By mid-1990, there had been approximately 24 major privatization initiatives handled by the EPU, and listed by the government as privatizations. The Malaysian government uses a broad definition of privatization, which includes various liberalization and deregulation measures and B-O-T projects, as well as asset sales. The first section will reflect all these initiatives, but the focus will be mainly on the asset sales and leases. The next two sections will describe the major privatizations in detail, and another section will identify key policy and design issues which have emerged.

Mainstream Privatization Initiatives

Table 5.1 summarizes the EPU privatizations to mid-1990.[2] Of the asset sales, the four largest are all in the transport and communications sector, although of these, only in the Klang Container Terminal sale did the government sell a majority of the equity.[3] There have been four public issues in the program, although only MAS and MISC were of any appreciable scale, and it is noticeable that these sales occurred early in the program (prior to the 1987 stock-market crash).

Since early 1987, although there have been a number of smaller EPU sales (including the public issue of equity in Cement Sarawak and the finance company Tradewinds), the emphasis has switched towards contracting-out and, in particular, the negotiation of B-O-T contracts—especially in the road sector and the provision of water treatment facilities. Included within this group of initiatives is the North–South Highway project which, at RM4.3 billion, is the single largest B-O-T project undertaken to date.

Table 5.1 also lists two major privatizations involving Jabatan Telekom, the government's Telecommunications Department, which was corporatized as a public company—Syarikat Telekom Malaysia Berhad—in 1987, and sold to the public after three years and LLN, the National Electricity Board, which was corporatized on 1 September 1990.

One of the striking features of the EPU privatizations is that the majority have been in sectors which are traditionally not tackled early in privatization programs elsewhere. Whereas in most programs, sales of utilities followed a period in which smaller, more competitive firms were sold, in Malaysia, the pattern seems to have been somewhat reversed. Transport, roads, telecommunications, and water supply have been sectors targeted for early attention. However, as discussed in greater detail below, this impression of monopoly privatization may not be entirely appropriate.

Though the overall scale of the EPU privatization process was small, the individual asset sales were important in defining the shape of future policy. The next section briefly describes the individual enterprise sales in chronological order, while another section considers, in detail, the key issues of policy implementation and program management, employment guarantees, risk sharing, and, in particular, the impact of the ownership objectives of the NEP.

Privatization Projects

Port Klang Container Terminal (1983–1986)

The privatization of container handling at Port Klang was central to the development of privatization techniques in Malaysia. Not only was it the first major privatization initiative following the government's explicit commitment to the policy, but it also served as a trial for future sales. It laid down guidelines in the areas of employment and pensions legislation, labor relations, and land sales, and provided the government and the civil service with the opportunity to acquire expertise in handling privatization efforts.

TABLE 5.1 EPU-Monitored Privatizations as of Mid-1990[a]

	Date	Sector	Method	Amt Sold[b]	Capitalzn[c] RMm.	Proceeds[d] RMm.	Adviser[e]	Completed
1. Completed Sales								
Klang Container Terminal (KCT)	1985	Transport	Private	51%	111.6	56.9	ASEAM	Yes
Sports Toto	1985	Services	Private	70%	30.0	35.5	AMMB	Yes
Malaysian Airline System	1985	Transport	Public	20%	350.0	63.0	MIMB	Yes
Aircraft Repair & Overhaul Dept (AIROD)	1984	Transport	Private	49%	6.8	72.8	EPU	Yes
Malaysian Int'l Shipping Corp. (MISC)	1987	Transport	Public	11%	500.0	136.3	AMMB	Yes
Tradewinds Berhad	1988	Finance	Public	7%	140.0	10.7	AIMB	Yes
Syarikat Gula Padang Terap Sdn. Bhd.	1988	Agric/Sugar	Private	100%	–	51.0	EPU	Yes
Cement Sarawak	1989	Manufact	Public	16%	32.0	6.4	AMMB	Yes
Cawangan Percetakan Keselamatan	1989	Printing	Private	100%	–	5.0	EPU	Yes
TOTAL PROCEEDS						437.6		
2. Licensing/Contracting/B-O-T								
TV3	1983	Services	Licence	–	–	44.1	CIMB	Yes
Kuching Interchange	1987	Roads	B-O-T	–	–	86.0	EPU	Yes
North Klang Bypass	1987	Roads	B-O-T	–	–	20.5	EPU	Yes
Kuala Lumpur Interchange	1987	Roads	B-O-T	–	–	300.0	EPU	Ongoing
Labuan Water Supply	1988	Water	B-O-T	–	–	126.5	EPU	Yes
North–South Highway	1988	Roads	B-O-T	–	–	4,300.0	EPU	Ongoing
Larut Matang Water Supply	1989	Water	B-O-T	–	–	339.0	EPU	Ongoing
Ipoh Water Supply	1989	Water	B-O-T	–	–	308.0	EPU	Ongoing

TABLE 5.1 (continued)

	Date	Sector	Method	Amt Sold[b]	Capitalzn[c] RMm.	Proceeds[d] RMm.	Adviser[e]	Completed
Labuan–Beaufort Interconnection	1989	Roads	B-O-T	–	–	80.0	EPU	Yes
Garbage Disposal	1990	Services	B-O-T	–	–	50.0	EPU	Ongoing
Marketing of Airtime	n.k.	Services	MC	–	–	–	EPU	Ongoing
RISDA Marketing	n.k.	Services	MC	–	–	–	EPU	Ongoing
Tube Wells	n.k.	Services	MC	–	–	–	EPU	Ongoing
Semenyih Dam	n.k.	Water	MC	–	–	–	EPU	Ongoing
Abattoir	n.k.	Livestock	Leasing	–	–	–	EPU	Ongoing
TOTAL CONTRACT VALUE						5,654.12		
3. Corporatizations								
Syarikat Telekom Malaysia Berhad (STMB)	Jan 1987	Telecoms	Public[f] 49%	equity[f]	500.0	4,000.0	EPU	Yes
Lembaga Letrik Negara (LLN)	1990	Power	Public[f] 49%	equity[f]	–	10,800.0	EPU	Ongoing
TOTAL						14,800.0		

[a]Excludes all divestitures handled by UPSAK.
[b]Amount of government equity to be sold.
[c]Paid-up capital as reported to CICU.
[d]Proceeds accruing to government only for asset sales. Value of contract for contracts/licenses and B-O-T.
[e]AMMB: Arab Malaysian Merchant Bank, AîMB: Asian International Merchant Bank, MIMB: Malaysian International Merchant Bank, CIMB: Commerce International Merchant Bank.
[f]Proceeds exclude costs of divestiture process.
Source: EPU.

The Privatization Process[4]

The Klang Port Authority (KPA) is a wholly government-owned enterprise which manages the largest port in Malaysia. It was established under the Ports Authority Act, 1963, and in 1973, established a container terminal. Throughout its history, KPA has been a profitable enterprise, though since 1973, the container terminal has been the most profitable part of the port. Despite this, KPA was perceived to be performing inefficiently, and concerns were expressed that Port Klang would be boycotted by international shippers, raising the uncomfortable specter of an even greater proportion of Malaysia's trade being routed through Singapore. Consequently, though the decision to privatize the container operations at Port Klang was taken very suddenly (allegedly in an attempt to find something to privatize in order to create some credibility for the program), there was a clear efficiency motive for it.

The privatization process began in November 1983, when the Prime Minister (personally) selected the container terminal as Malaysia's inaugural privatization transaction. In June 1984, a local merchant bank, Aseambankers, was selected as lead consultants in a team which included two UK firms with privatization experience, Price Waterhouse and Kleinwort Benson. The submission of the consultants' report to the government led to the immediate creation of the EPU (Main) Committee on Privatization to review it. Offers were subsequently invited, with four bids finally being accepted for consideration, all of which were joint ventures with foreign companies. The winning bid was accepted in March 1985, and came from a consortium, Konnas Terminal Kelang (KTK), which was specifically created as a joint venture between a Malaysian company, Kontena Nasional (80 percent), and P&O Australia (20 percent). Under an amendment to the Ports Authority Act 1963, a separate company, Klang Container Terminal (KCT), was created with an authorized capital of RM500 million. KCT issued the total equity to KPA for RM111.6 million (for the movable assets of the terminal, and a lease fee for the immovable assets, land and buildings of RM16.9 million per annum).[5] KTK then purchased 51 percent of these shares from KPA (for RM56.9 million), and became the managing partner of KCT. KCT began operating as a private company in March 1986.

Kontena Nasional is a Malaysian company in which a number of larger SOEs have an equity holding, and consequently, the change in ownership structure of the container terminal is as follows:

KCT Share Ownership

		Post-Sale	
Port Authority	100%	Klang Port Authority	49%
		Konnas Terminal Kelang	51%
		of which	
		Kontena Nasional 80%	
		P&O Australia 20%	
			100%

Kontena Nasional Share Ownership

Permodalan Nasional Berhad	82.0%
MISC	7.5%
Pernas Shipping	7.5%
Other	3.0%
	100.0%

Indirect Shareholding in KCT

Klang Port Authority	49.0%	(SOE)
Permodalan Nasional Berhad	33.5%	(SOE)
MISC	3.1%	(SOE)
PERNAS Shipping	3.1%	(SOE)
P&O Australia	10.2%	(FOREIGN)
Other Private Sector	1.1%	(PRIVATE)
	100.0%	

Clearly, in terms of ownership, there is very little by way of pure privatization, since KCT remains 88.7 percent owned by government-owned enterprises. The key issue was not the transfer of ownership of KCT to the private sector, but rather the fact that the equity injection from P&O Australia effectively purchased a management contract, through which P&O staff now occupy the posts of Chief Executive Officer, Acting General Manager, and Chief Engineer. The extent to which the efficiency turnaround can be attributed to this rather than the change in ownership per se is considered below.

Further Privatization of KCT

In the initial agreement between KPA and KTK, it was recommended that KCT should, within a period of two years, seek a public listing on the Kuala Lumpur Stock Exchange, involving a dilution of KPA's holding in KCT from 49 percent to 20 percent; that of KTK from 51 percent to 40 percent; the creation of a 5 percent employee participation scheme;[6] and the balance sold to the market (subject to the usual NEP provisos). The KCT, to be known as the West Port, would be given over exclusively to containerization, and under the management agreement/memorandum of understanding between KPA and KCT, the latter has a first-right-of-refusal on any new containerization activity within Port Klang. This clearly would establish KCT as the major operator within Port Klang, and, moreover, in proscribing competition in the port, would leave KCT in a domestic monopoly position.

Sports Toto Malaysia (August 1985 and July 1987)

Sports Toto Malaysia was established by the Government in 1969 for the purpose of running Toto (lottery) betting activities in terms of the Pool Betting

Act, 1967. The company started operations with an authorized share capital of RM1 million, and an initial paid-up capital of RM200. It performed successfully throughout the 1970s, and was not affected by the recession in the mid-1980s. In 1983, the share capital was raised to RM1,000,200 by a bonus issue of RM1 million out of retained earnings.

In August 1985, following an offer by interested private-sector investors (through first-come, first-served approach), the Minister of Finance (Incorporated) sold 70 percent of the equity to a private company, B&B Enterprises Berhad, for RM35 million. At the same time, B&B passed on 10 percent of the equity to Melewar Corporation Berhad. The sale conditions included payment in perpetuity of a 3 percent royalty to the government and 10 percent of pre-tax profits to the National Sports Council. In early 1987, a rights issue was made for RM29 million (29 for 1) paid in cash by all shareholders, raising total paid-up capital to RM30 million. Following this, Sports Toto sought and gained a public listing on the KLSE concurrent with a public offer of 5.25 million existing shares (17.5 percent) by the two private-sector shareholders, at RM2 per RM1 share. In accordance with practices in other public issues, the company also issued a Special Rights Share to the government, allowing it to be represented with observer status at AGMs, to grant or withhold prior consent on issues of merger, take-over, asset disposal, or amalgamation, and to appoint three directors, including the chairman, in addition to its rights as an ordinary shareholder.

Of the 5.25 million shares, 1.5 million (28 percent) were allocated to directors, employees, and Toto agents, 1.125 million to approved Bumiputera institutions, and 2.625 million to Malaysian companies and citizens, subject to the restriction that no single holding (other than by the government or anyone acting on its behalf) was to exceed 10 percent of total issued capital.[7] The public issue raised RM10.5 million, which accrued to B&B (RM9 million) and Melewar (RM1.3 million), leaving the post-sale share distribution as follows:

Sports Toto Share Ownership

	1983	1985 (Sale)	1987 (Pre-Listing)	1988 (Post-Listing)
Minister of Finance	1.0m. (100%)	0.3m. (30%)	9.0m. (30%)	9.0m. (30%)
B&B Enterprises		0.6m. (60%)	18.0m. (60%)	13.5m. (45%)
Melewar		0.1m. (10%)	3.0m. (10%)	2.3m. (7.5%)
Bumiputera Institutions				1.1m. (3.8%)
Employees and Agents				1.5m. (5.0%)
Other Malaysians				2.6m. (8.7%)
TOTAL	1.0m. (100%)	1.0m. (100%)	30.0m. (100%)	30.0m. (100%)

Interestingly, though the 1987 sale of Sports Toto equity is often referred to by the Malaysian authorities as a privatization, there has been no dilution of the government holding since its original sale in 1985, although the 1987 sale did provide for the issue of a "Golden Share."

Malaysian Airline System Berhad (MAS) (1985)

MAS was created in 1972 out of Malaysia-Singapore Airlines Limited (MSA) following the separation of the two countries in 1965.[8] Throughout the 1970s, the airline performed well, concentrating mainly on the domestic and regional network, although by 1978 it was beginning to expand its operations significantly, especially into the international market. The early 1980s were difficult times and, although capacity utilization remained reasonable (at around 66 percent), MAS was hit by high interest rates and high fuel costs, and in 1981/2, turned in a loss of RM35 million. It paid no dividend to the government during the five years to 1985 (Table 5.2).

In response to these conditions, the company decided to strengthen its capital base to boost cash flow and to finance fleet modernization. It approached the government with a request for RM250 million, which was not initially approved. However, and, it is argued, probably in response to the successful publicity surrounding the privatization of British Airways in the UK, the government later recommended that the MAS capital requirement should be met through a public share issue, part of which would consist of a sale of government equity in the airline. The privatization of MAS was thus embedded in a broader capital restructuring and listing of MAS shares on the KLSE.

The initial share capital of MAS at the time of its incorporation was 5 million shares, all held by the government. This was gradually increased to 70 million in 1979 through progressive cash injections from the government. Prior to listing, a revaluation was carried out on all assets, leading to a revaluation surplus which, along with RM131 million from the General Reserve, added a further 210 million shares, leaving the issued capital of the company prior to listing and the new issue at 280 million shares.[9]

The MAS capital issue/privatization occurred in October 1985 with the issue of the first privatization prospectus in Malaysia. It established the objectives of the sale and outlined the share allocation procedures to be adopted. According to the prospectus, the sale was to have four main objectives, namely: (i) to implement the government's policy of privatization; (ii) to provide an opportunity for government-approved institutions, Malaysian investors, and eligible employees of MAS and its subsidiaries to participate in the equity of the company in accordance with the objectives of the NEP; (iii) to raise capital for the MAS fleet expansion; and (iv) to obtain a public listing for the company.

The listing of MAS stock on the KLSE consisted of three elements. First, the company issued 70 million RM1 shares (priced at RM1.80). Second, the

TABLE 5.2 Malaysian Airline System: Financial and Operation Performance

	1979/80	1900/81	1981/82	1982/83	1983/84	1984/85	1985/86	1986/87	1987/88	1988/89
Total Revenue (RMm.)	581.5	825.7	995.3	1,183.5	1,237.3	1,314.4	1,326.0	1,432.7	1,613.9	1,939.2
Total Expenditure (RMm.)	562.5	817.1	1,028.9	1,170.8	1,140.1	1,179.7	1,218.8	1,316.9	1,458.5	1,738.9
Pre-tax Profit/(loss)	19.0	8.6	(33.6)	12.7	97.2	134.7	107.2	115.8	155.4	200.3
Rate of Profit (%)	3.3	1.0	-3.4	1.1	7.9	10.2	8.1	8.1	9.6	10.3
Passenger Load Factor	69.0	68.2	70.3	70.2	70.9	74.6	72.9	70.8	75.9	77.0
Overall Load Factor	67.5	67.3	70.9	65.1	69.8	73.8	74.0	72.9	77.0	76.9
Real Revenue per Employee (constant 1985 RM'000)	74.5	91.5	99.8	118.8	123.5	124.1	123.0	125.6	135.3	150.0

Source: MAS, Annual Report, 1988/89.

government sold 35 million of its own equity to approved institutions (through private placement). Finally, the company issued a RM1 Special Rights Redeemable Preference Share to the Government. This "Golden Share" gave the government the right of veto over the acquisition of the airline by a third party, the acquisition of other companies by MAS, and any major sale of assets. In addition, the Golden Shareholder also had the right to appoint six of the eleven board members.[10]

The share allocation was determined in line with Capital Issues Committee procedures established to ensure that, in the primary issue at least, the distribution of equity ownership accorded with the objectives of the NEP. The 70 million new share issue was distributed as follows: employees of MAS and its subsidiaries 17.5 million shares (25.0 percent), approved Bumiputera institutions 3 million shares (4.3 percent); and Malaysian companies and citizens 49.5 million shares (70.7 percent). The issue and sale (which was heavily oversubscribed) generated gross proceeds to MAS of RM126 million (RM121 million after expenses), while the government placement yielded RM63 million in privatization proceeds. Following the public issue, the distribution of shareholders was as follows:

Malaysian Airline System Share Ownership

	Pre-Sale	Post-Sale
Minister of Finance (Incorporated)	252m. (90%)	217.0m. (62%)
State of Sarawak	14m. (5%)	14.0m. (4%)
State of Sabah	14m. (5%)	14.0m. (4%)
Bumiputera institutions (PNB, etc.)		38.0m. (11%)
Employees of MAS		17.5m. (5%)
Other Malaysians and companies		49.5m. (14%)
	280m. (100%)	350.0m. (100%)

The government remains the single major shareholder and the public sector as a whole (including Bumiputera institutions) still controls 81 percent of the equity. Moreover, the shareholder control by government is underwritten further by the Special Rights share.

AIROD—Aircraft Maintenance (1985)

AIROD is a RM73 million joint-venture company, employing 200 people and providing maintenance and repair services for the Royal Malaysian Air Force. It was incorporated in late 1986, with the shareholding split between Lockheed Aircraft Services International of the USA, which holds the management contract and 49 percent of the equity, and Aerospace Industries of Malaysia (AIM), which holds 51 percent of equity. AIM is owned jointly by MAS (33.3 percent), the Minister of Finance Inc. (29.2 percent), and United Motor Works (Malaysia)

Holdings (37.5 percent).[11] Though initially involved only in repair work, AIROD has moved into commercial and overseas defense contracting, and has also begun "black-box" assembly for Lockheed. The company has a relatively short financial history and, though no comprehensive financial statistics are available, it is known that AIM's contribution to MAS group profits has been positive and rising over the period 1987/8 to 1988/9.

Malaysian International Shipping Corporation (1987)

The Malaysian International Shipping Corporation was incorporated in 1968 as a joint venture between the government, the public sector (the Lembaga Urusan & Tabung Haji)[12] and the private sector (Frank Tsao (Liberia) Ltd and Kuok Brothers Berhad). MISC has subsequently developed as the major shipping line in Malaysia, and indeed has acquired the status of the national shipping company.[13] Growth has been rapid and, prior to the public issue in January 1987, the MISC fleet consisted of 41 vessels with a deadweight tonnage of 1.38 million tons.

MISC's fleet expansion up till 1986 had been financed partly through increases in shareholder equity (from the original shareholders and new, principally public-sector shareholders) from RM7 million in 1969 to RM100 million by the eve of the public issue, but mainly through borrowings through the domestic financial sector. High interest rates, combined with the world trade recession of the early 1980s, severely depressed MISC's financial performance (Table 5.3). No dividends were paid from 1981 to 1985, losses were recorded in 1982 and 1983, and by 1984, the company's debt–equity ratio had reached an extremely high level of 22:1 (average debt to equity for all SOEs was only 2:1).

By 1986 though, the company had returned to a position of profitability (principally due to success in winning a lucrative 20-year LNG transportation contract with Japan, which accounted for 50 percent of total profit), it still required a significant equity injection to support its proposed RM1 billion fleet expansion. It consequently agreed with the government to the following financing proposal, only part of which involved the sale of government equity to the private sector:

i)   A special issue of 25 million RM1 shares to the Minister of Finance (Incorporated), "in appreciation of the Government's support for the company,"[14] fully paid and financed from retained earnings. This step raised the issued share capital from RM100 million to RM125 million;

ii)   A RM125 million one-for-one bonus issue to all shareholders, financed out of retained earnings. This raised the issued share capital to RM250 million;

iii) A RM250 million one-for-one rights issue at par to all existing shareholders (including the government). This raised issued capital to RM500 million and generated RM247 million net proceeds for MISC;

iv)   A RM1 Special Preference Share issued to the Minister of Finance (Incorporated) which allows the government to attend general meetings as a non-

TABLE 5.3 Malaysian International Shipping Corporation: Financial and Operation Performance (RM million)

	1979	1980	1981	1982	1983	1984	1985	1986	1987	1988
Total revenue (RMm.)	349.9	573.4	600.8	482.1	651.3	892.7	974.4	1,217.1	1,383.8	1,534.4
Pre-tax Profit/(Loss)	28.9	56.7	16.4	(58.5)	(60.9)	57.5	163.1	243.1	288.3	391.6
Rate of Profit (%)	7.3	9.9	2.7	(12.1)	(9.4)	6.4	16.7	20.0	20.8	25.5
Dividend	2.5	2.5	0.0	0.0	0.0	0.0	22.5	37.5	62.5	75.0
Debt–Equity Ratio	–	–	–	–	–	21.8	10.4	6.0	2.5	1.5
Earnings per Share (sen)	–	–	–	–	–	57.5	163.1	92.9	57.3	78.0
Real Revenue per Employee (RM'000)	–	–	–	–	–	351.0	347.9	435.6	522.1	577.0

Source: MISC, *Annual Report, 1988/89.*

voting member (above and beyond its rights as an ordinary shareholder), and to grant or withhold prior consent on issues of merger, take-over, asset disposal, and amalgamation;

v)   An application to the KLSE for the public listing of the entire equity of MISC;

vi) A public share offer by the 11 major shareholders in MISC of 84,985,000 shares, at an offer price of RM2.40 per share. The proceeds of the sale were to accrue directly to the shareholders and not to the company.

A number of objectives were achieved by this restructuring program. First, MISC raised an additional RM247 million towards its capital expansion program (step (iii)). Second, by expanding its capital base by 400 percent, the company dramatically improved its debt–equity ratio (steps (i), (ii) & (iii)). Third, the corporation achieved a public share quotation.[15] Fourth, the government divested some of its equity in the SOE (step (iv)), although through steps (i)–(iii), it had actually increased its equity in MISC. And, fifth, the government concurrently acquired a "golden share" in the company.

The mechanics of the share sale are complex, but to understand the way in which the Bumiputera and government-owned institutions are involved in the program, it is important to clarify the exact mechanics of the privatization element of the MISC transaction. The 84.985 million shares were to be allocated as follows: Bumiputera institutions (by private placement), 25.0 million (29.4 percent); Malaysian employees of MISC, 3.0 million (3.5 percent); Bumiputera institutions and individuals, 17.1 million (20.1 percent); other private sector, 39.9 million (46.9 percent).

Malaysian International Shipping Corporation Share Ownership

Name	Type	Pre-Sale (m.)		Post-Sale (m.)		Proceeds (RMm.)
Min. of Finance	Federal Govt	184.0	(36.8%)	147.2	(29.4%)	88.3
Sabah	State Govt	20.0	(4.0%)	16.0	(3.2%)	9.6
Sarawak	State Govt	20.0	(4.0%)	16.0	(3.2%)	9.6
Johor	State Govt	20.0	(4.0%)	16.0	(3.2%)	9.6
Pahang	State Govt	20.0	(4.0%)	16.0	(3.2%)	9.6
Penang	State Govt	20.0	(4.0%)	16.0	(3.2%)	9.6
AMMB	Bank	20.0	(4.0%)	16.0	(3.2%)	9.6
LUTH	Bank	46.1	(9.2%)	36.8	(7.4%)	22.3
Other Private		74.8	(14.9%)	59.9	(12.0%)	35.8
TOTAL		424.9	(85.0%)	339.9	(68.0%)	204.0

Source: MISC, *Annual Report, 1988/89.*

A comparison of their shareholdings before and after the share sale shows the number of shares that each sold. Of the shares sold, 66.8 percent were sold by the public sector, and 33.2 percent by the private sector. More than RM88 million accrued to the federal government, RM48 million to state governments, and RM68 million to the private sector. The most striking feature of the sale was that, though the public sector (i.e. the federal plus state governments) as a whole relinquished its majority shareholder position, the ownership structure of the company changed relatively slightly, with the federal government remaining the single major shareholder, and the public sector as a whole still controlling 45.4 percent of the equity. By 1989, that position had not changed, although it may be noted that the public sector institutions (ASN and the Employees Provident Fund) held a further 5.8 percent of the equity, bringing the consolidated public sector equity ownership in MISC to over 51 percent.

Tradewinds Malaysia Berhad (1988)

Tradewinds Malaysia Berhad is an investment holding company with interests in oil palm, cocoa, sugar refining, life and general insurance. It was incorporated in 1974 as a private limited company with a paid-up share capital of RM2.00 million (authorized RM500,000), held by Perbadanan Nasional Berhad (PERNAS), itself a 100 percent government-owned holding company.[16] During the subsequent decade, private-sector partners were attracted and by 1987, the issued share capital was RM140 million held by PERNAS (66.25 percent), Grenfell Holdings (Malaysia) (30.54 percent), and 3.21 percent held by employees of the company. The shareholders then sought a public share listing in line with the precedent established by MAS and MISC.

The KLSE listing, in February 1988, was accompanied by a sale of 15 million existing ordinary shares of RM1.00 each at RM1.10, with 10 million to be sold by PERNAS, and 5 million by Grenfell Holdings. The share allocation process followed the now standard pattern, with the 15 million shares being allocated: 6.7 percent to employees of Tradewinds and its subsidiaries; 28 percent to approved Bumiputera institutions; and the remaining 65.3 percent to Malaysian companies and citizens, subject to the standard restriction that no single holding, other than by the government or anyone acting on its behalf, could exceed 10 percent of the shares.

The sale generated net proceeds of RM16 million, of which RM10.7 million accrued to PERNAS, and RM5.3 million to Grenfell Holdings, and resulted in a post-sale share distribution as follows:

Tradewinds Share Ownership

	Pre-Sale	Post-Sale
PERNAS	92.75m. (66.25%)	82.75m. (59.11%)
Grenfell Holdings Sdn Bhd	42.75m. (30.54%)	37.75m. (26.96%)
Employees of Tradewinds	4.50m. (3.21%)	5.52m. (3.94%)
Bumiputera Institutions	–	4.20m. (3.00%)
Other Private Sector (including 30% to Bumiputera)	–	9.79m. (7.00%)
	140.0m. (100%)	140.0m. (100%)

Cement Manufacturers Sarawak Berhad (CMS) (1989)

CMS was incorporated in 1974 as a joint-venture company owned equally by the state economic development corporations of Sabah and Sarawak. The company manufactures Portland cement, and from 1978 to 1986, enjoyed a protected monopoly position in both Sabah and Sarawak. Following the establishment of a low-capacity cement mill in Sabah in 1986 (set up by the Sabah Development Corporation), CMS now supplies only the Sarawak market, where it enjoys a monopoly position, since high transport costs serve as effective external barriers to entry to Peninsular Malaysia despite its excess capacity. Though the sector was hard hit by the recession of 1985–1986, the company remained profitable, and has enjoyed an increasingly buoyant market since 1988, supported by high levels of spending by the state government in the tourism and construction sectors.

The decision to divest equity in CMS, and to seek listing on the KLSE, followed the same pattern as the other public-issue privatizations. The main objectives of the sale, cited in the prospectus, were not divestiture *per se*, but rather the wish to obtain a public listing and also to facilitate share distribution in accordance with the ownership objectives of the NEP. At the time of issue, the equity in CMS was held 35 percent each by the Sabah and Sarawak Development Corporations, and 30 percent by Permodalan Nasional Berhad. The share sale took place in January 1989, and involved (in addition to the public listing) the sale of 2.5 million shares (7.8 percent) by both the Sarawak and Sabah Economic Development Corporations, at a price of RM1.30 per RM1.00 share.

Allocation of shares was in accordance with now standard procedures, with 8.8 percent allocated to employees, 27.4 percent to approved Bumiputera institutions, and the remainder (63.8 percent) to Malaysian companies and citizens (of which 30 percent must be Bumiputera). The sale generated gross proceeds of RM6.5 million (RM6.347 million net) to the Sabah and Sarawak Economic Development Corporations, and resulted in the following post-sale share distribution:

Cement Manufacturers Sarawak Share Ownership

	Pre-Sale	Post-sale
Sarawak Economic Development Corporation	11.200m. (35%)	8.700m. (27.2%)
Sabah Economic Development Corporation	11.200m. (35%)	8.700m. (27.2%)
Permodalan Nasional Berhad (PNB)	9.600m. (30%)	9.600m. (30%)
Employees		0.444m. (1.4%)
Bumiputera Institutions		1.367m. (4.3%)
Malaysian Public		3.189m. (9.9%))
	32.000m. (100%)	32.000m. (100%)

Syarikat Gula Padang Terap and
Cawangan Percetakan Keselamatan (1989)

Two small private sales have also been undertaken directly by the EPU, both involving total equity sale to approved (i.e. Bumiputera) purchasers. Both were sales of companies in relatively competitive market sectors: sugarcane-growing and printing. Since both sales were undertaken as private "first-come, first-served" transactions, no publicly available data exist on the details of the transactions, the companies involved, or the post-sale performance of the enterprises. It may, however, be noted that both are relatively small concerns.

Build-Operate-Transfer Projects (1987–1990)

As noted above, one feature of the Malaysian privatization program is the extent to which methods other than direct asset sale predominate. In addition to a series of licensing agreements and deregulation activities (for example, TV3 and various marketing undertakings),[17] Malaysia has pioneered the use of Build-Operate-Transfer (B-O-T) contracts for infrastructural development. These schemes, which involve, in effect, an extension of standard public works tendering by transferring financing risks to the contractor rather than the client, have featured strongly in two sectors: road-building and water supply. Contracts have typically been extended on the "first-come, first-served" basis discussed earlier, and have embodied relatively standard conditions. The earliest B-O-Ts were in the roads sector and began following the passing of the Federal Roads (Private Management) Act 1984. Contracts generally involve local contractors (although foreign joint-venture contractors are also considered), with contract fees and toll-setting arrangements negotiated on a case-by-case basis.[18] Water-supply contracts, which cover only water treatment, with distribution and final consumer billing remaining a government activity, are relatively homogeneous, in terms of both contract conditions and also of the companies bidding for the contracts. Again, details on the structure of agreements are sparse.

Casual evidence suggests that the privatization effect of the B-O-T method has been severely compromised in Malaysia. B-O-T methods can really only be considered as privatization if there is a transfer of commercial risk from the government to the private sector. In the case of the road-sector B-O-Ts, the government's concern over creating credibility for the program resulted in high degrees of underwriting of the private sector contractors by the provision of revenue guarantees against falling toll collection. Clearly, in a situation of full underwriting, the B-O-T scheme merely represents a variation in funding schemes for public works projects. The contractor faces a different (but certain) payment process, while, in guaranteeing the toll, the government faces the same liability as if it was operating a standard user-cost recovery public road project. This problem is exacerbated in the Malaysian case by the apparent "capture" of the government by the contractors, especially on the larger projects. This was alluded to earlier in the discussion on cronyism. In 1990, contractors were forced to suspend toll collection on a highway serving as a major commuter link between a suburb and central Kuala Lumpur following violent opposition from the predominantly Chinese community who use the road. The government has compensated the toll contractor in full (Lim Siong Hoon, 1990).

The Federal Treasury and UPSAK Reforms

Running parallel to the EPU privatization program has been a smaller program of SOE reform and divestiture managed by the Federal Treasury through UPSAK. Starting in 1989, UPSAK prepared an audit on all the major ailing non-financial SOEs.[19] A total of 106 SOEs were identified, although 17 were excluded from the sample as they were either minority-owned, or were state- (as opposed to federal-) owned. Of the remaining 89, government-financed rehabilitation programs, executed under the direct aegis of the Federal Treasury, were instituted for the largest 10 major ailing companies—those with a capital base in excess of RM70 million.

Table 5.4 summarizes the ten major ailing enterprises. The rehabilitation programs are still under way and consequently no details are available on each individual reform, although most include management and production rationalization and financial restructuring, financed through renewed Government equity injections.[20] One particularly revealing aspect of this reform program is the particularly poor performance of large capital-intensive enterprises operating in the outlying states (Sabah, Kedah, Trengganu), all of which were created by state governments in the period of rapid expansion from 1970 to 1983.

The reform program of the remaining 79 enterprises has been carried out (without sizeable capital injection from the Treasury) by UPSAK (and its private-sector contractors). As noted above, UPSAK serves principally as an advisory and coordinating unit, and consequently, it only recommends that restructuring exercises be carried out. Implementation and, importantly, the financing of restructuring remain the responsibility of either the federal government (as in the case of the 10 major companies) or the relevant holding agency, and consequently, comprehensive details of the individual reform programs are not available. However, of the 79 companies covered, 17 required no further restructuring, 12 required further restructuring but were considered viable operations, 18 were recommended for sale, and 22 for closure. As at June 1990, 9 companies had been sold to the private sector, 2 had been leased, and 6 had been closed (Table 5.5). The proceeds (or costs) of the restructuring process are not known, nor are any details of the purchasers.

UPSAK's role widened as the review and appraisal procedures eventually covered all the SOEs[21] and the audit and restructuring work of UPSAK was integrated into the second phase of privatization heralded by the *Privatization Masterplan*.

TABLE 5.4 Federal Treasury Reform Program, 1989: Target Enterprises

Company	Kedah Cement	Perak Hanjoong Simen Bhd	Perwaja Trengganu Sdn. Bhd	Malaya-wata Steel Bhd	Malaysian Shipyard & Engineering	Sabah Forest Industries	Sabah Gas Industries	Kumpulan Fima Bhd	PERNAS Group	Perbadanan Nat. Shipping Line Bhd
Sector	Cement	Cement	Steel Billets	Steel Bars	Shipbuilding & Repair	Paper Manufacture	Methanol from Natural Gas	Investment Holding Co.	Investment Holding Co.	Shipping
Shareholding (%)										
Federal Govt	35.0	60.0	81.0	40.0	77.9	100.0	100.0	99.5	100.0	100.0
State Govt	25.0		19.0					0.5		
Domestic Private	30.0	40.0		36.0	7.4					
Foreign Private	10.0			24.0	14.7					
Financial Performance (1988) (RMm.)										
Turnover	108.1	92.9	143.0	157.6	187.0	257.6	449.8	178.0	39.9	77.1
Op. Profit/(Loss)	8.8	6.3	(184.0)	10.5	14.7	11.6	60.2	1.2	23.6	2.1
Interest	49.2	38.6	111.0	15.8	9.0	90.9	90.9	11.5	36.2	17.0
Net Profit/(Loss)	(73.2)	(55.3)	(295.0)	(5.0)	5.7	(137.5)	(27.2)	(35.2)	(20.6)	(16.5)
Paid-up Capital	180.0	149.6	250.0	67.2	100.0	388.2	371.9	189.3	751.0	49.0
Accum. Losses	(217.6)	(80.5)	(558.0)	(115.5)	(125.0)	(114.6)	(918.0)	(20.7)	(27.2)	(23.0)
Shareholders' Funds	(37.6)	69.1	(308.0)	(48.3)	(25.0)	273.6	(546.1)	168.6	723.8	26.0
Long-term Loans	592.6	428.8	1,370.0	44.1	212.0	1,113.7	1,226.0	166.4	588.9	222.1
Op. Profit/Turnover	8.1%	6.7%	-128.6%	6.6%	7.8%	4.5%	13.3%	0.6%	59.1%	2.7%
Interest/Turnover	45.5%	41.5%	77.6%	10.0%	4.8%	35.2%	20.2%	6.4%	90.7%	22.0%
Debt-Equity Ratio	3.2	2.8	5.4	0.6	2.1	2.8	3.3	0.8	0.7	4.5

Source: UPSAK, Snapshot Review of Major Ailing Companies 1989.

TABLE 5.5 UPSAK Restructuring Program, 1989

Company	Sector	Capital Acc. (RMm.)	Losses (RMm.)	Shareholders' Funds (RMm.)	UPSAK Recommendation	Action as at mid-1990
Pernas Holdings Chain (Selangor)	Services	67.6	52.9	14.7	No action required	–
Pernas Edar	Manufacturing	16.3	23.6	(7.4)	Restructure	Under way
Pernas Engineering	Manufacturing	10.0	67.7	(57.7)	Restructure	Under way
MKIC Security	Services	1.0	0.9	0.1	Sell	Sold
MKIC Amlak	Services	1.0	3.6	(2.6)	Wind-up	Wound-up
Bajakimia Industries	Manufacturing	2.7	2.7	0.0	Wind-up	?
Jean Simons Wigs	Manufacturing	0.2	0.3	(0.1)	Wind-up	?
Malaysia Timber Exports	Manufacturing	0.5	0.7	(0.2)	Wind-up	?
Malaysia International Palm Oil	Manufacturing	25.0	27.9	(2.9)	Wind-up	?
Pernas Hall Engineering	Manufacturing	0.5	2.5	(2.0)	Wind-up	Under way
Pernas Mining	Mining	12.5	18.6	(6.1)	Wind-up	Under way
Pernas Electronics	Manufacturing	2.5	13.9	(11.4)	Wind-up	Under way
Malaysian Titanium	Mining	20.0	63.7	(43.7)	Already in receivership	–
Associated Motors	Services	10.0	18.9	(8.9)	Sell	Sold
Berger Paints	Manufacturing	8.8	12.7	(3.9)	Sell	Sold
Kubota Agriculture Machinery	Manufacturing	10.0	10.8	(0.8)	Sell	Sold
Steelform Industries	Manufacturing	15.0	1.1	13.9	Sell	Sold
Fimajaya Foods	Ag. Processing	1.5	(3.5)	5.0	Restructure	Under way
Fima Mr. Juicy	Ag. Processing	0.1	0.2	(0.1)	Restructure	Under way
Ladang Fima	Ag. Processing	2.4	3.7	(1.3)	Restructure	Under way
Fima Fraser Hill	Ag. Proccssing	0.5	2.2	(1.7)	Lease	Undcr way
Makan Ternak Fima	Ag. Processing	1.3	3.4	(2.1)	Wind-up	Undcr way
Fraser's Hill Mushrooms	Ag. Processing	0.1	0.2	(0.1)	Wind-up	Under way
Ayam Fima	Ag. Processing	0.2	0.9	(0.7)	Wind-up	Under way

TABLE 5.5 (continued)

Company	Sector	Capital Acc. (RMm.)	Losses (RMm.)	Shareholders' Funds (RMm.)	UPSAK Recommendation	Action as at mid-1990
Cashew Industries of Malaysia	Ag. Processing	2.1	(10.1)	12.2	Wind-up	Under way
Fima Rantei	Ag. Processing	1.5	3.8	(2.3)	Wind-up	Under way
Fima Timuran	Ag. Processing	2.6	6.8	(4.2)	Already in receivership	?
Pembangunan Reality Corp	Finance	1.0	(2.6)	3.6	Restructure	?
Koko Malaysia	Finance	17.7	5.1	12.6	Sell	Sold
Syarikat Bandar Baru	Services	0.1	0.4	(0.3)	Restructure	?
Mardec Irving Moore	Manufacturing	4.3	4.7	(0.4)	No action required	–
MTIB Holdings	Ag. Processing	2.0	6.7	(4.7)	Wind-up	?
Pengkalan Eksport	Ag. Processing	0.2	1.9	11.7	Already in liquidation	–
Pengkalan Eksport Shapadu	Ag. Processing	1.3	2.4	(1.1)	Sell	Sold
Kima	Services	20.3	6.9	13.4	No action required	–
Ladang Mara	Services	17.1	10.3	6.8	No action required	–
Batek Malaysia	Services	8.5	7.1	1.4	No action required	–
Kenderaan Langkasuka	Services	0.1	0.2	(0.1)	No action required	–
Kenderaan Sri Kedah	Services	0.4	0.4	0.0	No action required	–
Molek Express	Services	0.2	0.2	0.0	No action required	–
Starise	Services	0.1	0.1	0.0	No action required	–
Kenderaan Manik	Services	0.8	0.6	0.2	Restructure	?
Masmara Tour & Travel	Services	4.2	2.8	1.4	Restructure	?
SKMK-Star	Services	0.1	0.4	(0.3)	Sell	?
Lori Malaysia	Services	10.6	17.5	(6.9)	Sell	?
Syarikat Mawar	Services	0.3	1.1	(0.8)	Wind-up	?
Sate Ria	Services	1.5	2.3	(0.8)	Sell	Sold
State Franchise	Services	3.2	2.9	0.3	Sell	Sold

TABLE 5.5 (continued)

Company	Sector	Capital Acc. (RMm.)	Losses (RMm.)	Shareholders' Funds (RMm.)	UPSAK Recommendation	Action as at mid-1990
Syarikat Perniagaan Peladang	Agriculture	0.9	0.9	0.0	No action required	–
Syarikat Perindustrian	Agriculture	0.0	1.3	(1.3)	No action required	–
Pempena	Tourism	41.7	5.3	36.4	Liquidate	?
Tanjung Jara Beach Hotel	Tourism	20.7	11.1	9.6	Sell	?
Motel Desa	Tourism	1.6	0.9	0.7	Sell	?
Holiday Village of Malaysia	Tourism	13.1	7.5	5.6	Sell	?
Pangkaut Rel Melaka	Tourism	0.1	0.1	0.0	Liquidate	?
TDC Duty Free	Tourism	0.5	0.8	(0.3)	Already in liquidation	–
Sawira	Manufacturing	35.0	6.3	28.7	No action required	–
Pahangbit	Manufacturing	3.8	7.8	(4.0)	Restructure	?
Pasarnika	Manufacturing	1.0	1.2	(0.2)	Restructure	?
Dara Ornamental Minerals	Manufacturing	0.7	1.1	(0.4)	Wind-up	?
Dara Wood	Manufacturing	1.0	6.8	(5.8)	Already in receivership	–
Kuari Kerisek	Manufacturing	0.6	1.0	(0.4)	Lease	Leased
Binadara	Manufacturing	0.9	3.6	(2.7)	Lease	Leased
Ladang Petri Tenggara	Agriculture	9.3	14.2	(4.9)	No action required	–
Pertanian Johor Tenggara	Agriculture	8.0	5.8	2.2	No action required	–
Kejora Avi	Tourism	9.0	11.3	(2.3)	Sell	?
Kejora Golf & Realty Devt.	Property	4.5	2.8	1.7	Sell	?
Desaru	Tourism	0.4	2.2	(1.8)	Sell	?
Johor Tenggara Hotel	Tourism	4.3	9.3	(5.0)	Sell	?
Rakyat Keteng	Agriculture	7.0	2.6	4.4	No action required	–
Ketengah Pewira	Agriculture	28.5	10.3	18.2	No action required	–
Ketengah Jaya	Agriculture	20.6	5.3	15.3	No action required	–

TABLE 5.5 (continued)

Company	Sector	Capital Acc. (RMm.)	Losses (RMm.)	Shareholders' Funds (RMm.)	UPSAK Recommendation	Action as at mid-1990
Kesedar Inn	Tourism	1.1	0.1	1.0	No action required	—
Syarikat Majutani	Manufacturing	1.1	8.5	(7.4)	Liquidate	?
Kedawan Engineering Corp.	Manufacturing	0.1	0.2	(0.1)	Wind-up	?
Keda Pallet	Manufacturing	0.2	0.3	(0.1)	Wind-up	?
Syarikat Gabungan Risda	Ag. Processing	7.0	5.1	1.9	Restructure	?
Smallholders Aqua Farm	Ag. Processing	3.2	3.8	(0.6)	Lease	?
Narsco Properties	Ag. Processing	0.8	0.2	0.6	Wind-up	?
TOTAL		536.6	539.2	(2.7)		

SUMMARY	Recommendation	No.	Action
	No action[a]	22	11
	Sell[b]	22	–
	Liquidate	3	–
	Wind-up	19	9
	Restructure	13	5
	TOTAL	79	25

[a] Includes those already in liquidation.
[b] Includes lease.
Source: UPSAK.

Assessment of the Privatization Program, 1983–1990

The first seven years' experience of privatization in Malaysia provides a considerable body of information with which to assess privatization policy. The experience reveals much about the relative importance of the various objectives cited in the *Guidelines for Privatization*, and raises some more fundamental issues relating to ownership and performance in Malaysia.

Privatization Outcomes and Objectives

Table 5.6 details the gross cash flow generated by EPU privatizations over the period 1984-1989, expressed in comparison to the government revenue and GDP. Even ignoring the costs to the government in pre-sale rights issues, the immediate impression from the table is that, as a percentage of GDP, the proceeds from privatization have been surprisingly small. Even in 1985 and 1987—the high points in the privatization program during the 1980s—total proceeds from asset sales amounted to only 0.2 percent of GDP, while the cumulative proceeds from all asset sales from 1984 to 1989, totalling RM437.6 million, are equivalent to less than 0.1 percent of GDP. When one considers that SOE-sector output is estimated to be approximately 25 percent of GDP, the EPU privatization program was of only very modest size in terms of revenue-raising divestiture—despite its relatively high profile. The position in terms of government revenue is, not surprisingly, similar, with proceeds reaching a maximum of only 0.75 percent of total revenue; and, in cumulative terms, proceeds amounted to only 0.35 percent of total revenue over the period 1984–1989.

The picture is somewhat different when the other privatizations are considered. In reviewing these figures, it should be borne in mind that the full contract value for B-O-Ts and licensing agreements is reported here for the year the contract was signed. The reason for taking the contract value as a measure of "proceeds" is that it represents the amount which would have had to be raised out of the public development budget had the contract not been undertaken by the private sector. Moreover, since details of the payment arrangement are not known with any degree of certainty, the total contract value is recorded in the year in which it was awarded, which clearly tends to overstate the impact of these contracts in their initial year, especially in view of the fact that a number of the road contracts have a long gestation period. However, notwithstanding these points, it is clear that the B-O-T program eclipsed the asset sale program in the period 1987–1990, and represented a significant private-sector contribution to the overall development budget, in line with the commitment made in the Fifth Malaysia Plan.

In order to assess these outcomes, it is helpful to summarize, in a stylized manner, what the objectives of each sale were.[22] This is represented in Table 5.7. Most striking is that, with the exception of the KCT sale—which was a flagship sale—the only majority asset sales have been those in which the Government has responded to direct bids from the private sector. Government-managed sales

TABLE 5.6 Privatization Cash Flow, 1984–1989 (EPU Privatizations Only)

		1984	1985	1986	1987	1988	1989	Cum. Tot.
Asset Sales	RM million	72.80	155.40	0.00	136.30	61.70	11.40	437.60
	% Revenue	0.35	0.74	0.00	0.75	0.34	0.05	0.35
	% GDP	0.09	0.20	0.00	0.17	0.07	0.01	0.09
Licensing/B-O-T/Contracting	RM million	0.00	0.00	0.00	406.50	4,426.50	727.00	5,153.50
	% Revenue	0.00	0.00	0.00	2.24	24.40	3.31	4.11
	% GDP	0.00	0.00	0.00	0.51	4.87	0.72	1.03
Total	RM million	72.80	155.40	0.00	542.80	4,488.20	738.40	5,454.80
	% Revenue	0.35	0.74	0.00	2.99	24.74	3.36	4.35
	% GDP	0.09	0.20	0.00	0.68	4.94	0.73	1.09
Memorandum Items	RM million							
	Federal Govt. Revenue	20,805	21,114	19,518	18,143	21,967	23,863	125,410
	GDP (Market Prices)	79,550	77,547	71,729	79,711	90,806	100,650	499,993

Contracts included at full value in year of commencement.
Source: Economic Planning Unit.

TABLE 5.7 Malaysian Asset Sales: Analysis of Stated Objectives

Enterprise	Nature of Sale						Sale Objectives					
	First-Come[a]	Direct Sale	Public Issue	Majority Sale	Minority Sale	Golden Share[b]	Privatization[a]	NEP[b]	ESOP[c] (%)	Balance Sheet[d]	Listing[e]	Improved Efficiency[f]
Klang Container Terminal		X		X			X					X
MAS			X		X	X	X	X	5.00	X	X	
MISC			X		X	X		X	0.00	X	X	
AIROD	X	X			X							X
Sports Toto	X	X		X		X		X				
Tradewinds			X		X			X	0.70		X	
Cement Manufacturers Sarawak			X		X			X	1.40		X	
Gula Padang Terap	X	X		X								
Cawangan Percetakan Keselamatan	X	X		X								

Nature of Sale:
[a]First-Come: asset sold following direct approach by private sector.
[b]Golden Share: sale accompanied by issue of Special Rights share to government.

Sale Objectives:
[a]Privatization: implementation of privatization cited as specific objective of sale.
[b]NEP: pursuit of asset ownership in terms of NEP objectives cited as objective of sale.
[c]ESOP: percentage of total equity in enterprise reserved for application by employees.
[d]Balance Sheet: improvement in balance sheet gearing cited as objective for share issue.
[e]Listing: share listing on KLSE cited as objective of sale.
[f]Efficiency: improved operating efficiency cited as reason for sale.
Source: Sale Prospectuses.

(which have been predominantly through public issues) have generally involved the sale of only a minority equity holding, have involved the creation of Special Rights Shares for the government, and have tended to emphasize the pursuit of NEP objectives and a capital market listing as the principal objectives of the sale. Striking, however, is the extremely limited role of employee share participation which is present in only three sales, and then, only in the case of MAS was the allocation of shares a significant percentage of the total equity. In the following subsections, an attempt will be made to analyze the cause and effect of these stylized effects.

Program Management and Implementation

The government cut its teeth on the KCT privatization. For the 1980s, it remained the only sizeable asset sale which involved a considerable degree of management change, but as will be noted below, many of the issues raised and lessons learnt from the KCT privatization were of more relevance to the privatization proposals for the large utilities than for the asset sales during the 1980s. Although the initial sale plan envisaged a transfer of the fixed assets and land from KPA to the new company, KCT, it later emerged that this was impossible since the land was not in fact owned by KPA, but had been granted to it by federal government fiat. Further investigation revealed this to be the case with most SOEs. As an interim measure for the KCT sale, a leasing agreement was therefore drawn up pending a constitutional amendment. This amendment was eventually passed in 1989 and allowed statutory bodies to transfer or lease land to private operators through privatization. At the same time, a further constitutional amendment was passed to allow statutory bodies to transfer their operations to non-statutory bodies. This again was an issue which had been overlooked in much of the thinking about privatization, which had initially been conceived in terms of equity dilution in public limited companies.

Employment Policy

A coherent policy on employment and privatization emerged in an *ad hoc* manner from the KCT sale, although the publicity associated with it has entrenched the arrangements in the canon of privatization practice in Malaysia. Again, the issue did not arise in the partial privatizations that succeeded the KCT sale,[23] but has become central to the corporatization/privatization programs for the utilities.

In the negotiations over the KCT sale, CUEPACS, the civil service union congress, and the unions which represented the workers at KPA, initially took a strong anti-privatization line, and consequently, negotiations were protracted. The underlying principle behind the policy which emerged strongly supported employees and stated that "employees will not lose in any way the benefits they enjoyed while being employed by Government." Three options were available to all employees:

i)   Depending on their employment status, workers could opt to retire with generous lump-sum severance pay and entitlement to early pension benefits.
ii) Employees could opt not to join the KCT, regardless of their function. The KPA would be obliged to retain these people without loss of pay, conditions, grade, etc.
iii) Workers could choose to terminate their contract with the KPA (and the civil service) and join the KCT, the new company, on terms no less favorable than before. The KCT employees could not be dismissed for a period of five years, except in disciplinary cases.

In addition to option (iii), the government amended the Pension Act of 1980 to ensure that employees of the new company would not lose accumulated civil service pension rights. Given these conditions, 99 percent of all container terminal employees opted to join the KCT, with the support of their former union (in which they were entitled to remain).

In view of the fortuitous improvement in trade volumes from 1986 onwards, the agreement reached with the unions did not pressurize the financial performance of the KPA or the KCT, since the demand for labor has remained high. However, many of the privatization proposals in the pipeline—in particular, electricity and railways—are of enterprises which are grossly overstaffed. Sale of such assets under the above employment conditions is likely to prove extremely difficult, and it was this factor which led the Finance Minister to announce in 1986 that the government was prepared to sell the entire railway system for one ringgit (RM1) on condition that it was operated as a going concern without employment cuts (*Malaysian Business*, 15 May 1989). The Railwaymen's Union of Malaya (RUM) demanded the KCT employment conditions as a minimum in the debate over the privatization of KTM, the national railways. The delay in bringing STMB to a public issue was due in part to high labor costs (STMB employed 28,000 people).

The second issue related to employment policy concerns the role of employee share participation in the case of public share issues. As noted in Table 5.7, the use of employee share participation is relatively limited, and seems to be used more as a management incentive scheme than as an employee incentive. Employee share participation in Malaysia does not involve free share allocations, share discounts, or soft financing for equity participation. To date, shares have been allocated in minimum lots of 1,000 shares at issue prices ranging from RM1.10 to RM2.40, with applications generally payable in full; this represents a high proportion of average wages in the non-managerial sector. As discussed below, a link between privatization and wealth distribution does exist, but the mechanisms employed to achieve wider share participation were such that employee shares (ESSs) were hardly used.

Enterprise Performance

Identifying causal effects in efficiency gains from privatization is difficult. In general, changes in performance can emanate from three sources: changes in demand conditions; changes in market structures as determined by the degree of competition and/or regulation; and changes in the internal efficiency of the enterprise brought about by changes in ownership and management. It is the third that is relevant in assessing the impact of privatization.

In the case of all the privatizations surveyed above, available evidence points to improved performance following privatization, although frequently the improvement preceded the actual sale. Such improvements can be seen not only in financial measures (profits, turnover, dividend payments, etc.), but also in a variety of operating and productivity measures. For example, improved operating efficiency in the KCT is most easily measured by the reduction in turn-around times for container operations; in 1985, it was 11.6 hours; by 1989, it had fallen by 23 percent to 8.9 hours. Similarly, for the port as a whole, the average stay has fallen from 8 to 3.8 days, throughput was up, and Port Klang moved up from 11th to 7th position in terms of worldwide container port performance. In MAS, load factors have risen steadily since 1985/6, while revenue per employee rose by 20 percent in real terms between 1985/6 and 1988/9. Similar improvements are evident in MISC, where real revenue per employee rose by 32 percent in the two years following privatization, and the company began to pay dividends for the first time since 1981 (Tables 5.2 and 5.3).

The problem of separating the causes of these improvements is difficult since most sales have occurred during a period of rapid economic recovery following the 1985-1986 recession. Given also the fact that a number of the enterprises sold are in sectors with high pro-cyclical elements (cement, external trade, investment, finance), the ability to discern measurable efficiency improvements is made more complex. Finally, it must also be noted that in only four cases was the privatization more than partial, such that it involved a change in ownership and control. In fact, only in the cases of Sports Toto, Port Klang, and the two 100 percent sales have there been any change in management.

These caveats notwithstanding, there are clear areas where the privatization process has had an impact. The first is in the financial structure of companies. As noted, a number of the privatizations stated that capital restructuring, along with the pursuit of a KLSE listing, was a motivating factor. Reduced dependence on government funding gives the enterprise greater financial flexibility, while the process of asset sales (in particular, through public sales) tends to impose an external discipline on the balance sheet, enables the company to improve its debt–equity ratio, and therefore improve its access to credit from the financial sector. This factor prompted the capital issues by MISC and MAS, and in the former case, assisted the company in reducing its debt–equity ratio from 22 : 1 in 1984 to 1.5 : 1 in 1989. In addition to the initial stimulus or capital injection, the simple fact of being listed and actively traded on the KLSE provides disciplining forces through which the company's performance can be measured. The monitoring and disciplining role of a capital market listing can thus be a major advantage by removing control from the hands of a traditionally passive shareholder (i.e. the government).

A partial indicator of post-privatization performance may be found in the share performance of the public issue sales relative to the overall market index, the KLSE composite index. Figure 5.1 and Table 5.8 show the performance of these shares relative to the KLSE. In general, all the companies' share prices have outperformed the market average, although the results are distorted quite dramatically by the worldwide stock-market crash in October 1987. The market as a whole fell dramatically at this time but MISC and MAS share prices stayed relatively steady, driving up the index of relative performance shown in Figure 5.1. Post-1987 share performances are less dramatic, although privatization shares have all consistently outperformed the market. The performance of MAS has been the most dramatic, outperforming the market index by 100 percent over the first five years since its listing, even though its privatization did not bring a change in management. MISC, on the other hand, despite the significant capital injection it enjoyed at the time of privatization/public listing, has seen its share price converge back towards the market average.

The second major area where privatization has had an impact is its effect on management incentives, and the extent to which the change of ownership can solve the principal–agent problems which frequently characterize SOEs. Evidence

FIGURE 5.1   Privatization Share Performance
(Share Price v. KLSE (KLSE=100))

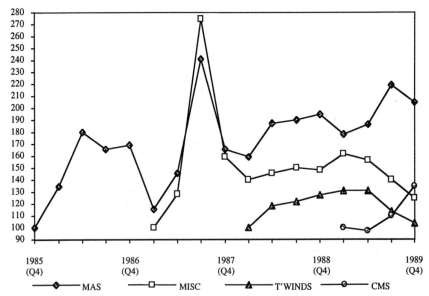

TABLE 5.8 Post-privatization Share Price Performance Relative to KLSE Index, 1985–1989

	Issue Price	1985 Q4	1986 Q1	1986 Q2	1986 Q3	1986 Q4	1987 Q1	1987 Q2	1987 Q3	1987 Q4	1988 Q1	1988 Q2	1988 Q3	1988 Q4	1989 Q1	1989 Q2	1989 Q3	1989 Q4
MAS — Price (RM)	1.80	2.24	2.81	3.12	3.38	4.06	4.36	6.05	5.80	4.10	5.00	6.50	6.20	6.65	6.90	7.95	10.50	11.10
Index		100.0	125.4	139.3	150.9	181.2	194.6	270.1	258.9	183.0	223.2	290.2	276.8	296.9	308.0	354.9	468.7	495.5
Price/KLSE		100.0	133.1	180.7	163.8	167.6	113.6	145.0	241.8	163.6	157.4	185.6	190.7	193.9	175.5	186.0	220.6	204.6
MISC — Price (RM)	2.40						5.25	7.30	8.95	5.40	6.00	6.90	6.65	6.95	8.65	9.05	9.15	9.10
Index							100.0	139.0	170.5	102.9	114.3	131.4	126.7	132.4	164.8	172.4	174.3	173.3
Price/KLSE							100.0	127.9	272.8	157.5	138.1	144.0	149.5	148.2	160.9	154.8	140.5	122.6
Tradewinds — Price (RM)	1.10										1.65	2.12	2.05	2.26	2.67	2.90	2.78	2.88
Index											100.0	128.5	124.2	137.0	161.8	175.8	168.5	174.5
Price/KLSE											100.0	116.5	121.4	126.9	130.7	130.6	112.4	102.2
Cement Sarawak — Price (RM)	1.30														2.20	2.30	2.90	4.06
Index															100.0	104.5	131.8	184.5
Price/KLSE															100.0	96.1	108.9	133.7
KLSE (1977=100)		233.5	220.0	180.0	215.0	252.4	400.0	435.0	250.0	261.2	331.0	365.0	338.8	357.4	409.7	445.5	496.1	565.3
		100.0	94.2	77.1	92.1	108.1	171.3	186.3	107.1	111.9	141.8	156.3	145.1	153.1	175.5	190.8	212.5	242.1
							100.0	108.8	62.5	65.3	82.8	91.3	84.7	89.4	102.4	111.4	124.0	141.3
											100.0	110.3	102.4	108.0	123.8	134.6	149.9	170.8
															100.0	108.7	121.1	138.0

Source: KLSE Research Department.

following the KCT privatization (the only important sale in the 1980s which altered management structures) suggests that a major impact was indeed felt through changes in management attitudes and structures (including payment structures), following the replacement of a public-sector management structure with a commercial-form management system. It is less clear, however, that the new ownership structures in Malaysian privatizations so far have addressed the principal–agent problem. This is due principally to the extent of institutional shareholding, and the particular nature of ESSs. This will be further discussed in the next section, but in general, the process of share-pricing has tended to result in many shares reverting to large, frequently passive, state-owned institutions. Even those shares reserved for management—which might be thought to provide financial incentives for managers to perform efficiently—were rapidly traded as the initial recipient exploited the extremely high potential capital gains in early trade in privatization stocks.

Privatization and Government Policy

Many governments view privatization as a means of raising short-term finance through capitalizing future revenue streams from the sale of assets. This becomes a particularly relevant option in an environment such as Malaysia (see World Bank, 1989c), where there exist concerns about the limits to domestic debt-financing. Combined with the fact that the privatization program began when the government was experiencing sizeable fiscal deficits, it may have been expected that asset sales would be used to support short-term revenue-raising efforts. However, in general, the percentage of equity sold in each public issue in the 1980s was low—the only exception being MAS, where 30 percent was sold—even though there is no evidence that the capital market's absorptive capacity was a constraint. The government could easily have raised a significantly larger amount of revenue through public sales. Moreover, as will be noted below, there has been a tendency on the part of the government to discount new share issues heavily on the KLSE, thereby further reducing the potential revenue flow. Short-term revenue considerations thus seem not to have been a feature of the Malaysian privatization program.

A feature almost unique to Malaysia is the relatively widespread use of the Special Rights or "Golden Share" in privatization sales. The "Golden Share" concept, which has been a feature of a number of UK privatizations, operates in principle as an entrenched provision allowing the holder powers of veto over fundamental decisions of the company (usually involving any major change to the basic orientation and scope of the enterprise) irrespective of the Special Shareholder's ordinary shareholding. It is essentially a guarantee which becomes operable when the holder is a minority shareholder, and is usually prevalent in cases where the enterprise is deemed to be of strategic or social importance. In Malaysia, three of the assets sales have involved the use of Golden Shares—MAS,

MISC, and Sports Toto. With MAS and MISC, however, the entrenchment of Golden Shares would, possibly, indicate the government's intention to dilute its shareholding further, so that it indeed becomes a minority shareholder. If this is not likely, the so-called privatizations of MAS and MISC become very difficult to rationalize: the government sells a very small part of its equity, such that there is no change whatsoever in the effective ownership structure of the enterprise and no change in the management, yet strengthens its control on an otherwise commercial company through the creation of a special share. In the case of Sports Toto, even though the government sold a majority of its equity holdings (it still holds 30 percent), the rationale for a Golden Share is much less clear.[24]

One final issue which is of relevance to understanding the government's objectives is the restriction on all public share sales that no one shareholder (other than the government) can hold more than 10 percent of the stock. This is echoed by the 1985 *Guidelines on Privatization* which states: "as far as possible the ownership of share capital of companies involved in privatization should be equitably distributed so that no one interest will hold an absolute majority." While this constraint is, presumably, driven by a need to limit concentration away from Bumiputera investors, it raises the familiar problem of shareholder free-riding and the failure of the shareholders to adequately monitor and control the enterprise management. If each shareholder has a small equity stake, then no one shareholder will be prepared to assume the costs of monitoring management since the benefits will be shared by other shareholders. It is conceivable, then, that, rather than exposing enterprises to the rigors of shareholder monitoring by profit-maximizing shareholders, privatization through public issue with ownership restrictions may in fact ensure the perpetuation of sub-optimal shareholder monitoring, particularly as ownership is re-concentrated in the hands of state-owned institutions.

The NEP

The evidence of the first seven years of privatization in Malaysia suggests that privatization has been driven almost entirely by the NEP. It was noted at the beginning of this section that the *Guidelines* stated clearly: "Privatization will be implemented within the context of the NEP, indeed, privatization is expected to open up new opportunities for furthering the progress of the NEP."

The asset sales to date (with the possible exception of the KCT sale) have consisted, to a large degree, of the distribution of equity to the Bumiputeras or their institutional representatives. Privatization thus represents a second phase in the NEP, through which the asset accumulation by the government on behalf of the Bumiputeras is redistributed to individual Bumiputeras and Bumiputera institutions. In all the public share issues, a tranche of the issue is reserved specifically for Bumiputera institutions (and in many cases is allocated through private placement), while the "open" sale is subject to the requirement that a further one-third of shares are taken up, in the primary issue, by Bumiputera individuals and institutions. This segmentation of the share allocation process may explain to a degree the "limited" emphasis put on employee ownership as a means of widening share ownership. Unlike other economies, the instruments that influence the asset distribution already exist and the share allocation process uses these institutions rather than, for example, ESSs or other options. Apart from special allocations, employees can further increase their shares themselves through the open market.

The striking conclusion that emerges from this review of the first decade of privatization in Malaysia is how widespread the subjugation of the objectives set out in the *Guidelines* is to those of the NEP, and consequently it is difficult to conclude that the privatization process itself has elicited any fundamental efficiency changes. However, recent developments in the design of the second phase of privatization may serve to dilute this conclusion.

Telecommunications

Prior to 1987, telecommunications services in Malaysia were supplied almost exclusively by the government through Jabatan Telekom Malaysia (JTM) on the basis of the Telecommunications Act 1950. Early in the privatization program, and again, as with the decision to privatize MAS, following the lead set by the UK, the decision was taken to embark on the eventual privatization of telecommunications. Arab-Malaysian Merchant Bankers were contracted as consultants and proposed that privatization be carried out as a two-stage process, starting with the "corporatization" of JTM, to be followed later by a public issue of shares. Corporatization was executed in terms of the Telecommunications Services (Successor Company) Act 1985, which established the encompassing legal framework for the creation of the new telecommunications enterprise. JTM was eventually corporatized on 1 January 1987, and became known as Syarikat Telekom Malaysia (STM).

Many of the legal technicalities surrounding the corporatization of STM had been previously encountered during the sale of the container facilities at Port Klang—most noticeably the transfer of pension rights and landholdings from the public to the corporate sector—although the introduction of the instrument of the "Successor Company" Acts was pioneered with telecommunications, and was also employed with the corporatization of electricity and railways, and other future privatizations.

Following corporatization, the bulk of the 30,000 former JTM employees were transferred to the new company, STM, with a small group remaining with JTM to form the putative regulatory body for telecommunications. Employees were transferred in terms of the conditions established by the KCT sale, with STM being committed to provide each individual with terms of service at least as good as conditions enjoyed in the public service, and agreeing to a five-year moratorium on retrenchment.

TABLE 5.9 Telecommunications Pre-corporatization Performance, 1975–1986

	1975	1976	1977	1978	1979	1980	1981	1982	1983	1984	1985	1986
Financial Indicators (RMm.)												
Total Earnings	221.4	282.7	296.3	368.2	439.4	522.7	636.1	771.7	970.9	1,231.9	1,430.4	1,558.7
Operating Profit	90.8	139.1	107.1	165.5	199.0	225.3	272.5	344.8	316.1	509.3	585.7	565.9
Interest	4.9	8.2	6.7	27.5	19.9	14.5	13.1	80.7	116.8	227.6	284.3	405.9
Net Profit	85.9	130.9	100.4	138.0	179.1	210.8	259.4	264.1	199.3	281.7	301.4	160.0
Rate of Return (%)			12.3	13.7	13.3	11.6	11.2	11.7	9.4	15.4		
Return on Capital (%)			11.0	14.0	16.0	16.2	16.3	18.0	18.7	26.3		
Debt-Equity (%)			42.0	57.0	63.0	83.1	78.8	89.0	153.5	128.4		
Operational Indicators												
Subscribers ('000)	169.5	194.2	227.6	271	325.1	395.6	488.7	585.4	700.1	849.1	958.6	1,042.8
Revenue per Sub (RM)	936.8	997.4	940.9	960.8	969.9	983.6	1,003.8	1,022.9	1,056.4	1,126.2	1,185.4	1,226.6
Lines/Employee	9.94	11.07	12.82	14.85	15.22	15.65	18.12	19.64	23.49	28.08		

Source: Salim (1990a).

TABLE 5.10 Malaysian Privatization Share Performance

Company	Trading Date	Issued ('000)	Issue Price (RM)	Traded Day 1 ('000)	Turnover (%)	Opening Price, Day 1 (RM)	Closing Price, Day 1 (RM)	Premium (%)	Price, Week 1 (RM)	Premium (%)	Price, Month 1 (RM)	Premium (%)	Price, Month 3 (RM)	Premium (%)
Malaysian Airline System Berhad	16/12/85	70,000	1.80	2,390	3.41	3.50	2.45	36.11	2.20	22.22	2.35	30.56	2.63	46.11
Malaysian International Shipping Corporation	23/02/87	84,985	2.40	15,809	18.60	5.00	5.00	108.33	5.05	110.42	5.25	118.75	7.20	200.00
Sports Toto Malaysia Berhad	29/07/87	5,251	2.00	1,833	34.91	7.15	9.55	377.50	9.95	397.50	10.00	400.00	7.70	285.00
Tradewinds Malaysia Berhad	23/03/88	15,000	1.10	2,600	17.33	2.30	1.83	66.36	1.65	50.00	1.83	66.36	1.93	75.45
Sistem Televisyen Malaysia	25/04/88	6,618	2.00	1,228	18.56	6.10	6.05	202.50	5.00	150.00	5.10	155.00	5.30	165.00
Cement Manufacturers Sarawak	02/02/89	5,000	1.30	1,001	20.02	2.48	2.17	66.92	2.25	73.08	2.12	63.08	2.05	57.69

Source: KLSE Research Department.

TABLE 5.11 Malaysian Public Share Issues

Company	Issue Price	Price, Day 1	Issue P/E[a]	Day 1 P/E[b]	CIC Pricing Guideline
MAS	1.80	2.45	5.90	8.03	4–8
MISC	2.40	5.00	4.90	10.21	4–8
Tradewinds	1.10	1.83	5.50	9.15	6–10
Sports Toto	2.00	9.55	5.00	23.88	4–8
TV3	2.00	6.05	5.00	15.13	4–8
Cement Sarawak	1.30	2.17	6.28	10.48	5–9

[a]Based on forecast dividend quoted in prospectus.
[b]As note (a) but calculated at first-day trade price.
Source: KLSE Research Department.

STM has embarked on significant reforms of its operations, most noticeably in the areas of billing, bad debt recovery, and marketing. Repair and service backlogs have been dramatically reduced and cashflow substantially improved, while capital expenditure is expected to be reduced to approximately 75 percent of its pre-corporatization levels (Table 5.9). Competition has also been introduced, with private firms competing with STM in the supply of corporate value-added networks, such as computer lines and systems.

Electricity

Privatization of the Lembaga Letrik Negara (LLN), the National Electricity Board, was not as well advanced as for telecommunications, although the general pattern for privatization was similar: the department was corporatized, staff transferred on the newly established terms—with a number retained in the public sector to manage the regulatory structure for the industry—and, following a period of financial restructuring, the enterprise was listed in November 1991.

Capital Market

The use of public share issues as a means of asset sales has played a significant role in the Malaysian privatization program. Proceeds from public sales totalled RM216.4 million out of a total of RM437.6 million (see Table 5.1), including the two largest sales up to mid-1990, MISC and MAS. Prices have been set by the CIC more or less within their recommended P/E ratio guidelines, and have subsequently been oversubscribed with high initial premia in secondary trading (Tables 5.10 and 5.11). More importantly, these initial premia were maintained over a significant period; after three months, the average premium

TABLE 5.12 Pre- and Post-sale Share Distribution (%)

Company	Pre-Sale Distribution							Post-Sale Distribution						
	Federal Govt	State Govt	Bumi Insts	Other Insts	Employ-ees	Other Private	Total	Federal Govt	State Govt	Bumi Insts	Other Insts	Employ-ees	Other Private	Total
MAS	90.0	10.0	0.0	0.0	0.0	0.0	100.0	60.0	10.0	11.0	0.0	5.0	14.0	100.0
MISC	36.8	20.0	8.0	5.2	0.0	30.0	100.0	29.4	16.0	14.8	4.2	0.6	35.0	100.0
Sports Toto	30.0	0.0	0.0	0.0	0.0	70.0	100.0	30.0	0.0	3.8	0.0	5.0	61.3	100.0
Tradewinds	66.3	0.0	0.0	30.5	0.0	3.2	100.0	59.1	0.0	4.2	27.0	0.7	9.0	100.0
Cement Sarawak	30.0	70.0	0.0	0.0	0.0	0.0	100.0	30.0	54.4	4.3	0.0	1.4	9.9	100.0

Sources: KLSE and Prospectuses.

over the issue price was still close to that which emerged in initial trading, as prices tended to stabilize towards the market P/E ratio, rather than revert to the CIC issue P/E ratio.

Aside from the high initial capital gains, it is also worth noting that in the case of Malaysia, there has only been a relatively modest transfer of equity ownership to the private sector. In no case has there been a significant dilution of public-sector control through privatization, and in fact, when the role of the "Golden Share" is taken into account, it seems as if public share issues have done nothing to transfer ownership and control to the private sector (Table 5.12). Unfortunately available data refer only to the distribution of shareholders following the primary issue but prior to the start of secondary market trade. Casual evidence does, however, point to a dramatic contraction in the number of individual shareholders through the realization of capital gains, and a consequent concentration of equity in the hands of the Bumiputera and non-Bumiputera institutions. For example, company accounts for MISC report a contraction in the number of shareholders from 60,000 at point of issue to only 5,000 following the first three months of secondary trading. This phenomenon is not unusual in share markets when systemic underpricing is prevalent; the same share behavior is prevalent in the UK share sales through the stock exchange. However, one of the more striking features of the Malaysian capital market is that concentration tends to revert back towards public, or quasi-public, shareholders. Given the earlier comments about the issue of risk absorption by these institutions, and their closeness to the Government in the implementation of the NEP, it raises the issue once more of the extent to which the privatization program is in fact opening the economy to greater private-sector control.

Conclusion

Privatization in Malaysia during the 1980s presented an enigma. In terms of the baldest statistics, the privatization program during the 1980s only had a minimal impact on the balance between public and private, and in only a very small number of cases has there been any noticeable shift in the pattern of resource control. However, the program seems relatively firmly entrenched in the policy matrix of the government, and, if implemented, the *Privatization Masterplan* may indeed involve a radical shift towards the private sector. The early evidence from the sale of STM would indicate that this process is now under way.

There are, however, a number of features of the Malaysian program which distinguish it from most others. The first is that the basic structure of the Malaysian economy, and in particular, its relatively open trade and capital orientation, mean that it has the potential to provide a structurally competitive environment within which the gains from privatization can be realized. The private sector is relatively competitive, both domestically and internationally; the supply of skilled labor is good; and the macroeconomic regime is conducive to strong economic performance. In addition, there exists a high level of savings and a sophisticated financial sector capable of mobilizing these savings into risk capital.

Second, there exists capacity to manage a privatization program professionally. Management expertise and regionally specialized consultancy services are available to undertake privatization, while the government itself commands sufficient human resources to suggest that a capacity to manage and regulate privatization exists.

However, thirdly, and most importantly, privatization in Malaysia does not exist within a vacuum. It is most accurately seen as a key element of the second phase of the New Economic Policy, and as such operates within the constraints established by the NEP. Within this environment, the primacy of public-sector intervention, particularly in the intermediation of risk, remains entrenched, and thus the real benefits of privatization are being compromised by continued public-sector intervention in the private management of commercial risk.

Notes

1. "Why Malaysia Means Business", *Euromoney*, February 1985.

2. After completion of the research for this study, two large sales were carried out by the Malaysian government. One was EON motor distributors, which raised RM56 million through public issue. The second was the sale of 24 percent of the equity in Syarikat Telekom Malaysia (STM) in November 1990; STM raised RM2.35 billion—almost five times the value of all other privatization issues put together—and was the biggest single listing ever on the KLSE (amounting to approximately 10 percent of the entire market's capitalization). However, no further details were available to the authors.

3. Although, as noted below, the purchasing company was majority-owned by the government.

4. This section draws heavily on Leeds (1989).

5. According to the KPA management, the initial RM111.6 million included an amortized amount for common services and overheads, although a fee is still paid for security and fire services supplied by KPA.

6. Despite their initial opposition to privatization in principle, the main civil service union, CUEPACS, has negotiated a deal whereby non-KCT employees of KPA can participate in any future employee participation in the share issue.

7. The ownership restriction apparently applies only to the 5.251 million shares issued on the KLSE, and not to the holdings of B&B Enterprises and Melewar.

8. The Malaysian government forced a distribution whereby MAS retained all the fixed assets of the joint airline and the regional and domestic routes, leaving Singapore International Airways (SIA) with only the international routes. SIA subsequently built up a modern fleet and one of the strongest international airlines in Asia.

9. Held 90 percent by the Minister of Finance (Incorporated), 5 percent by the State of Sarawak, and 5 percent by the State of Sabah. The authorized share capital was raised to RM1 billion in September 1985.

10. The Chairman, Managing Director, Finance and Transport Ministry representatives, and the representatives of Sabah and Sarawak.

11. The government also has a 40 percent equity stake in United Motor Works Berhad.

12. The Muslim Pilgrim Trust—an Islamic financial institution.

13. According to the CICU database, there are 20 SOEs in the shipping subsector. Of these, 9 are active, including two shipping companies (MISC and Perbadanan Nasional Shipping Line) and a number of associated companies.

14. Quoted by the Assistant Company Secretary in an interview.

15. Also, as will be noted later, since MISC shares traded at a significant premium over their issue price, the market value of the company increased.

16. PERNAS is the largest of the SOE holding companies, accounting for 99 SOEs (CICU database).

17. TV3 was incorporated in 1983 and granted a license to operate as Malaysia's only commercial TV station. The station serves Kuala Lumpur and the surrounding valley, and currently local production accounts for 40 percent of its output. It was established by a group of private-sector investors (the main one of which was the *New Straits Times*, the leading newspaper in Malaysia). The company was listed in March 1988.

18. Only three of the smaller road-sector B-O-Ts have been completed and are charging toll fees. Unfortunately, full details on the toll schemes and structures are not available.

19. Ailing enterprises are defined as those which had been making consistent losses over the previous five financial years.

20. Perwaja Steel, by far the worst performing of the ten, received an initial RM200 million capital injection.

21. The total nominal capital of the companies covered by the first UPSAK study totalled RM536 million—only 2 percent of the total paid-up capital of the SOE sector as a whole.

22. This is, in general, only possible for the sales involving public share issues as the objectives of the sale are listed in the Sale Prospectus.

23. Only in the case of Port Klang did the sale involve a statutory body as opposed to an SOE established in terms of the Companies Act. In the case of corporate SOEs, employees are not covered by government employment legislation.

24. Indeed, as one commentator noted to the author: "It is difficult to understand what the purpose of the privatization program is when the only majority sale has been of a betting company, and even then the government felt it necessary to issue itself a 'Golden Share'!"

PART TWO

Issues

6

Management Buy-Outs

EDMUND TERENCE GOMEZ

Economic reforms in Malaysia, whether to alleviate poverty and reduce unequal wealth distribution or to promote economic growth, tend also to have important political implications, often related to the multi-ethnic nature of the country's population. This interlinking between politics and economic restructuring is particularly manifest in the area of privatization. While promoting privatization as a means to address Malaysia's fiscal and debt problems, exacerbated by the deteriorating economic situation in the mid-1980s, Prime Minister Datuk Seri Dr Mahathir Mohamad was compelled to add that privatization "would not negate the objectives of the New Economic Policy (NEP). The Bumiputeras will get their share, both in terms of equity and in employment" (Gomez, 1991b).

The NEP, a 20-year redistributive program for 1971–1990, was aimed at reducing poverty and eliminating the association of race with economic roles. The policy aspired, through "restructuring," to increase Bumiputera ownership of Malaysian corporate wealth to at least 30 percent and to alter employment patterns by placing more Bumiputeras in more lucrative jobs.

The NEP's implementation, however, has been severely criticized because the main beneficiaries of the policy have been Bumiputera individuals enjoying close ties to leaders of Mahathir's United Malays National Organization (UMNO), the dominant party in the governing Barisan Nasional coalition. Privatization, actively implemented since the mid-1980s, has come under fire for similar reasons.

The introduction of privatization in 1983 was significant as it marked a major change in Government policy, involving a departure from its earlier reliance on the use of public enterprises to provide infrastructure and public utilities, to bolster economic growth and redistribute wealth and employment. To a large extent, the performance and accomplishments of most public enterprises had been unimpressive. They appeared heavily dependent on Government funds and preferential access to business opportunities, as well as immunity from the discipline of financial constraints and competitive forces of the market, and the knowledge that, because of the supposed social functions they served and the substantial funds invested in them, there was little likelihood of liquidation even if performance was poor and losses mounted.[1] Virtually unbridled public-sector expansion under the NEP had also led to a bloated bureaucracy, inferior and unsatisfactory services, economic inefficiency, high production costs, low productivity, and constraints to innovation (Paul, 1985). Apart from this, public enterprises were subject to political interference by politicians eager to utilize these enterprises to purvey benefits in return for or to augment electoral support; in many instances, politicians used their influence over the bureaucracy to influence decisions favorable to their supporters, even though detrimental to the interest of the enterprises themselves.

While the impetus for privatization may have been justified by the poor performance of such public enterprises, the shift towards more market-oriented development policies has also been influenced by the election to power of strong conservative governments and the ascendancy of their intellectual supporters in major industrialized countries in the late 1970s and early 1980s. These new governments have strongly advocated policies of denationalization. Swayed by this new disposition towards market-led development, major multilateral financial agencies and their supporters, such as the World Bank, the Asian Development Bank (ADB), and the International Monetary Fund (IMF), also argued against extensive government involvement in the economy (Cook and Minogue, 1990: 390).

In Malaysia, the main argument for privatization has been that by placing public assets under private ownership, and by allowing for competitive market decision-making over Government planning, Government control over the economy would be reduced, and productivity and efficiency increased (Mahathir, 1989: 10). Furthermore, with ownership and control in the private sector, resource allocation would be optimized, because in comparison to Government ownership, private enterprises generally have more efficient incentive structures (Jones, 1991).

Other rationales for privatization were that divestiture of public enterprises would accelerate development of the domestic capital market,[2] which would in turn help broaden share ownership. The freeing of capital to compete in the market, coupled with limited Government presence and intervention in the economy, would compel the private sector to bear greater corporate social responsibility, and thus play a bigger role in policy formulation and economic development (Moore, 1990: 54, 68). This would also ease public spending and diminish the administrative burden of the bureaucracy (Moore, 1990: 54).[3]

Despite arguments for the expediency of privatization, the policy has a crucial political dimension because it involves changing ownership patterns, which unavoidably affect income distribution, employment patterns, and control of crucial economic sectors (Jones, 1991). Public political sensitivities are also involved because privatization, in itself, does not eliminate monopoly profits. Another criticism is that public assets may be sold off at discounted prices to selected individuals who later resell them at huge premiums. Government projects can also be contracted out at high rates to politically influential rentiers, who in turn sub-contract them at much reduced rates, thus securing substantial rents. The Malay-sian Government's privatization policy has been subject to such criticisms (see, for example, Toh, 1989; Jomo, 1990: 211–28; Gomez, 1991b; Milne, 1991, 1992).

Such criticisms also abound when privatization of government entities has been implemented through management buy-outs (MBOs), although this method has been utilized, to date, on only two occasions.[4] Although limited empirical data impedes a precise assessment of the extent to which the objectives of privatization have been fulfilled through MBOs, the case studies here throw much light on the factors involved in the implementation of the policy in Malaysia, particularly the political linkages of executives controlling the newly privatized companies. The studies also provide insights into how or on what basis companies are selected for privatization.

The Management Buy-Out (MBO)

Coyne and Wright (1985: 1) define an MBO as an occasion when "some representatives of the management of the company, usually a small buy-out team, have negotiated to purchase the company from its current owners (including the receiver) and organized the finance to support the purchase. The transfer of own-ership should be completed with the former owners having no substantial further ownership interest in the newly formed company." They add that such buy-outs relieve the management from previous constraints which may have hindered in-dependent managerial and financial decisions; this, in effect, "remarries ownership and control within industry, and encourages independent, entrepreneurial decision-making" (Coyne and Wright, 1985: 3).[5]

One factor that has promoted MBOs is that generally, it is not the owners, but the management—particularly in the case of government-owned or quoted companies—who knows more about the assets of a company and is thus able to influence the value of these assets (von Thadden, 1990: 642). This strengthens arguments for private enterprises to have managers who are owners because it enhances the motivation for greater private returns, which helps increase effi-ciency,[6] a contention of some arguments in support of MBOs.

Public-choice school theorists, for example, point out that the managers of public enterprises, unlike those of private entities, seek to maximize different objectives; while the former may be interested in fulfilling certain social goals, profit maximization is the latter's primary focus (see Ahmad Galal, 1986). The principal-agent argument, which is of greater relevance here, maintains that the divorce of ownership from management in public enterprises provides little in-centive for the management (or agents) to perform in a manner that maximizes the benefits to owners (or principals) (White, 1988: 19). This theory's main proposition is that agents wish to maximize their own welfare rather than that of their principals and that owners of large companies tend to be unable to control the decisions made by their managers (Vining and Poulin, 1989). Another major point made by De Alessi is that since ownership of public enterprises is not transferable, this "rules out specialization in their ownership," which will inhibit "the capitalization of future consequences into current transfer prices and reduces the owner's incentives to monitor managerial behavior" (quoted in Vining and Poulin, 1989).

These drawbacks, however, can be curtailed in privatized entities because managerial behavior can be conditioned by shareholders through the share market. Managers are greatly influenced by shareholders' interests to ensure their continued support for the company, thus enhancing the value of the stock. The trust of stockholders in a company's management also provides the managers with an avenue for further generation of funds, thus reducing the probability of bankruptcy, hostile takeovers and, most importantly, attempts to replace the management (White, 1988: 19).

In Malaysia, two public enterprises were sold in 1990 through a privatized management buy-out—the property development concern, Peremba Bhd, and Kumpulan Fima Bhd, a food processing company. In early 1993, two major publicly-listed and media related companies, The New Straits Times Press Bhd (NSTP) and Sistem Televisyen (M) Bhd (or TV3), were bought over by their management for a massive RM800 million—the largest MBO in Malaysian corporate history to date.

Four senior executives of NSTP, reportedly close allies of Finance Minister Datuk Seri Anwar Ibrahim, had acquired a majority 48 percent stake in NSTP and 43 percent stake in TV3 from Renong Bhd, UMNO's main publicly-listed company. Using an obscure private company, Realmild Sdn Bhd, which had a paid-up capital of only about RM100,000 and hardly any asset base, these executives then undertook a reverse takeover of Malaysian Resources Corporation Bhd (MRCB), an ailing property development company whose chairman was Tan Sri Wan Azmi Wan Hamzah, a close associate of Anwar and of former Finance Minister and UMNO Treasurer Tun Daim Zainuddin. The reverse takeover gave the four NSTP executives majority control of MRCB, which was now responsible for Realmild's RM800 million rights and obligations. These NSTP executives later divested some of their equity in MRCB to minority shareholders, a move which helped them to fund the reverse takeover and yet retain control of MRCB. Anwar, meanwhile, secured editorial control of NSTP and TV3, crucial for him to gain the post of Deputy President in the November 1993 UMNO election.[7] Despite the significance of the NSTP and TV3 MBO, the case studies here, however, involve public-to-private divestment.

Case Study: Kumpulan Fima Bhd

Kumpulan Fima Bhd, a product of Malaysia's NEP, was incorporated on 23 February 1972 and had a paid-up capital of RM190 million. Its equity was once almost wholly-owned, with a 99.95 percent stake, by the Ministry of Finance

Incorporated, a holding company of the Finance Ministry.[8] Although food processing was the company's main area of activity, the Kumpulan Fima group has also been involved in trading, manufacturing, plantation agriculture, and general services. Kumpulan Fima, thus, functioned primarily as a holding company for its 16 subsidiaries, 7 associate companies, and 3 publicly-listed companies (*Malaysian Business*, 1 October 1990; *New Straits Times*, 25 March 1991).

Among Kumpulan Fima's former directors were Mahathir (who resigned in 1981, when he assumed office as Prime Minister), Tengku Razaleigh Hamzah, a former Finance Minister and now leader of the opposition Semangat 46, Lorrain Esme Osman, who was involved in the opprobrious BMF scandal,[9] and Tan Sri Eric Chia, a prominent Chinese businessman with long-standing close ties to Mahathir (Gomez, 1990: 32–4).

Among Kumpulan Fima's most important assets was its stake in publicly-listed Fima Metal Box Bhd. Formerly known as Metal Box and under British control until 1981, Kumpulan Fima had successfully taken majority ownership of the company, through a share-for-asset swap by injecting a major subsidiary into Fima Metal Box (Gomez, 1990: 33–34).[10] In December 1989, just before it was involved in the MBO exercise, despite little previous relevant experience, Fima Metal Box was the beneficiary of the privatization of the Government's security printing operations (*The Star*, 2 December 1989).[11] In September 1990, the MBO was announced on the eve of the October general election when Mahathir's future was more strongly challenged than ever before. Kumpulan Fima then had a dominant 33 percent stake in Fima Metal Box. At that time, two other publicly-listed companies were associated with Kumpulan Fima—United Plantations Bhd and Nestle (M) Bhd, in which Kumpulan Fima had a 19.08 percent and 3.4 percent stake respectively. Following the buy-out, Kumpulan Fima divested its stake in United Plantations for RM125 million (*Malaysian Business*, 15 October 1990 and 1 December 1992). This was more than half the price of Kumpulan Fima's MBO, which was valued at RM190 million.

Kumpulan Fima's MBO was led by Tan Sri Basir Ismail, a close associate of Mahathir, who had replaced him as director of the company in 1981 and become chairman in 1986. After making his reputation in the Johor State Economic Development Corporation, Basir was involved in other Government-owned entities established under the NEP, most notably as chairman of the Government-owned Bank Bumiputra from 1985 to 1990, and as chairman of Petroliam Nasional (Petronas), the national petroleum company. Basir is also chairman of Malaysian Airport Corporation, another corporatized entity, and a number of publicly-listed companies—United Plantations, Cold Storage (M) Bhd, Cycle & Carriage Ltd and Cycle & Carriage Bintang Bhd. Despite his active involvement in these public and private business entities, Basir was the powerful chairman of the Capital Issues Committee (CIC), a Government regulatory body which was responsible for monitoring and approving corporate exercises until the estabishment of the Securities Commission in early 1993 (*The Star*, 13 July 1991; *Malaysian Business*, 1 December 1992).

Since the late 1980s, Basir has emerged as a major corporate player. In 1989, he was disclosed as one of the main owners of Hong Kong-based Yung Pui Co Ltd, which had acquired a substantial stake in Cycle & Carriage Ltd from Government-controlled Permodalan Nasional Bhd (PNB). Another owner of Yung Pui was Wan Azmi Wan Hamzah (*Eksklusif*, 30 April 1989). Cycle & Carriage was later used to acquire a stake in Cold Storage. Through his main holding company, Kegiàtan Makmur Sdn Bhd, Basir also acquired a minor stake in publicly listed Roxy Bhd, later renamed Technology Resources Industries (TRI), and controlled by Tajudin Ramli, who is also closely linked to UMNO Treasurer Daim. Interestingly, both Cold Storage and TRI were once majority-owned by Daim. In fact, Daim's equity in Cold Storage had been acquired from Kumpulan Fima (Gomez, 1991a: 25–6). Through Kegiatan Makmur, Basir also owned a stock-broking firm, Capitalcorp Securities Sdn Bhd. In 1991, Basir bought into Jernih Insurance Corporation Sdn Bhd, a company controlled by the Hong Kong-based Kuok Group (*New Straits Times*, 11 October 1991).

Under the terms of Kumpulan Fima's management buy-out, the company was sold to Kegiatan Makmur, whose major shareholders then were Basir, Datuk Mohamed Noor Ismail, the managing director of Kumpulan Fima, and Mohd Fauzy Abdullah, a former employee of Bank Bumiputra and a director of Capitalcorp Securities. The RM200 million loan for the MBO was arranged by Bumiputra Merchant Bankers Bhd, a subsidiary of Bank Bumiputra, of which Basir had been chairman until earlier that year (1990). The loan was provided by Government-controlled United Malayan Banking Corporation, Bank of Commerce Bhd, an UMNO-controlled bank, Public Bank, and Pacific Bank. The collateral for the loan was the entire Kumpulan Fima equity and 2.8 million TRI shares (*Malaysian Business*, 1 December 1992).

Basir later divested part of his 80 percent equity in Kegiatan Makmur to Subur Rahmat Sdn Bhd, a company controlled by Mohamad Azlan Hashim, a former merchant banker, probably to relieve part of his debt burden taken to acquire Kumpulan Fima. Kegiatan Makmur also plans to divest part of its Kumpulan Fima equity to the company's employees, ostensibly to promote their ownership and participation in the development of the company (*New Straits Times*, 25 March 1991; *The Star*, 13 July 1991; *Malaysian Business*, 1 December 1992).

Although it was speculated that the takeover of Kumpulan Fima would be worth at least RM300 million because the company then had investments worth almost RM232 million—Kumpulan Fima's stake in its listed entities alone amounted to RM226 million at that time—and was registering sales totalling more than RM150 million per year (see *Malaysian Business*, 1 October 1990), the MBO was surprisingly priced at a mere RM190 million. Even though the MBO meant that Kegiatan Makmur would take over Kumpulan Fima's liabilities totalling RM138 million (*New Straits Times*, 25 March 1991), the buy-out was severely censured by various quarters. Allegations of favoritism were made by the opposition Democratic Action Party (DAP), while other critics alleged that profitable

Government entities were being privatized to businessmen with close connections to top UMNO leaders (see *Malaysian Business*, 1 December 1990; Gomez, 1991a: 23–7).

Since the MBO of Kumpulan Fima in 1990, the group has continued to register an increase in turnover and profits, as indicated in Table 6.1. However, despite this continued increase in group turnover and profits after the MBO, a segmental breakdown of Kumpulan Fima's major activities in 1991 indicates that there has been no major increase in percentage turnover (see Table 6.2). The figures in Table 6.2 also reveal that Kumpulan Fima's continued profitability was particularly due to its involvement in the manufacturing sector, one of the fastest-growing sectors since the late 1980s; even here, there was a decline in turnover from its manufacturing activities. This suggests that Kumpulan Fima's profits may be a reflection of the Malaysian economy's buoyancy, rather than a result of improved managerial performance following the MBO. Furthermore, the figures in Table 6.2 do not suggest that the diminished or limited improvement in Kumpulan Fima's major activities was because of its involvement in new business sectors.

TABLE 6.1 Kumpulan Fima Group Performance, 1989–1991 (RM million)

	1989	1990	1991
Turnover	205.7	251.7	281.5
Profit before tax	8.9	6.3	6.5
Profit after tax	4.5	6.5	2.9

Source: *Malaysian Business*, 1 December 1992.

TABLE 6.2 Segmental Turnover of Kumpulan Fima, 1989–1991 (percentage)

	Turnover		
	1989	1990	1991
Agriculture	1.3	1.4	1.6
Manufacturing and Trading	89.9	90.3	88.9
Bulk Handling	2.9	3.5	3.6
Investment Holding	6.2	4.8	6.0

Source: *Malaysian Business*, 1 December 1992.

Case Study: Peremba Bhd

Peremba was incorporated on 3 May 1979 as the commercial and construction arm of a Government-owned entity, the Urban Development Authority (UDA). Another by-product of the NEP, UDA was established to assist Bumiputeras expand their businesses in small manufacturing, retailing, and services by providing premises in urban commercial areas (Gale, 1981: 141).

Following the incorporation of Peremba, more than 30 UDA subsidiaries, involved in land and development ventures, were channeled into the company. Within just 18 months of its establishment, Peremba was described by its founding chairman, Daim Zainuddin, as "one of the largest property companies in South East Asia" (*Asian Wall Street Journal*, 8 November 1980).

Daim, Finance Minister from 1984 to 1991, was a founder director of Peremba, along with Mohd Desa Pachi; both men were then also directors of Fleet Group Sdn Bhd, UMNO's main holding company. Daim remained a director of Peremba until 1984, when he was appointed Finance Minister. In 1985, an attempt was made by Fleet Group to acquire Peremba; the deal eventually fell through following a downturn of the property market, precipitated by the mid-1980s economic recession, which badly affected Peremba (Gomez, 1991a: 24–5).

During Daim's tenure as Peremba's chairman, a number of now prominent Bumiputera businessmen 'close' to Daim were then in the employ of the company. Among them were Wan Azmi Wan Hamzah of publicly listed R.J. Reynolds Bhd and Land & General Bhd; Datuk Halim Saad, the chairman of UMNO's main listed company, Renong; Mohamad Razali Mohamad Rahman, a shareholder of Hatibudi Sdn Bhd (another UMNO holding company which bought into United Engineers (M) Bhd (UEM), the listed company which was awarded the controversial privatized multi-billion ringgit North-South Highway Project); and Samsudin Abu Hassan, who leads Aokam Perdana Bhd (formerly Aokam Tin), a quoted company once majority-owned by Waspavest Sdn Bhd, another UMNO holding company.

The management buy-out of Peremba was ostensibly spearheaded by its chairman, Mohamad Razali, its chief executive, Abu Bakar Noor, and Hassan bin Chik Abas, the managing director of Landmarks Bhd, Peremba's main publicly quoted company in which it had a 40 percent stake. Apart from having been a director of UMNO's Hatibudi, Mohamad Razali had also served as a director of a number of private holding companies owned by Daim, including Sykt Maluri Sdn Bhd, Taman Bukit Maluri Sdn Bhd, Pradaz Sdn Bhd, Daza Sdn Bhd, and Baktimu Sdn Bhd; he also served in an executive capacity at the Malaysian French Bank Bhd and was appointed a director of the United Malayan Banking Corporation (UMBC) at the time when Daim's companies owned a majority stake in these banks (Gomez, 1990: 108).

Hassan Abas was also involved as director and shareholder of companies linked to Daim, the most prominent of which was Sri Alu Sdn Bhd. Sri Alu had a 35 percent stake in Seri Angkasa Sdn Bhd, which was awarded the privatized

Jalan Kuching-Jalan Kepong interchange project despite the company having no previous experience in construction projects. Daim's brother, Abdul Wahab Zainuddin, was another director-cum-shareholder of Seri Angkasa, while his nephew, Mohd Amir Mohamed Senawi, served as a director (*Asian Wall Street Journal*, 31 May 1988). The interchange was eventually subcontracted to a Japanese company for construction, and Seri Angkasa later exchanged its rights to operate the interchange for a substantial interest in a then minor publicly listed company, Kamunting Bhd (Gomez, 1991a: 24–5).[12]

Peremba's MBO was estimated at around RM350 million, with all of the company's equity used as collateral for the buy-out (*Malaysian Business*, 16 May 1992). Not having recovered from the mid-1980s economic—especially real property—slump, Peremba did not appear as profitable as Kumpulan Fima; it was also smaller in terms of corporate structure. Peremba, however, had an extremely lucrative asset base. By the late 1980s, apart from its majority stake in Landmarks and its large land banks, some of which are in Kuala Lumpur's Golden Triangle area, Peremba had an interest in Saujana Resort (golf course and hotel) and UBN Holdings (hotel, office, and apartments) and was also involved in the Wangsa Maju township project, a major development venture on the outskirts of Kuala Lumpur (*Malaysian Business*, 16 May 1992).

Before the MBO in 1990, Peremba's total assets were worth RM374 million, while its liabilities amounted to RM65.4 million. Peremba had also begun to show signs of recovery, its turnover having increased from RM139 million in 1989 to RM208 million in 1990. In 1990, Peremba had also declared a pre-tax profit of RM4.7 million in contrast to its RM28 million loss the previous year (*Malaysian Business*, 16 May 1992).

Landmarks was controlled by Tan Sri Chong Kok Lim and his family before Peremba obtained a major 43 percent stake in 1989, following a reconstruction scheme to revive the afflicted listed company faced with the threat of imminent liquidation. To revive Landmarks, Peremba sold some of its important subsidiaries to the ailing company including Saujana Resort, Golf Associates Sdn Bhd, and part of its equity in the highly lucrative UBN Holdings (Cheong, 1991: 137–9). Apart from these companies, Landmarks also owned the Parkroyal Hotels in Kuala Lumpur and Penang and the Sungai Wang Plaza, a large shopping mall in the heart of the capital. Buoyed by these new assets, and with the recovery of the property development sector by the end of the 1980s, Landmarks' performance recovered appreciably. By 1991, just a year after Peremba's MBO, Landmarks' turnover and pre-tax profits had almost doubled (*Malaysian Business*, 16 May 1992).

Most of Peremba's assets which had been taken over by Landmarks were paid for through the issue of new Landmarks shares, which increased Peremba's stake in the company to more than 60 percent. Around one-fifth of these Landmarks shares were then sold to the listed company's minority shareholders, reducing Peremba's stake in the company to around 42 percent. Despite this divestment which has helped broaden ownership of Landmarks, Peremba maintained majority control of the listed company and raised almost RM152 million, which helped ease its own debts and revive its poor financial standing (*Malaysian Business*, 16 May 1992).

Since the MBO in 1990, Landmarks has obtained a 60 percent stake in Teluk Datai Resorts Sdn Bhd—the remaining 40 percent is held by the Kedah State Economic Development Corporation—to construct a holiday resort in Pulau Langkawi, a major tourist location in Kedah. Through another wholly owned subsidiary, Landmarks Engineering & Development Sdn Bhd, Landmarks has also been the beneficiary of a number of minor privatized projects; the listed company is, in the words of its managing director, Hassan Abas, "still trying for bigger privatization projects" (*Malaysian Business*, 16 May 1992).

Although the property development sector recovered significantly in the late 1980s, deft maneuvering of shares and assets by Peremba, rather than active participation in this sector, seems to have helped revive the ailing company and its almost moribund flagship, Landmarks. Furthermore, most of the restructuring to revive Peremba and its subsidiaries seems to have transpired before the MBO, a strong indication that the company was sold only after its previously dire financial position had already been sorted out. Meanwhile, by being a beneficiary of other privatized projects, the growth potential of Landmarks and Peremba cannot be attributed to improved management after privatization.

Conclusion

From the case studies, there appears to be little basis to make a case that the MBOs of Kumpulan Fima and Peremba have significantly advanced the objectives of the Government's privatization policy. Rather, the divestiture of these two public enterprises provides further grounds for criticism of the implementation of this policy. Apart from evidence of apparent preferential treatment in the selection of entities for privatization through MBOs, both these companies appear to have returned to profitability before the MBOs, thus fueling arguments that patronage was a crucial factor at play in both cases. Furthermore, even though Peremba and Kumpulan Fima have registered increased profitability since the MBOs, there does not appear to be any evidence of substantial increase in productive efficiency in either instance. The post-privatization performances of Kumpulan Fima and Peremba probably reflect the generally improved economic environment since the late 1980s, rather than major management improvements following the MBOs.

In both cases, the MBOs were made possible with substantial loans from financial institutions, with the shares of the companies involved pledged as collateral. Although Kumpulan Fima and Peremba had already shown signs of recovery before the MBOs, their managements' access to private-sector financing seems to have been due to their political linkages, particularly with former Finance

Minister Daim Zainuddin. These political associations, thus, cloud proper assessment of whether the funds provided to them were primarily due to the professional confidence of the financial institutions in the management of the companies. The availability of such financing also raises doubts as to whether these managers are truly subject to the discipline of the financial market, as argued by proponents of privatization. The threat of takeover and bankruptcy appears remote, thus allowing managers to be indifferent to the possibility of market discipline, which supposedly enhances the efficiency of these companies.

While the Government has incurred high costs, including opportunity costs, by propping up inefficient, loss-making public enterprises set up under the NEP, these problems do not seem to have been satisfactorily addressed by privatization either. Instead, patronage is still being practiced in placing previously public enterprises in the ownership of private businessmen who are proxies of political leaders. Both Kumpulan Fima and Peremba have had access to other lucrative privatized projects just before and after their MBOs. Also, whatever little obligation to public accountability there may have been in the case of public enterprises is undermined with the privatization of public enterprises. In addition, the public-sector deficit will only be exacerbated by the privatization of profitable public enterprises, leaving the public sector with the responsibility of running and financing the remaining unprofitable ones. By allowing privatized public enterprises the benefits of preferential access to finance—sometimes from Government sources at discounted interest rates—and Government-influenced business opportunities, including those associated with other privatizations, the political patronage prevalent during the NEP period appears only to have taken on new forms, through new institutional arrangements and with new implications, not necessarily less adverse in terms of the public interests.

Such patronage also means that political interference in business continues despite, or rather, through such privatization. Since Kumpulan Fima and Peremba are currently controlled by politically influential businessmen, the possibility that such political ties will continue to undermine economic competition and consumer welfare appears inevitable. Furthermore, these changes of ownership appear to have advanced the interests of politically well-connected Bumiputera rentiers, who are not even likely to be potential entrepreneurs. The rents accruing to them— including those from improved management, in the event that that should be the case—are therefore unlikely to be deployed productively, let alone innovatively. Instead, some are most likely to enhance the resources and power of their political benefactors, while much of the balance is likely to be channeled to mergers, acquisitions, and other paper-shuffling portfolio investment activities, which seems to be the stuff of much of what passes as entrepreneurship in Malaysia, after deducting, of course, for the conspicuous consumption closely associated with Malaysia's political business elite.

The fact that Kumpulan Fima and Peremba displayed signs of recovery before the MBOs suggests that public enterprises can be profitable entities despite, or even because of Government ownership. On the other hand, the case studies demonstrate that in spite of the change of ownership from the public to the private sector, competition does not appear to have increased in either case. The case studies also suggest that there is no evidence that private ownership has significantly enhanced efficiency or improved productivity. This supports the contention that it is competition and management, and not ownership per se that promotes efficiency. This would also mean that in the long term then, the Government's immediate income from divestiture of such profitable enterprises does not necessarily outweigh the loss of future revenue inflows if ownership had been retained.

There is also little evidence to support suggestions that new market opportunities have emerged because of these MBOs promoting economic development with greater private-sector participation. What is obvious, however, is evidence of skewed wealth concentration exacerbating income inequality. Thus, despite the apparent decline of direct and blatant Government intervention in the economy— associated with the NEP period—with privatization, there appears to be a marked parallel or similarity between the two policies in at least one sense—i.e. the attempt to concentrate corporate ownership in the hands of Bumiputera rentiers who enjoy close ties with influential politicians.

Notes

1. Heavy losses have been registered by a number of Malaysia's most heavily capitalized public enterprises, particularly those involved in Mahathir's pet heavy industry projects. Such public enterprises have also been major contributors to the national debt (see Gomez, 1991b; *Asian Business*, August 1990).

2. By June 1992, 13 privatized entities were listed on the Kuala Lumpur Stock Exchange; they had a total market capitalization of RM201.09 billion, which accounted for 8 percent of total market capitalization (Mohd. Sheriff, 1991; *Investors Digest*, November 1992).

3. By 1992, it was estimated that due to privatization, public-sector personnel had been reduced by almost 65,000 (Gomez, 1992: 76–7).

4. A number of other methods have been used to implement the privatization policy. While the most popular method has been the sale of Government-owned equity, other means include build operate transfer (B-O-T) arrangements as well as the lease and sale of assets.

5. MBOs are not limited to the sale of public entities to their managements. Coyne and Wright (1985: 11) list five major circumstances in which MBOs will generally arise:

a) receivership of an independent company, in which the buy-out may be the only means of continuing the company;
b) receivership of the parent company, in which the viable subsidiary (or group of subsidiaries) is bought out, while the remainder of the parent is liquidated;
c) retirement or death of the current owners;
d) divestment of a subsidiary by a parent company still operating;
e) privatization of all or part of a nationalized industry, where a MBO is a more attractive or feasible proposition than immediate flotation on the Stock Exchange.

6. However, it cannot be denied that apart from having to register a profit, the administration of a public enterprise generally has certain other social or strategic considerations to fulfill. In the private sector, the profit motive may far supersede the public service aspects of a privatized enterprise, thus increasing costs to consumers, especially if it is a monopolized industry (Bruce, 1986: 203).

7. For an account of the political and economic implications of the management buy-out of The New Straits Times Press and TV3, see Gomez (1993).

There have been two other minor MBOs in the private sector. In March 1989, Hagemeyer's manufacturing division was taken over by a management team for RM3.7 million. In April 1990, Harrison & Crosfield sold its trading arm for around RM10 million (*Malaysian Business*, 1 October 1990).

8. The Sabah State Economic Development Corporation owned the remaining 0.05 percent of Kumpulan Fima's equity (*Malaysian Business*, 1 October 1990).

9. The BMF scandal involved questionable loans amounting to RM2.5 billion by Bank Bumiputra's Hong Kong subsidiary, Bumiputra Malaysia Finance (BMF). The scandal implicated a number of top UMNO politicians, including Mahathir and Razaleigh. See Lim Kit Siang (1986) for details of the controversy.

10. Gomez (1990: 33–5) provides a detailed study of how Kumpulan Fima maneuvered the takeover of Metal Box with the Government's help.

11. Under this privatization exercise, Fima Metal Box took over the Security Printing Branch of the National Printing Department for RM7 million. Fima Metal Box is thus responsible for the printing of all Government security documents, except currency (*The Star*, 2 December 1989).

12. Hassan Abas and Daim's relatives later divested their stake in Seri Angkasa to Datuk Lim Ah Tam and his family. Kamunting later acquired a substantial stake in publicly listed Multi-Purpose Holdings Bhd, the investment arm of the MCA.

7

Efficiency and Consumer Welfare

WINNIE GOH and JOMO K.S.

Privatization is supposed to enhance enterprise efficiency. There are two relevant aspects of efficiency to be considered here, namely productive and allocative efficiency. Productive efficiency is attained when a firm's output is produced at minimum resource cost. Allocative efficiency is achieved when the consumer's marginal valuation of the product equals the marginal cost of production, assuming no externalities. (However, this does not imply allocative efficiency in terms of satisfying consumer preferences for quality services.) To achieve both productive and allocative efficiency, privatized enterprises generally need to be exposed to greater competition, liberalization, marketization and deregulation, notwithstanding scale economies and other "extenuating" circumstances.

In so far as allocative efficiency may be best achieved through greater competition and deregulation—which have not been important in the Malaysian privatization experience thus far—it is doubtful that consumer welfare has been significantly enhanced through privatization. In fact, there is considerable evidence to the contrary with increases in consumer charges for utilities and services in anticipation of, or soon after privatization, as shown in Table 7.1.

The Government has been preoccupied with getting privatization off the ground. It has sought to ensure public acceptance for the policy by selecting profitable or potentially profitable entities for privatization and by share under-

TABLE 7.1 Recent Consumer Charge Increases Associated with Privatization

Utility/Service	Old	New	Year	Increase
Telephone call unit charge (sen)	10	13	1987	30%
Toll (sen per km)	5	7.5	1993	50%

pricing. It had also minimized employee opposition by providing job security and improved terms and conditions of service (especially incomes). The authorities have ensured that the politically well-connected and reliable have secured control of the privatized entities. In pursuing these other goals, efficiency and consumer welfare concerns have been compromised. Efficiency here is broadly understood to involve gains to consumers, employees, (private) buyers, (Government) sellers and competitors.

Given the privatization process, the motivations for the privatization policy and the nature of the privatized entities in Malaysia, competition for most of the entities privatized has been limited, implying the transformation of public monopolies into privatized monopolies. In all cases, user costs have not been lowered, and in most cases, consumer prices have been significantly increased, ostensibly to reflect the better services provided. This is hardly suggestive of greater efficiency, though it has certainly ensured greater profitability.

Kelang Container Terminal

In Malaysia, the case of the Kelang Container Terminal (KCT) has been much celebrated as proof of the success of Malaysia's privatization policy. This is no accident as KCT was carefully chosen as the pioneering entity for privatization to ensure success and acceptance for the policy besides profits for the shareholders. There have been several studies of KCT's privatization—Nankani (1988), Leeds (1989), Ismail (1991), Adam and Cavendish in this volume, and Jones and Fadil (1992a)—all claiming to find significant efficiency and welfare gains in that case. Of these studies, Jones and Fadil have analyzed KCT's performance before and after divestiture more carefully than the other researchers. A critical review of their findings provides a better idea of the actual gains from that privatization.

Divestiture

The Klang Port Authority (KPA), a government statutory body, previously had the financial autonomy to manage the entire port facility, including the container terminal. With this financial autonomy, it was expected to raise funds for its investments and to pay corporate taxes. Financially, KPA has never been in the "red," and soon after its container terminal went into operation, it became the primary source of earnings for the KPA.

The container terminal was a good candidate to become Malaysia's first privatized project as it met a number of criteria. The authorities apparently felt that the first privatization project had to be successful to secure public support for the policy. Therefore, it was important to choose an entity that was not politically sensitive. Also, the enterprise to be privatized needed to have a track record of profitability (Leeds, 1989: 746).

The KPA container terminal satisfied the above criteria, but was functioning at a low level of efficiency by international standards. Pilferage was disturbingly high and terminal security lax. The below par performance of the container terminal was believed to be the result of too many bureaucratic controls. It was felt that if it had the freedom and flexibility to manage and operate its facilities on a more commercial basis, performance would undoubtedly improve.

TABLE 7.2   Kelang Container Terminal Distributional Impact Statement (RM million, 1985 present values)

	Operation by		Gains
	Private	Public	Privatization
Domestic			
Consumers	1539	1481	58
Government	1887	1530	357
Taxes	1650	967	683
Net Quasi-Rents	185	563	-378
Share Sales (less transaction costs)	52	0	52
Debt Subsidy/Take-over	0	0	0
Others	0	0	0
Shareholders	109	0	109
Diversified	0	0	0
Concentrated	109	0	109
Employees	0	0	0
Miscellaneous	284	330	-47
Employees (as inputs)	66	0	66
Competitors	217	330	-113
Providers	0	0	0
Citizens	0	0	0
Domestic Total	3818	3341	477
Foreign			
Consumers	770	740	29
+ Shareholders	27	0	27
+ Competitors	54	83	-28
+ Others	0	0	0
Foreign Total	851	823	28
World Total	4669	4164	505

Source: Jones and Fadil (1992a).

In October 1985, KPA incorporated Kelang Container Terminal as its wholly-owned subsidiary. KCT was awarded a 21-year licence to operate the KPA container terminal. In March 1986, KPA sold 51 per cent of KCT to Konnas Terminal Kelang Sdn Bhd (KTK), retaining the remaining 49 per cent. KTK is a joint venture between Malaysian and foreign interests, with Kontena Nasional (KN) owning 80 per cent and P&O Australia Limited (POAL) holding the remaining 20 per cent of KTK (see the table in the Adam and Cavendish chapter of this volume). Most importantly, KCT autonomy thus involved handing management over to KTK, and especially to POAL, which had some experience of container terminal management.

Welfare Gains

Jones and Fadil (1992a: Table 13.17) also offer an analysis of the welfare impact of the KCT privatization, which is summarized in Table 7.2. According to Table 7.2, summarizing the distribution of welfare gains from the KCT privatization, buyers enjoyed a positive welfare impact. They had paid RM57 million for an income stream worth RM193 million, thus obtaining a net gain of RM136 million. Of this, domestic shareholders enjoyed a net gain of RM109 million, with RM27 million going to the foreign shareholders.

Who were the shareholders? Ninety percent of the KPA shares were still in the hands of the government (see the Adam and Cavendish chapter in this volume). P&O Australia, the foreign buyer, has the remaining 10 percent of KCT shares, through its 20 percent share in KTK, which has a 51 percent share in KCT. P&O's management of the KCT is widely credited for the welfare gains. If this is truly the case, the welfare gains could presumably have been achieved without divestiture, e.g. by awarding a management contract. It is not self-evident that divestiture was necessary for the change in management. It is also not clear that P&O offered the most competitive management contract available since there never was any competitive (e.g. tender) process involved in determining the new managers of KCT. Such a competitive process may well have resulted in a Malaysian firm securing the management contract, thus reducing payment outflows for securing improved management. If necessary, foreign expertise could be secured by hiring foreign consultants as and when needed, instead of allowing foreign management control.

Performance

KCT's performance since privatization has been quite impressive. Prior to privatization, the terminal handled 244,120 TEUs in 1985, compared to 273,335 TEUs in 1987. The average turnaround time also improved from 13.4 hours in 1985 to 11.3 hours in 1987, while the average length of time that each container remained on the dock declined from 8 to 3.8 days.

Public profitability—defined as Benefits minus Variable Costs divided by Fixed Costs—at constant market prices grew at an annual average compound rate of 4.7 percent in the pre-divestiture period and at 17.7 percent thereafter.

$$\text{Public Profits} = \frac{\text{Benefits - Variable Costs}}{\text{Fixed Costs}}$$

or $$\text{Public Profits} = \frac{X - II - R - rk^w - W}{K^f}$$

where
- X – value of output
- II – value of intermediate inputs
- W – employee compensation
- R – factor rentals
- rk^w – working capital
- K^f – fixed costs

Since fixed assets were stable from 1982 to 1987, the improved performance can be attributed to the numerator. Also, the costs of energy, working capital, and rentals did not experience any significant changes in the same period. The only major change was apparently due to wage increases as average workers' compensation rose at an average compound rate of 12 percent after privatization. This may be due to overtime payments and increased incentive payments, which may have contributed to considerably greater increases in labor productivity.

Although it has been claimed that there has been no change in service charges, "free" storage time was decreased from seven to five days in late 1986. This has effectively meant a 28.6 percent increase in storage costs to customers, which in turn contributed to a 3.9 percent increase in overall costs from 1986 to 1989. Clearly, the increase in turnover (output growth) has been the main source of improved profitability for KCT.

Since output growth has been the main source of improved profitability, could output growth be due to privatization *per se* or to exogenous demand shifts? To assess whether output growth was a result of increased demand, Jones and Fadil (1992a: Fig. 13.7) compared real GDP and KCT output indices. From 1983 to 1986, output growth seemed to grow with real GDP, but after divestiture, it grew faster. They then concluded that since output growth after divestiture exceeded real GDP growth, the difference could be attributed to efficiency gains from privatization. However, the export-led nature of the economic recovery of the late 1980s has involved proportionately greater increases in imports and exports compared to GDP growth, which the authors did not take into consideration.

Throughput has been on the increase since 1987, and from 1989 to 1991, it registered more than 20 percent growth in each year (see Table 7.3). However, it is misleading to attribute this increase to improved efficiency due to privatization.

TABLE 7.3 Relationship between Growth of Output to GNP, Exports and Imports Before and After Divestiture

Year ended 31 Dec.	Throughput (TEUs[a])	Percentage Increase (%)	Turnover ('000)	Percentage Increase (%)	GNP (RM mil.)	Percentage Increase (%)	Exports of Goods (RM mil.)	Percentage Increase (%)	Imports of Goods (RM mil.)	Percentage Increase (%)
1985	244,120		n.a.	n.a.	72,039		44,184		45,716	
1986	241,182	-1.0	75,185	–	66,814	-7.0	41,824	-5.3	42,240	-7.6
1987	273,335	13.0	91,089	21.0	74,679	12.0	52,939	27.0	46,639	10.0
1988	319,557	17.0	107,756	18.0	85,777	15.0	64,114	21.0	59,774	28.0
1989	393,954	23.0	127,221	18.0	96,630	13.0	78,204	22.0	79,011	32.0
1990	494,978	26.0	151,370	19.0	110,505	15.0	94,331	21.0	98,882	25.0
1991	603,257	22.0			123,530	12.0	109,827	17.0	122,595	24.0

[a]twenty-feet equivalent units.
n.a. — not available.
Source: Jones and Fadil (1992a).

After the 1985–1986 recession, the Malaysian economy picked up tremendously from late 1986, with export-led industrialization using imported components and equipment. Exports and imports continued to grow rapidly in the late 1980s and early 1990s. From 1987 to 1990, annual growth of exports as well as imports was in excess of 20 percent (see Table 7.3). Thus, KCT's increased turnover may be due to the growth in̂ international trade, and may therefore be wrongly attributed to privatization.

Government

According to the Jones and Fadil study, the government enjoyed the bulk of the positive welfare impact from the KCT privatization. Although it gave up a profit stream of RM378 million, it received RM52 million from share sales (less transaction costs) and substantial tax gains of RM683 million inclusive of the rental payment plus a variable payment based on throughput. This impressive positive welfare impact was primarily a result of increased taxation revenue from higher profitability after privatization.

However, the authors beg the question of how much more benefits could have been obtained if the KCT was still fully KPA-owned. Prior to the KCT privatization, KPA had never been in the "red." Although its performance was considered inefficient, the container terminal—the most lucrative KPA operation—was contributing a positive net cashflow. It is quite possible that if the KPA had been given the freedom and flexibility to operate the terminal on a commercial basis, the government may have benefited just as much or even more than by allowing P & O to take a share in KCT and to take over KCT's management. Unfortunately, such counterfactual analysis is not possible, especially since the relevant information is not available and cannot be meaningfully inferred. However, other studies of KCT's privatization suggest that efficiency and productivity gains and improvements in performance have primarily been the result of managerial and organizational reforms by the new private management team, rather than due to the ownership change *per se*. After all, there is not much change in ownership as KCT remains 88.7 percent owned by government-owned enterprises.

As noted earlier, there has been a distinct tendency for the government to sell their "most lucrative enterprises" first in order to create a positive public impression of privatization. Economically, however, this policy undermines the potential gains from privatization for the government. If the "worst-run enterprises"—presumably, therefore, in greatest need of privatization—had instead been sold first, the welfare outcome might have been quite different.

Employees

According to Jones and Fadil, employees also gained from higher wages by an estimated RM66 million. This is in line with the government's assurance that employees would be rewarded for greater productivity, with terms and conditions not worse than those they were enjoying while serving the government.

But were there real gains? Although wages increased, real welfare gains may have increased by less than the full amount of the wage increase. Workers may have to work harder, for longer hours. Also, future compensation and promotion prospects are supposed to be directly linked to work performance, rather than seniority. In the privatized KCT, lifetime job security is no longer guaranteed. Instead, the government only required the KCT to guarantee that "no employee would be fired or retrenched for a period of five years." Hence, the immediate welfare gains are primarily of a short-term nature, with some non-monetary long-term losses not adequately reflected in typical welfare analysis. It is also expected that the union may lose its ability and influence to negotiate better terms and conditions for its members in dealing with a completely profit-oriented private-sector employer, instead of a public-sector employer; this does not seem to figure in Jones and Fadil's welfare accounting.

Consumers

According to Jones and Fadil, consumers gained from improved services by about RM88 million. There has been significant progress in terms of reduction of turnaround times as well as crane handling movements, and the increasing number of vessels calling at the port.

The expected operation of the second container terminal, Klang Port Management (KPM), from mid-1993 has provided some competition to KCT (Mazida, 1992). KPM is expected to offer a wider range of services, including container handling. This should be beneficial to consumers as competition should enhance efficiency, though actual welfare gains are difficult to predict without further information about the nature of the expected duopoly. While consumers' welfare has been enhanced in the case of KCT, this is not necessarily true in all cases of divestiture.

Malaysia Airlines (MAS)

In the early 1980s, Malaysia Airlines (MAS) suffered losses due to high interest rates and fuel costs. The government's own financial difficulties and other priorities also limited the funds available to MAS for expansion. An attractive solution to the problem was partial divestiture, regarded by some as a form of privatization. In the case of MAS, therefore, privatization only involved partial divestiture as majority ownership remained in the hands of the government. With its "golden share," ultimate control will continue to remain with the government even if it loses majority ownership.

MAS's post-divestiture experience has been different from KCT's. Management style has not changed significantly as virtually the same people are still in charge. There is no evidence of any change in managerial autonomy as the government seems to be still very much in control. However, investment increased to meet anticipated future demand. This resulted in an apparent decline in productivity due to the greater rise in capital relative to output, and also to the increase in non-fuel intermediate input costs (mainly advertising and marketing expenditure).

MAS has been operating in two different market conditions. The airline faces an oligopolistic market internationally while enjoying a domestic monopoly. Hence, prices (fares) have been largely exogenously determined internationally, while domestic fares are subject to government regulation. Domestically, fares have been adjusted within a designated band to maintain profitability. If deregulation accompanies divestiture, such an arrangement could easily be abused to the disadvantage of domestic consumers. Of course, increased competition on domestic routes can be generated by allowing foreign carriers or even other domestic carriers to compete, but this has not been allowed. For example, Singapore International Airlines (SIA) wanted to fly between Singapore and Sarawak. However, MAS retained its virtual monopoly, invoking its claim to cross-subsidization of commercially unprofitable routes.

According to Jones and Fadil, domestic consumers have been net losers as they have had to pay higher prices and have received only a small fraction of the benefits of the increased investments. Instead, the bulk (four-fifths) of the welfare gains have accrued to foreign shareholders, competitors, and consumers, with consumers benefiting most due to lower airfares in the international market.

Postal Services

The corporatization of the Postal Services Department (PSD) took place on 1 January 1992 with promises to provide better quality and more efficient services. As with other privatized utilities and natural monopolies, it is important to ask if there is a need to privatize to achieve such improvements. The PSD has

TABLE 7.4 Comparison of Malaysia's Domestic Postage Rates with those of Singapore, Thailand, Indonesia, Japan, and India as at 1 May 1991 (RM)

Weight/Country	Malaysia	Singapore	Indonesia	Thailand	India	Japan
Up to 20 gm	0.20	0.30	0.31	0.22	0.14	1.24
21–50 gm	0.30	0.45	0.61	n.a.[a]	0.41	1.44
51–100 gm	0.45	0.75	0.76	0.35[b]	0.47	3.50

[a]Not available as rate is based on a combined system, part of a marketing strategy.
[b]Surface service only, does not involve air service.
Sources: Postal Services Department; Rodhiah, 1991.

TABLE 7.5 Postage Rates by Destination

	Within Malaysia			To Singapore and Brunei			To Other Countries		
	Old Rates	New Rates	% Increase	Old Rates	New Rates	% Increase	Old Rates	New Rates	% Increase
Up to 20 gm	0.20	0.30	50	0.20	0.40	100	0.40	0.50	25
21 – 50 gm	0.30	0.35	17	0.30	0.70	133	0.80	1.00	25
51 – 100 gm	0.45	0.50	11	0.45	1.20	167	1.20	1.50	25
101 – 250 gm	0.85	1.00	18	0.85	2.50	194	2.50	2.80	12
251 – 500 gm	1.50	2.00	33	1.50	4.50	200	4.50	5.30	18
501 – 1000 gm	2.50	3.50	40	2.50	8.00	220	8.00	10.00	25
1001 – 2000 gm	4.00	6.00	50	4.00	15.00	275	14.50	18.00	24

Source: Postal Services Department.

been financially stable with an impressive track record in recent years, showing increasing profits yearly without any increases in postage rates in almost 10 years. In 1988, its revenue was RM186.3 million and profits were RM11.3 million. In 1989, revenue was RM202.3 million and profits were RM15.9 million. In 1990, revenue increased to RM252 million with profits more than doubling to RM44 million (*Business Times*, 31 December 1991). With such impressive earnings, it cannot be argued that the privatization of the PSD is to reduce the financial burden of the government. Furthermore, government departments and agencies had been enjoying free postal services all along. With corporatization, however, the government had to begin paying between RM5 million and RM20 million a year to Pos Malaysia Berhad (PMB) (Kartini, 1991).

As Table 7.4 shows, Malaysia's domestic postage rate for a letter of up to 20 gm was only 20 sen, the lowest in the region after India. Also, Malaysian postal services have long been among the best in developing countries, featuring its low charges and relative efficiency. With the core of postal services constituting a natural monopoly, there is not much room for enhancing competition. Hence, it is unclear how privatization *per se* is expected to contribute towards productive efficiency.

Table 7.5 compares postage rates before and after corporatization with postage rates rising tremendously in 1992 with corporatization. For letters (weighing less than 20gm) posted to destinations within Malaysia, the postage rate increased by 50 percent; for those posted to Singapore and Brunei, the postage rate increased by 100 percent. A detailed comparison of the tables will show that some of the postage rates increased by more than 100 percent in 1992.

The Postal Services Department has been a monopoly, and with privatization, it is likely to become a private monopoly. Corporatization of the PSD has already involved hefty increases in consumer charges. It may also involve increased labor costs in the form of bonuses and increased salaries for staff, as well as increased expenditure for overheads for assessment rates and quit rent.

Telephone Services

The corporatization of the Telecommunications Department (Jabatan Telekom Malaysia) has seen the introduction of some better services such as improved counter-services; the option of a detailed billing system reducing errors (for which one has to pay more), and quicker responses to applications for telephone installations. There is no doubt that there has been some efficiency increase and better services, but not without higher charges. Since corporatization of the telecommunication services in 1987, even basic telephone charges have increased. For example, a three-minute call unit used to be charged 10 sen, but such a call has been charged 13 sen since corporatization, i.e. a 30 percent increase.

It is highly unlikely that these improvements in services could not have been achieved at much lower cost than the additional consumer charges. Hence, it can hardly be argued that the consumers are better off on the whole since the improvements cost much less than the extra they have to pay. This does not mean that Telekom Malaysia is less efficient than its predecessor, but rather that it is able to capture an enhanced rent from the private monopolistic position it enjoys.

Passenger Railway Services

The corporatization of Keretapi Tanah Melayu (KTM) on 1 August 1992 has been seen as a step to ease its financial burdens. Compared to other corporatized or privatized monopolies (e.g. Tenaga Nasional Bhd and Pos Malaysia), KTM Bhd faces more competition from road (as well as sea and air) transport.

KTM Bhd has to show a track record of profitability before it can be publicly listed on the Kuala Lumpur Stock Exchange (KLSE). One obvious option available to KTM to cut its losses is to increase its fares (Philip, 1992). On 1 January 1993, five months after corporatization, KTM increased fares for the second time in three months, as shown in Table 7.6. While railway services are said to have improved after corporatization, as in many of the other cases reviewed earlier, these generally marginal improvements cannot be said to justify the fare increases, implying a definite decline in consumer welfare.

Highway Tolls

Another item that has affected the public adversely is the highway toll charges. Until the mid-1980s, the construction and maintenance of public roads in Malaysia were the sole responsibility of the public sector. As part of the government's privatization thrust, the construction and operation of toll roads by

TABLE 7.6 Railway Passenger Fare Increases

	From 1/8/84 (sen/km)	Effective 1/10/92 (sen/km)	Increase	Effective 1/1/93 (sen/km)	Increase (compared to fare of 1/8/84)
First-class coach	12.14	13.96	15%	15.00	24%
Second-class coach	5.47	5.74	5%	6.50	19%
Third-class coach	3.36	3.53	5%	3.65	7%
Supplementary charge for air-conditioned coach[a]	RM3	RM4	33%	RM4	33%
Berth charge for first-class coach[a]	RM15	RM25	67%	RM25	67%

[a]This is a standard charge irrespective of distance.
Source: Passenger Division, KTM Berhad.

the private sector were introduced in the mid-1980s. In existing and proposed road privatization projects, the method for private sector involvement is the build-operate-transfer (B-O-T) approach. Under this system, the private company finances the construction—in some cases merely involving the widening or improvement—and operation of public roads for a specific period, and collects tolls over the concession period.

The concession period varies from the 9 years for the Jalan Kuching/Jalan Kepong Interchange and Jalan Kuching Upgrade projects to 30 years in the case of the North-South Highway. The concession period varies with the time the concessionaire ostensibly needs to recoup the investment. In some B-O-T projects, the toll charges are fixed for the duration of the concession. In the case of the North-South Highway, there is explicit provision for a toll revision after 1996 (see Naidu's chapter in this volume).

On 1 January 1993, effective toll charges were increased by 50 percent for the North-South Highway, from 5 sen to 7.5 sen per kilometer. For example, the original toll charge from the Sungei Besi toll-gate to the Tangkak toll-gate was RM7.10, while the new toll charge is RM10.60. With the increased toll charges, consumers will be adversely affected through higher prices charged for transportation, goods and other services, with a negative impact on real incomes and welfare.

Underpricing of Government-owned Enterprise Share Issues

One of the declared aims of privatization is to reduce the financial burden of the government. The sale of government-owned enterprises is therefore meant to raise revenue for the government. Such one-off proceeds may relieve the

TABLE 7.7 Proceeds from the Sale of Equity

Company	RM million
Sports Toto Sdn Bhd	113
Malaysian Airlines System Berhad	469
Malaysian International Shipping Corporation	90
Edaran Otomobil Nasional	29
Malaysian Shipyard and Engineering	247
Syarikat Gula Padang Terap	51
Perusahaan Otomobil Nasional (PROTON)	177
Tenaga Nasional Berhad (TNB)	248
Syarikat Telekom Malaysia Berhad	639
Total	2,063

Source: *Economic Report, 1993/94*, Ministry of Finance, Malaysia.

government's financial burden in the short run, but may result in forgone income in the long run. Table 7.7 sums up the proceeds to the government derived from the sale of equity of some government-owned enterprises.

In all cases of public flotation of government-owned enterprises, there has been substantial underpricing of shares in the initial public offerings. Table 7.8 reveals that high initial premiums were obtained on the first day of secondary trading. As a consequence, the government has forgone considerable revenue, amounting to nearly RM4.25 billion for the 14 companies.

In the case of Sports Toto, the first 70 percent was sold for RM28 million to Vincent Tan's B&B Enterprise, said to be 60 percent Bumiputera-owned, of which 10 percent was subsequently sold to Tunku Abdullah's Melewar Corporation. The remaining 30 percent was later sold for RM85 million to the Daim-connected Raleigh Berhad (26 percent owned by Bumiputeras). While the second sale involved a share price seven times that of the first, when Sports Toto was listed on the KLSE, it traded at a much higher price on the first day (see Table 7.8), implying underpricing even in the second instance, and hence, gross underpricing in the initial sale. Since Berjaya Corporation (B&B's holding company) had almost 56 percent of Sports Toto at the end of the 1990–1991 financial year, and was about 42 percent Bumiputera-owned, Jones and Fadil (1992c) conclude that private Bumiputera interests had relinquished control by selling out—while presumably realizing very considerable capital gains—to non-Bumiputera interests.

Such underpricing of initial public offerings seems to have been deliberately done to improve the likelihood of the share offer's success since failure could have adverse consequences. Another reason advanced for such "undervaluation" of assets is to promote wider share ownership in line with the government's redistributional objectives. Unfortunately, this politically popular objective of wider share ownership may not be sustained as there is widespread stagging (selling a share almost immediately for profit) (Toh, 1989). This can be seen in Table 7.8, which shows that turnover has been relatively high for MISC, Sports Toto, and KCT.

However, some writers have argued that there has been no underpricing of the public offerings, which are, according to them, only initially and temporarily, priced higher than their intrinsic value by the market due to speculative demand. As evidence, they cite the considerable variation in the degree of underpricing with different share issues. For example, the listing of Syarikat Telekom Malaysia Berhad occurred during the Gulf Crisis, resulting in a relative modest premium of only 22 percent on the first day of trading. In contrast, the initial premium for TNB, listed in May 1992, was 94 percent! When Hicom Holdings Berhad (HHB) was formed from Hicom Berhad's reverse takeover of New Serendah Rubber Company Berhad in December 1993, when the stock market was very bullish, the stock traded at RM12. Just before the public share issue in March 1994, the stock traded at around RM8.50. Based on its own 1994/5 forecast earnings per share of 18 to 20 sen, HHB was trading at a huge price-earnings (P/E) ratio of

TABLE 7.8 Estimated Revenue Foregone and Initial Premia on the First Day of Secondary Trading

Company	Volume of Shares (million)	Issue Price (RM)	Vol. Traded on Day 1 (million)	Turnover (%)	Price on Day 1[a]	Premium (%)	Revenue[b] Foregone (RM million)
Malaysian Airlines Bhd (MAS)	70	1.80	2.390	3.4	2.45	36.1	45.50
Malaysian International Shipping Corporation (MISC)	85	2.40	15.809	18.6	5.00	108.3	221.00
Sports Toto Malaysia Bhd	5.2	2.00	1.833	35.0	9.55	377.5	39.26
Tradewinds	15	1.10	2.601	17.3	1.83	66.4	10.95
Cement Manufacturers Sarawak	5	1.30	0.828	16.3	2.17	66.9	4.35
Cement Industries of Malaysia	8.8	1.00	–	–	1.91	91.0	8.00
Kedah Cement Holdings	29.2	2.00	15.770	54.0	2.60	30.0	17.52
Perusahaan Otomobil Nasional	30	5.00	21.000	70.0	6.60	32.0	48.00
Edaran Otomobil Nasional (EON)	36	5.00	3.302	9.2	8.15	63.0	113.40
Syarikat Telekom Malaysia Bhd	470.5	5.00	29.895	6.4	6.10	22.0	517.55
Tenaga Nasional Bhd	625	4.50	51.932	8.7	8.75	94.4	2,656.25
Kelang Container Terminal	50[c]	3.10	19.962	74.0	8.40	171.0	265.00
Petronas Dagangan Bhd	66.15	2.80	–	–	6.95	148.2	274.52
Hicom Holdings Bhd	82	2.10	–	–	–	–	–
Total							4,221.30

[a]Closing prices.
[b]The difference between the issue price and the price on Day 1 multiplied by the volume of shares.
[c]Allocation for the Malaysian public.
Source: KLSE Research Department.

about 63 (*Malaysian Business*, 16 February 1994). The Capital Issues Committee (CIC) apparently sets share issue prices rather conservatively, based on a P/E ratio of between 3.5 and 8.0.

Interestingly, Bumiputera interests have divested RM1,794.7 million worth of shares in publicly listed companies up to 1993, of which 53 percent were shares of companies listed during 1990–1992. At the average market prices quoted for the earlier part of 1993, these shares were valued at RM14,147.8 million, of which 68 percent were accounted for by the companies recently listed in 1990–1992. This clearly reinforces the impression of general underpricing of recent share issues, much of which is accounted for by privatizations, suggesting private capture of rents due to the underpricing of public assets. The difference between the market price and the par value of the shares divested by Bumiputeras was RM12,353.1 million, i.e. 688 percent of the par value of the shares, which provides some indication of the enormity of the rent capture associated with underpricing (Malaysia, 1993: 69) .

As Table 7.9 shows, the actual Bumiputera allocations in share issues associated with privatizations have increasingly been in excess of the much-mentioned and often-presumed 30 percent. More ominously, a great proportion of this is allocated by the government through procedures which are not transparent, and which are popularly presumed to favor those well-connected with the dominant faction of the ruling party, or even the Minister of Finance himself. Whereas some such allocations were done by the Ministry of Trade and Industry in the 1980s, this prerogative has been increasingly exercised by the Ministry of Finance in the 1990s. In this period, there have also been corresponding increases in both actual Bumiputera share allocations as well as those selected by the government, including non-Bumiputera interests, suggesting the increasing politicization of such share allocations, and therefore greater politically-determined privatization-related rent capture.

Since these types of allocations greatly overlap, it suggests that political influence and access are very important determinants of such rent capture among politically influential Bumiputeras. However, in so far as they do not coincide, it suggests that there are important non-Bumiputera beneficiaries from such government allocations. The magnitude of these allocations suggests that the 1993 furor over the diversion of 90 percent of ten million Telekom Malaysia shares allocated to Maika Holdings—controlled by the Malaysian Indian Congress (MIC), a non-Bumiputera component member of the ruling coalition—to companies personally selected and believed to be controlled by the MIC President, only reflects the tip of the iceberg of such possible "abuses" involving personal aggrandizement ostensibly on behalf of party political interests. It may seem almost incredible that the very fact of such political allocations coupled with underpricing in themselves have not been the subject of investigative scrutiny (see *Sunday Times* (London), 13 March 1994).

The likelihood of such abuses is exacerbated by the lack of transparency in these allocations. A glance at the share ownership profile of some recently pri-

TABLE 7.9 Allocations of Share Issues Associated with Privatizations

Company	Date of Offer	Offer Price (par value = 1.00) (RM)	Govt Selected Institutions/ Investors	Directors and Employees	Malaysian Citizens, Companies, Societies, Institutions	Minimum Total Bumiputera Share Acquisition[a]	Total
Cement Industries of Malaysia Bhd (CIMA)	7.5.1984	1.00	–	1,409,000	7,391,000[b]	–	8,800,000
Malaysian Airline System Bhd (later Malaysian Airlines Bhd) (MAS)[c]	18.9.1985	1.80	35,000,000[d]	17,500,000	52,500,000[e]	(36.1%)	105,000,000
Malaysian International Shipping Corporation Bhd (MISC)[c]	29.12.1986	2.40	25,000,000[d] (29.4%)	2,992,000	56,993,000	42,097,900 (49.5%)	84,985,000
Tradewinds (M) Bhd	23.2.1988	1.10	–	1,016,000	13,984,000[a]	(30%)	15,000,000
Sistem Television Malaysia Bhd (STMB/TV3)	March 1988	2.00	–	2,205,000	4,413,000[a]	(30%)	6,618,000
Cement Manufacturers Sarawak Bhd (CMS)	Jan. 1989	1.30	–	444,000	4,556,000[a]	(30%)	5,000,000
Edaran Otomobil Nasional Bhd (EON)	8.6.1990	4.30	12,000,000 (33.3%)	3,483,000	13,072,000[a]	15,921,600 (44.2%)	36,000,000
Syarikat Telekom Malaysia Bhd (STM/Telekom Malaysia)[c]	26.9.1990	5.00	252,100,000[f] (53.6%)	70,500,000	147,900,000	304,000,000 (64.6%)	470,500,000
Kedah Cement Holding Bhd (KCHB)	9.12.1991	2.00	n.a.	n.a.	n.a.	n.a.	29,240,000
Perusahaan Otomobil Nasional (PROTON)	Jan. 1992	5.00	88,800,000[g]	5,772,000	55,428,000	90,464,400 (60.3%)	150,000,000
Tenaga Nasional Bhd (TNB)[c]	29.2.1992	4.50	300,000,000[h] (48.0%)	84,925,000	240,122,000	372,036,600 (59.5%)	625,047,000
Kelang Container Terminal (KCT)	25.9.1992	3.10	12,400,000[h]	5,000,000[i]	27,178,000	20,553,400 (59.5%)	50,000,000
Heavy Industries Corporation of Malaysia (later Hicom Holdings Bhd) (HICOM)[c]	Feb. 1994	2.10	309,562,000[d]	24,592,192	82,550,000	334,327,000	416,704,192

[a]Usually at least 30% is set aside for Bumiputera individuals, companies, etc. approved by Ministry of Trade and Industry (MTI).

[b]No 30% Bumiputera allocation was mentioned in the prospectus.

[c]"Golden Share" held by government.

[d]These shares were reserved for Bumiputeras as approved by MTI.

[e]Three million from this amount had been reserved for an approved institution.

[f]From this amount, 100,000,000 was reserved for Bumiputeras.

[g]A total of two million was reserved for PNB with the rest given to Bumiputeras approved by MTI.

[h]This amount was approved by MoF for Bumiputeras.

[i]This amount was approved by MoF.

vatized companies shows that large, politically-favored, predominantly Bumi-putera, institutional investors and nominee companies have emerged as the major shareholders. According to Telekom Malaysia's 1991 Annual Report, for example, as of March 1992, the Ministry of Finance Incorporated (MoF Inc.) still held 78.1 percent of the company's paid-up capital, followed by Permodalan Nasional Berhad (PNB) with 4.6 percent, Hongkong and Shanghai Bank (HSB) Nominees with 2.8 percent, Citibank Nominees N.A. with 2.5 percent, Cartaban Nominees with 1.8 percent and Chase Manhattan (Malaysia) Nominees with 1.1 percent. According to TNB's 1992 Annual Report, as of October 1992, MoF Inc. still held 73.2 percent of its paid-up capital of RM3,000,000,001, followed by PNB with 6.0 percent and HSB Nominees with 1.2 percent.

Conclusion

Privatization advocates usually claim that enhanced efficiency will be achieved through the interaction of private ownership and competition. In the Malaysian context, however, privatization has not been accompanied by significantly increased competition. For example, MAS, Pos Malaysia Berhad, Tenaga Nasional Berhad, Telekom Malaysia, and MISC remain virtual monopolies. In all these cases, the transfer of ownership from public to private hands has not involved reduced user costs or significantly enhanced quality of services. Instead, user costs have generally risen quite significantly, resulting in net consumer welfare losses. Hence, efficiency gains have not been significant, though they have nevertheless been exaggerated by proponents of privatization in Malaysia. And in so far as they have occurred, they are unlikely to have been the result of privatization *per se*, but have been mainly due to managerial and organizational reforms which do not require privatization.

8

Employee Welfare

KUPPUSAMY S.*

This chapter evaluates the impact of privatization in Malaysia, for employees involved in the newly privatized companies formed from the public sector. Prior to the change, these employees would have held certain perceptions, opinions and, in some cases, apprehensions of what they might encounter after joining the privatized entity. This chapter will examine the effects of privatization on employees, looking at expectations held before and actual conditions encountered after privatization in the two cases of Tenaga Nasional Berhad (TNB, or National Power Limited), and Projek Lebuhraya Utara-Selatan (PLUS, or North-South Highway Project).

Effects of Privatization on Labor

Employees involved in the transition from public to private service have been known to fear retrenchment or reduction of benefits. These feelings emerge because the public sector is widely believed to be overstaffed, and since privatization advocates improved efficiency and productivity, employees believe employers may reduce the size of their workforces. Although the government assures job security for the first five years (e.g. for Telekom Malaysia, TNB, etc.) following corporatization, employees are nonetheless concerned about job security after the fifth year.

The reduction in the public-sector workforce has been a primary objective and important consequence of Malaysia's privatization program. Table 8.1 indicates that 53,886 employees were transferred to the private sector by the end of 1990 under the privatization program. Another consideration is that allocations

*The author would like to express his gratitude to the employees and management of PLUS and TNB for their cooperation with his research for his Master of Public Administration thesis entitled "The Impact of Privatization on Employees: Perceptions and Opinions of Tenaga Nasional Berhad and Projek Lebuhraya Utara-Selatan," submitted to the Faculty of Economics and Administration, University of Malaya, Kuala Lumpur, 1992, on which this chapter is partially based.

TABLE 8.1 Number of Personnel Transferred to Private Sector due to Privatization Programs

Name of Company	Number of Employees
Projek Lebuhraya Utara-Selatan (PLUS)	750
Aircraft Overhaul Depot (AIROD)	223
Kelang Container Terminal (KCT)	763
Government Security Printing	167
Telekom Malaysia (STM)	28,983
Tenaga Nasional Berhad (TNB)	23,000
Total	53,886

Source: Sheriff Kassim, Mohd. (1990).

for government pensions will be smaller when the size of the public sector is reduced.

Records from the Public Services Department show another interesting finding. Employment figures for the proposed privatization projects given in Table 8.2 indicate that the employment shares in Grades A and B are relatively low while those of Grades C and D are relatively high, indicating that most of the employees involved in privatization are in the lower grades.

Private managements are generally eager to reduce the number of employees transferred from the civil service to increase productivity and profits (Mustafa Johan Abdullah and Shamsulbahriah Ku Ahmad, 1987: 71). Staff redundancy by the government is expected to be overcome through normal attrition, redeployment, and expansion (Kharmazan, 1992: 6). The government generally has not allowed any corporatized or privatized company to lay off workers on the regular payroll during the first five years except on the grounds of disciplinary action by the company, though ostensibly disciplinary actions in corporatized entities have seen an increase in recent years. For example, Syarikat Telekom Malaysia Berhad, which was corporatized from the old Telecommunications Department in 1987, has not retrenched any staff so far, though the union claims disciplinary actions against employees have increased considerably.

In the pioneering case of the Kelang Container Terminal (KCT) divestiture, employees gained so substantially that they have advocated privatizing the Kelang Port Authority (KPA) as a whole. Job security (no lay-offs) for five years was assured, while employees had the choice of retiring early, staying on with KPA or joining KCT on terms no less favorable than those previously enjoyed. These

TABLE 8.2 Employment by Grade Category in Projects Earmarked for Privatization (some of which have already been implemented)

Name of Department	A	B	C	D	Total
National Film Dept	15	34	96	150	295
Factories & Machinery Dept	45	45	91	52	233
Road Transport Dept	130	212	1,939	1,008	3,289
Social Security Dept	77	58	142	169	446
National Printing Dept	24	7	417	969	1,417
Postal Services Dept	134	100	4,331	6,684	11,249
Public Trustee	8	40	131	75	254
Business Registration	2	11	149	65	227
Companies Registration	42	52	105	90	289
Malayan Railway	98	154	1,772	6,887	8,911
National Electricity Board	911	400	4,365	18,687	24,363
Johor Port	53	37	264	671	1,025
Kelang Port	127	141	1,291	4,792	6,351
Penang Port Authority	2	5	15	14	36
Bintulu Port	24	2	101	404	531
Govt Toddy Shop	–	–	6	118	124
Perak Water Dept	24	16	145	872	1,057
Penang Water Dept	20	10	127	1,055	1,212
Telecoms Dept	840	1,154	18,619	9,942	30,555
Total	2,576	2,478	34,106	52,704	91,864

Source: Central Records Office, Public Services Department, cited by Ismail Muhd. Salleh (1991).

features of the first Malaysian divestiture became precedents in dealing with employees in subsequent major divestitures.

According to Jones and Fadil (1992c: 10), real hourly compensation for KCT employees rose by 60 percent between 1985 and 1990 in return for working longer hours (6 percent more), harder, and "smarter," producing about 75 percent more work. While arguing that job security is not a first-best solution, they acknowledge that efficiency gained has accrued primarily from increased labor flexibility. Although in most cases privatization reduced overtime work opportunities, this has not been the case for KCT. Hence, productivity is now considered high, using a reduced turnover time criterion, mainly due to employees working round the clock. Such opportunities to earn extra income have motivated employees to work longer hours. It appears that more customer-oriented management, more flexible work schedules, incentive payments, and extra overtime work have been mainly responsible for the gains in terms of throughput and turnover as well as reduction of turnaround time discussed by Goh and Jomo elsewhere in this volume.

Through privatization, the government is disposing off specific state-owned assets, while at the same time trying to protect the rights and privileges of public-sector employees (Ismail Muhd Salleh, 1991: 100). While privatization seeks to promote efficiency, competition, and productivity, employees have been assured that they will not lose the benefits they enjoyed when they were employed by the government. Privatization has thus promised employees terms and conditions not less favorable than those offered by the government, at least in the short term.

In other respects, an employee who starts afresh with a private employment scheme is offered gratuity and EPF savings at the end of service, besides bonuses which may be given yearly. In most cases, other perks—such as medical benefits for employees, spouses and children—are also maintained.

There are two basic options offered to an employee upon privatization, i.e. either to join or not to join the privatized entity (Kharmazan, 1992: 6). Employees who opt to quit will retire, with benefits paid immediately. On the other hand, those who opt to join the privatized entity will be required to choose whether to continue with the government's scheme of service or to opt for the new, more commercially-oriented private alternative. Since only the latter offers employees special privileges such as ownership of company shares and bonuses based on the performance of the entity, most have opted for it.

Generally, employees in privatized entities are adversely affected by the possibility of losing their jobs, a weakening of union bargaining strength as well as poorer pay and poorer employment conditions for new recruits (Ragunathan, 1990: 213). Other effects of privatization on employees have not been so clear-cut. For example, the early 1992 TNB industrial action organized by middle management executives is a good example (*New Straits Times*, 1 February 1992). Although the main objective was to demand better bonuses, an underlying issue was the executives' call to restrict the board of directors' powers over senior and middle executives.

Upon joining the corporatized company, public-sector employees will have the right to join a private-sector union. Prior to privatization, the provisions of section 27 of the 1959 Trade Union Act and section 52(1) of the 1967 Trade Union Act deter employees from becoming union members and from practising collective bargaining (Lobo, 1992: 3). The Trade Union (Amendment) Act, 1980 further restricted public officers from joining the trade unions unless exempted by the sovereign (Yang Di-Pertuan Agong) through a notification in the *Government Gazette* (Lobo, 1992: 5). However, under section 27(2) of the 1959 Trade Union Act, such gazetted exemptions are not applicable to public servants involved in the security services (such as the police force, prison service, and armed forces).

For statutory bodies, section 27(3) of the 1959 Act stipulates that employees can join a trade union whose members are exclusively confined to the particular statutory body, i.e. an in-house union.

However, after privatization, the employees will no longer be bound by the restrictions in section 27 of the 1959 Act. Besides, the trade unions of the privatized entity will now be free to refer trade disputes to the Industrial Court, on condition that the privilege is not extended to employees engaged in state administration. Lobo (1992) concluded that "the greatest impact of privatization of the public sector will be: (i) the right to trade union membership free from statutory restrictions; (ii) the right to carry out trade union activities; and (iii) the right to collective bargaining, having its consequent impact on individual contracts of employment of trade union members in the private sector."

We now turn to the two privatized companies, looking at the background to and circumstances of their privatizations.

Tenaga Nasional Berhad (TNB)

After World War II, it was felt that a central body was vital to integrate and operate electricity generation and distribution projects. This resulted in the formation of the Central Electricity Board (CEB) in 1949. The Board owned 34 power stations generating power equivalent to 39.88 megawatts. Special provisions also entitled private companies to operate via licenses, e.g. the Penang Municipality, the Kinta Electrical Distribution Co. Ltd, the Perak River Hydro Electric Power Co. Ltd. and Messrs. Huttenbachs Ltd. In 1955, the Board bought over the assets of the Penang Municipality and Messrs Huttenbachs, bringing about a significant development in the power supply of the country. On 22 June 1965, the National Electricity Board (NEB), or Lembaga Letrik Negara (LLN), replaced the CEB. By the end of 1969 (i.e. after 20 years), there were about 900 miles of transmission of 66 kV and above, and about 500 miles of transmission of 33 kV, compared with only 150 miles of 33 kV transmission in 1949. Net assets of the Board were RM37 million in 1950, RM56 million in 1960, RM791 million in 1970, RM2,526 million in 1980, and RM14,967 million in 1992.

On 1 September 1990, LLN was corporatized through the formation of Tenaga Nasional Berhad (TNB) under the Companies Act, 1965. Pursuant to Section 3 of the Successor Act, all properties, rights, and liabilities to which LLN was entitled or subject were transferred to TNB, thereby corporatizing the generation, transmission, and distribution of electricity in Peninsular Malaysia (TNB, 1992: 17). A license had been issued by the Ministry of Energy, Telecommunications and Post to TNB to operate for an initial period of 21 years effective from the day of TNB's formation. This license charges RM1.50 per kilowatt annually, of available installed capacity of electricity (TNB, 1992: 19).

Like its net assets, the number of LLN staff was large. Staff numbers grew from 724 in 1951 to 2,725 in 1952; 5,130 in 1960; 9,405 in 1970; 19,248 in 1980;

and 23,065 in 1991; before declining marginally to 22,752 in 1992. Of these, only 5 underwent staff training in 1952; 47 in 1960; 768 in 1970; 1,190 in 1980; and 4,026 in 1989. During the 1980s, LLN financed many students pursuing degrees in certain disciplines in Malaysian as well as overseas universities. However, not all of them were absorbed into LLN's service upon completion of their studies.

Projek Lebuhraya Utara-Selatan (PLUS)

The Malaysian Government privatized the North-South Inter-Urban Toll Expressway Project (better known as the North-South Highway, or PLUS) to United Engineers Malaysia Bhd (UEM) in March 1988. The move drew strong protests from the public as well as from opposition MPs in Parliament, who claimed that nearly half of the 1000-km expressway (PLUS claimed the figure was only 254.5 km; see Table 8.3) had already been completed at a cost of more than RM3 billion while the remainder would cost RM3.4 billion. Of this, PLUS was expected to raise RM1.75 billion, while the government would provide the balance of RM1.65 billion through concessionary loans.

A letter of intent was issued by the Public Works Department (PWD) for the contract on 29 December 1986. The Democratic Action Party (DAP), Malaysian Trades Union Congress (MTUC) and academicians alleged favoritism in business activities and conflicts of interest on the part of the Mahathir administration in this award, since UMNO held a majority share in UEM through Hatjbudi Sdn Bhd (Gomez, 1990: 128). Lim Kit Siang (1987: iv) alleged that the government had sold the documentation and plans for the highway project to UEM three months ahead of the tender announcement date on 4 April 1986. He claimed that

TABLE 8.3 Sections of NSE Taken Over by PLUS from MHA

Section	Length (kilometers)	Date of opening to traffic
Bukit Kayu Hitam-Jitra	24.0	1985
Jitra-Alor Setar	24.0	1988
Alor Setar-Gurun	35.6	1987
Changkat Jering-Ipoh	53.9	1987
Kuala Lumpur-Seremban	51.0	1977
Seremban-Ayer Keroh	66.0	1987
Total	254.5	

The sections of the Expressway above have been listed to reflect the sequence from north to south Peninsular Malaysia.

Source: UEM, *Annual Report*, 1988.

UEM therefore had an edge and extra time compared with the others to prepare its tender submission. The controversy intensified when the DAP revealed that Pilecon and Hashbuddin (M) Sdn Bhd had offered more competitive bids than UEM. UEM received the contract despite requiring the most in terms of tolls and government loans, compared to the other two companies. UEM also demanded a higher toll rate of 7.5 sen per km compared to 7 sen per km by Pilecon and 5 sen per km by Hashbuddin. Therefore, the total toll collection is expected to increase to RM54 billion. This means that UEM is able to collect an average of RM1.8 billion per year over 30 years, compared to RM740 million annually by Pilecon over 25 years and RM814 million yearly by Hashbuddin over 22 years. UEM will profit from higher charges and for a longer period of time, compared to the other bidders.

Awarding the contract to UEM was clearly politically motivated. This was later confirmed by the Prime Minister, Mahathir Mohamad, who stated that UEM was chosen in order to finance the UMNO headquarters complex costing RM360 million (*The Star*, 29 August 1987). The then Minister of Youth and Sports, Najib Tun Razak, elaborated: "In the case of the North-South Highway Project, it is a means of UMNO solving its problems by repaying loans taken for the new UMNO headquarters building. As big projects are hard to come by now, I feel it is alright in the case of UMNO to be involved in a company's bid for the highway project. This project will ensure income for repaying the loan for the UMNO building" (*The Star*, 30 August 1987).

The DAP filed an injunction to prevent UEM from signing the contract, but the injunction was lifted upon appeal to the Supreme Court, and the contract was signed on 18 March 1988 (Gomez, 1990: 130). A Concession Agreement was concluded between the government and UEM on 31 May 1988. Subsequently, PLUS was formed as a private company and became a subsidiary of UEM. Once the construction of the highway is completed, PLUS will seek listing on the KLSE (*Investors Digest*, July 1988).

Though PLUS was given seven years to complete construction of the Highway, it tried to complete the roads quickly so as to collect toll as soon as possible. PLUS obtained materials through bulk purchases with stable price, including a long-term contract with Pemasaran Simen Negara in 1988, two contracts in 1989 with Hume Industries (M) Bhd to supply pre-cast products and quarry materials, and another with Time Engineering Bhd to supply toll equipment, guardrails, lamp posts, and other highway related materials. These transactions have resulted in the creation of what is arguably the biggest business group in the country (Gomez, 1990).

In order to complete the projects in time, PLUS also awarded parts of the project to other private companies in related fields. Thirteen major contracts were made in 1989 for a total length of 171 kilometers for a total value of RM1,242 million, while another ten were awarded in 1990 for 120 kilometers valued at RM966 million.

In 1989, PLUS decided to accelerate construction of the remaining stretches of the North-South Expressway (NSE) and the New Klang Valley Expressway (NKVE) by reducing the initial 7-year plan to 5 years. Both expressways were completed and open for traffic by February 1994, i.e. one year ahead of the original 7-year schedule.

The first phase of this construction, covering a total length of 129 kilometers, comprised the Gurun-Sungai Petani, Pagoh-Yong Peng, and Kuala Lumpur-Tanjong Malim sections. The second phase and the third (and final) phase were expected to cover 175 and 152 kilometers respectively. Besides, PLUS was also engaged in widening the Federal Highway into a six-lane expressway with separate motorcycle lanes.

Given the desire to complete the expressways ahead of schedule, more man-power—especially professional manpower—was required. This project has brought significant revenues to PLUS and the UEM group of companies. Revenue from toll collection totalled RM28.6 million in 1988, RM72.873 million in 1989, RM87.420 million in 1990, RM119.6 in 1991 and RM148.8 million in 1992 (Table 8.4). Simultaneously, recorded net assets increased very significantly from RM65.3 million in 1989 to RM86.2 million in 1990, 127.9 million in 1991 and RM373.0 million in 1992. A total of 356 kilometers of the expressway was completed and duly tolled in 1989, while the figures for 1990, 1991 and 1992 were 21.1, 45.9 and 152.7 kilometers respectively (UEM, *1992 Annual Report*: 30).

The completed sections of the North-South Expressway—for which PLUS took over toll collection from the Malaysian Highway Authority (MHA) and assumed responsibility for maintenance on 30 November 1988—are shown in Table 8.3. Another stretch of the highway, the 54.9-km Ayer Keroh-Pagoh section, was handed over by MHA to PLUS on 5 April 1989. Apart from these, under the terms of the Concession Agreement, PLUS is required to construct new expressways as listed in Table 8.5. Construction of these sections will complete the entire length of the NSE from the border with Thailand, through Kuala Lumpur, to the Johor Causeway on the border with Singapore.

TABLE 8.4 PLUS: Development, 1988–1990

	1988[a]	1989	1990	1991	1992
Toll Revenue (RM mil)	28.6	72.9	87.4	119.6	148.8
Profit Before Taxation (RM mil)	10.9	16.4	21.9	27.8	31.0
Net Assets (RM mil)	–	65.3	86.2	127.9	373.0
No. of Employees	749	927	1,050	1,207	1,558

[a]Operations for 1988 covered only 8 months.
Source: UEM, *Annual Reports*, 1988–1992.

TABLE 8.5 Sections of the NSE to be Constructed by PLUS

Section	Length (kilometers)
Gurun-Butterworth	53.3
Butterworth-Changkat Jering	79.5
Ipoh-Bidor	66.7
Bidor-Tanjong Malim	54.6
Tanjong Malim-Kuala Lumpur	64.8
Pagoh-Ayer Hitam	59.8
Ayer Hitam-Skudai	65.2
Skudai-Johor Bahru	18.3
Total Length of Expressway to be Constructed	462.2

Source: UEM, *Annual Report*, 1988.

The construction of the New Klang Valley Expressway provides a new highway link in the central Klang Valley region, offering an alternative route to traffic travelling north or east. Currently this traffic uses Federal Highway Route 2 and the traffic dispersal scheme network in Kuala Lumpur. The total length of the NKVE including the Damansara link road is 34.8 kilometers. The Prime Minister officially opened the New Klang Valley Expressway on 11 January 1993, running from Bukit Lanjan to Tanjong Malim (*The Star*, 12 January 1993). Efficiency in providing services ahead of schedule has been achieved by the prospect of increased toll collection.

PLUS was also given the concession to improve and charge tolls on the Kuala Lumpur-Kelang highway, which has been designated as Federal Highway Route 2, by:

(a) widening it from a dual two-lane to a dual three-lane carriageway for 15 kilometers between the Subang Airport Interchange and the Berkeley Roundabout near Kelang with the provision of separate motorcycle lanes all of which had already been completed by mid-1994, and

(b) the construction of five new interchanges at the 7-legged Roundabout, Berkeley Roundabout, North Klang Straits By-pass Junction, Shah Alam North, and Batu Tiga which was still in progress in mid-1994.

Further to this, the government has already agreed in principle to award PLUS in principle the contract to build the second link to Singapore, for which UEM submitted its proposal in March 1990. The RM1.6 billion work to construct the second link between Gelang Patah in Johor and Tuas in Singapore is expected to begin in early 1995 (*Straits Times* (Singapore), 9 March 1994). This indicates the prospect of further privatization of transport services and road construction after 1994, by which time PLUS had already completed the NSE and NKVE.

The government has made the following support available to PLUS:

i)   a supportive loan amounting to RM1.65 billion;
ii) a supplementary loan, if actual traffic volume falls below the agreed traffic volume; and
iii) external risk supplements, if adverse foreign exchange movements are in excess of 15 percent on offshore debts and if adverse interest rate movements are in excess of 20 percent (UEM, *Annual Report*, 1988).

The government support loans involve interest at a fixed rate of 8 percent per annum. A commercial loan for RM2.5 billion signed on 21 November 1989 was a breakthrough in the history of Malaysian loan syndication by a private company. This was considered necessary in order to eliminate the foreign exchange risk.

Survey

To enable a proper evaluation of before and after perceptions of the effects of privatization, TNB employees who had served the NEB prior to corporatization and a sample of PLUS employees who had served the MHA prior to privatization were surveyed. A list of names and particulars of such PLUS employees who had served MHA was selected, from which a random sample was obtained. For TNB, 4 executives and 6 non-executives were chosen as respondents from each of the 103 regional offices. With the cooperation of headquarters, the internal mailing system was used to facilitate this study. A period of 45 days was allowed for respondents to respond to the questionnaire.

The study was carried out in December 1991. TNB had about 1,600 executive officers and about 21,000 non-executives in employment at the time of the survey. Of these, 412 executives (25 percent) and 618 non-executives (31 percent) were selected. Only 491 (47 percent) valid responses, comprising 190 executives and 301 non-executives, were received. PLUS, on the other hand, had 71 executives and 790 non-executives. Of these, 19 executives (26.8 percent) and 206 non-executives (26.1 percent) responded. The discussion which follows is based on the opinions expressed by these samples.

The ages of the respondents from TNB were somewhat evenly distributed, i.e. 13.9 percent were 30 years or younger, 28.3 percent between 30 and 34 years, 21 percent between 35 and 39 years, 11.7 percent between 40 and 44 years, while the rest were 45 or above. The majority of the respondents were male (79.1 percent), reflecting the actual composition of the organization's labor force. By ethnic origin, 77.9 percent were Malays, 11.5 percent were Chinese, while Indians and Others constituted the rest. Slightly more than half the respondents (53.6

TABLE 8.6 Educational Attainment of Respondents in PLUS and TNB

	PLUS		TNB	
Educational level	No.	%	No.	%
Primary schooling only	–	–	8	1.5
Lower secondary (Form 1 to 3)	7	3.0	45	9.3
Upper secondary (Form 4 to 6)	203	90.4	262	53.6
Technical/vocational schooling	6	2.6	38	7.7
College	4	1.9	76	15.5
University	5	2.1	60	12.3

percent) had upper secondary education, 7.7 percent had technical or vocational education, while 27.8 percent had college or university education.

Corresponding to the age distribution, 33.9 percent had served LLN for more than 15 years, 27.2 percent had served between 10 and 15 years, 29.5 percent between 5 and 10 years, while only 9.4 percent had served less than 5 years. On the other hand, the majority from PLUS were aged less than 30 years (72.1 percent), while 15.8 percent were aged between 30 and 34, 6.0 percent between 35 and 39, 4.0 percent between 40 and 44, and the remaining 2.2 percent accounted for those above 50 years of age. This reflects the age distribution in the organization itself, formed about three years prior to this study. The majority of respondents in PLUS were Malays, constituting 88.4 percent, while Chinese and Indians constituted 3.8 percent and 6.9 percent respectively.

It is probable that PLUS absorbed only younger members of the Malaysian Highway Authority upon privatization. The picture was different in TNB. In many ways, TNB still "acts" like the NEB because the organizations are basically similar, with almost the same number of staff upon corporatization; the main difference was that TNB was under a different management.

As Table 8.6 shows, a majority of respondents had only secondary schooling while less than 30 percent had tertiary education.

Perceptions

The immediate concerns of employees upon hearing that their enterprise was going to be privatized were basically apprehensions over (i) job security, (ii) heavier workloads, (iii) reduced overtime opportunities, and (iv) loss of pension eligibility. As explained earlier, the Malaysian government has sought to protect the welfare of established public-sector employees affected by privatization, especially by ensuring at least five years of job security.

The three statements listed in Tables 8.7 and 8.8 seek to capture these fears among the TNB and PLUS employees surveyed. Of the PLUS sample, 54.6 percent expected the job to be tougher, while the rest expected otherwise. After privatization, 65.8 percent of the sample found their jobs to be tougher, while the others found it otherwise. Some 60.1 percent of the TNB respondents expected their jobs would be tougher after joining TNB, while 79.9 percent found them to be tougher. This suggests that in both organizations, work has become more difficult after privatization, probably due to the increased workload in both organizations.

The respondents were also asked about their expectations of overtime work opportunities since private entities will presumably try to reduce operational costs to increase profits. Of the PLUS respondents, 60.9 percent expected less overtime work opportunities after privatization, while the figure for TNB was 80.3 percent. However, only 54.6 percent in PLUS found their expectations realized, while the figure for TNB was 61.5 percent.

Although there has been some reduction of overtime work opportunities after privatization, 45.4 percent of the respondents in PLUS and 38.5 percent in TNB still had overtime work opportunities. This can be explained by PLUS wanting to complete the North-South Highway as quickly as possible and having to maintain the existing highway in order to collect toll from users. Meanwhile, TNB has faced a rapidly increasing demand for electricity.

On the issue of job security, 60.3 percent of the PLUS sample and 67.2 percent of the TNB sample expected greater job insecurity upon joining the private company. After three years of working in PLUS, 16.5 percent still felt insecure, while more than a year after being corporatized, 32.8 percent of TNB employees still felt the same. Job dismissals in these two organizations could only take place five years after the corporatization or privatization of the organization.

Not surprisingly in view of government conditions for privatization, the study found that almost everyone had better salaries after privatization. In most cases, the employees received at least one increment in their respective pay scales. There was a minimum increment of between RM20 and RM40 in TNB, while a majority of those sampled received between RM200 and RM300 in increments. This includes a bonus increment which was seen as an incentive to encourage public servants to join the new companies upon privatization. This is consistent with 95.4 percent of the sample's expectations of privatization benefits. Employees who were doubtful about their futures, e.g. over job security, probably opted to stay on with the government department. The government offer of choice and assurance of better remuneration meant that there was almost no fear of income loss after joining the private firm.

Promotion Prospects

Although officially imposed conditions for privatization preclude retrenchment, there is no provision which stipulates certain clear criteria for promotion.

TABLE 8.7 PLUS: Perceptions of Work, Security, and Overtime Work Opportunities Before and After Privatization

Perceptions	Before				After			
	A	B	C	D	A	B	C	D
a. More difficult job after privatization	14	106	89	11	20	126	68	8
	6.4	48.2	40.4	5.0	9.2	56.6	30.5	3.7
b. Less overtime work opportunities after privatization	21	111	79	6	10	113	85	17
	9.7	51.2	36.4	2.7	4.5	50.1	37.9	7.5
c. Better job security after privatization	8	70	114	4	30	154	36	1
	4.2	35.5	58.3	2.0	13.6	69.9	16.1	0.4

TABLE 8.8 TNB: Perceptions of Work, Security, and Overtime Work Opportunities Before and After Privatization

Perceptions	Before				After			
	A	B	C	D	A	B	C	D
a. More difficult job after privatization	34	247	179	8	61	313	89	5
	7.3	52.8	38.2	1.7	13.0	66.9	19.0	1.1
b. Less overtime work opportunities after privatization	81	282	85	4	58	215	123	48
	17.9	62.4	18.8	0.9	13.1	48.4	27.7	10.8
c. Better job security after privatization	16	117	265	11	25	260	120	19
	3.8	28.5	64.6	2.6	5.9	61.3	28.3	4.5

A = Strongly agree; B = Agree; C = Disagree and D = Strongly disagree.
First set of figures in the table are actual frequencies. The second set represents percentages.

As such, promotions remain the prerogative of the organizations concerned. Of the PLUS sample, 82.2 percent expected promotion, while the corresponding figure for the TNB sample was only 50.2 percent. Of the respondents in PLUS, 85.4 percent said they had good opportunities for advancement, though only 39.7 percent felt that promotional prospects in PLUS had turned out to be as expected prior to joining; a further 31.5 percent felt there were limited promotion and advancement prospects, partly due to their perceptions of their jobs as being "dead-end" in nature.

PLUS promises promotions and perks, such as housing and vehicle loans, only to employees absorbed from the MHA during privatization. New appointments in PLUS do not enjoy these benefits (only respondents who had served MHA before being transferred to PLUS were interviewed for this study). Although a remarkable 90.5 percent of the sample mentioned that promotion in PLUS is expected to be based on ability, achievement, and performance, a small proportion reported unhappiness over allegedly unfair promotional practices; 11.0 percent of respondents felt that there were hardly any promotion prospects and that they had not advanced at all since working in PLUS. Interestingly, only a very small proportion (1.9 percent) felt that promotions were given on racial grounds.

In TNB, only 37.3 percent acknowledged having good opportunities for advancement, while only 21.7 percent said that promotion prospects were as expected prior to joining TNB. A significantly large proportion (48.2 percent) indicated that promotion prospects were limited in TNB. Furthermore, while 52.9 percent indicated that employees were promoted based on their ability and achievement, a smaller proportion of the sample (17.5 percent) expected little advancement because they were involved in "dead-end jobs."

Judging by the responses from both samples, it appears that PLUS has provided better promotion prospects since only a few there had grouses over the matter. As for TNB, only a small proportion were optimistic about their prospects, with the majority pessimistic. This is consistent with their expectations on this subject prior to joining the private company, as 82.2 percent in PLUS and 50.2 percent in TNB respectively had expected better promotion prospects.

Organizational Characteristics and Red-tape

Tables 8.9 and 8.10 reflect differences in goal-setting in the PLUS and TNB work environments. In the case of PLUS, there was not much difference in all areas with the exception of the subject of red-tape: 68.6 percent in the PLUS sample felt there were few efforts to reduce red-tape in MHA prior to privatization, whereas 46.1 percent felt the situation changed after privatization. This suggests that there has been a significant reduction of red-tape in PLUS, which may be attributable to the higher degree of autonomy, decentralization, and delegation.

Table 8.10 indicates that there were not many perceived differences in the work environment, although independent studies suggest that there have been

TABLE 8.9 Work Environment in PLUS

Perception	After Joining PLUS				Before Joining PLUS			
	A	B	C	D	A	B	C	D
a. The organization expects me to work harder than before	118 52.7	105 46.7	– –	1 0.6	28 12.4	177 78.5	20 9.1	– –
b. The organization often has social activities to please its employees	20 8.7	139 61.7	63 27.8	4 1.7	19 8.4	152 67.6	52 23.1	2 0.9
c. PLUS encourages everyone to be involved in sports	26 11.7	173 76.8	22 10.0	3 1.5	23 10.2	175 78.1	25 11.2	1 0.4
d. Employees are not given opportunities to make suggestions	3 1.3	17 7.6	164 73.2	40 17.9	3 1.3	31 13.8	163 73.0	27 11.9
e. Red-tape is kept to a minimum in PLUS	7 3.4	99 50.6	83 42.6	7 3.5	2 1.2	59 30.1	122 62.0	13 6.6

TABLE 8.10 Work Environment in TNB

	After Joining TNB				Before Joining TNB			
Perception	A	B	C	D	A	B	C	D
a. The organization expects me to work harder than before	220 44.9	261 53.4	7 1.4	2 0.3	91 18.8	356 73.3	39 8.0	– –
b. The organization often has social activities to please its employees	23 4.7	192 39.4	242 49.5	31 6.4	13 2.6	258 52.8	203 41.5	15 3.1
c. The organization encourages everyone to be involved in sports	15 3.0	291 59.6	175 35.9	8 1.5	18 3.6	333 68.1	131 26.8	7 1.4
d. Employees are not given opportunities to make suggestions	7 1.4	94 19.2	353 72.4	34 7.0	13 2.6	107 22.0	345 70.9	22 4.4
e. Red-tape is kept to a minimum in TNB	24 5.3	259 57.6	137 30.5	30 6.6	43 9.5	224 49.4	171 37.8	15 3.3

TABLE 8.11 Need for Training and Retraining Opportunities

	PLUS				TNB			
Perception	A	B	C	D	A	B	C	D
a. There is a great need for acquisition of further education/training to cope with increased work pressure	21 9.3	134 59.9	67 30.2	1 0.6	71 14.9	274 57.5	128 26.8	4 0.8
b. There is a need for more training for most of the present staff	31 13.8	136 61.3	53 23.8	2 1.1	94 19.5	312 64.9	72 14.9	3 0.6

many changes in the work environment. Statistically, a t-test analysis shows that the difference between apprehension about red-tape before and after privatization is very significant in PLUS, but only marginally significant in TNB (the respective t-test values were 6.0 and 1.76 at a 5 percent level of significance for the PLUS and TNB samples respectively). It is possible that the difference here can be attributed to the period since privatization or the more basic organizational and managerial changes associated with PLUS being a more "business-oriented private entity" compared to TNB.

Training

Privatization is said to have increased work and other pressures on the affected employees. As such, the need arises for employees of both companies to acquire training and retraining to keep in touch with the latest technologies. The need for training was expressed by a majority in both organizations, i.e. 63 percent in PLUS and 64.9 percent in TNB. There is also a perceived need to acquire higher education or enhanced training or retraining to cope with increased work pressure according to a majority of 59.9 percent in PLUS and 57.7 percent in TNB.

Should More Public Departments be Privatized?

The government expects privatized companies to provide training to employees for them to have greater job satisfaction, productivity and a sense of achievement as well as better remuneration. With privatization, the company is expected to introduce better and faster technology in order to improve quality and productivity. This is because the privatized organization is small in size compared to the government machinery, which is often quite impossible to monitor, let alone effectively allocate resources including technology; the smaller organization should be able to ensure better deployment of capital for the development of human resources. Better incomes and bonuses are also expected to motivate the employees concerned, and should result in greater work satisfaction and quality, especially if employees are efficient and effective in performing their duties.

Privatization appears to be encouraging as well as threatening to government servants. Employees are generally concerned about their future, should their department be privatized. This is in sharp contrast to the claim made by Prime Minister Mahathir Mohamad (*New Straits Times*; *The Star*, 6 February 1992) that employees from many other government departments which had not been privatized were urging the government to privatize their departments as soon as possible. Tables 8.12 to 8.14 summarize various responses to the question of whether employees feel more public enterprises should be privatized. PLUS employees, who support privatization, said that they had better facilities at work, and were providing better quality service to the public. They also felt that they were generally better equipped, more efficient, professional and productive in their work after privatization.

TABLE 8.12 Main Reasons for Privatization According to Affected Employees[a]

| | PLUS | | TNB | |
Reason	Non-executives	Exe-cutives	Non-executives	Exe-cutives
1. Better facilities at work	56	2	32	20
2. Better quality service/work	39	–	31	3
3. Efficient and professional	28	2	10	16
4. Increased productivity	26	–	21	2
5. Better national development	20	1	13	3
6. Reduced govt. expenditure	17	1	24	9
7. More dedicated workers	13	–	25	7
8. To achieve Vision 2020	10	–	2	–
9. Better employee performance	10	–	6	3
10. Good for firm	9	–	26	23
11. Revenue for the country	9	–	9	1
12. Increased earnings/income	9	–	8	3
13. Employment opportunity	8	–	2	1
14. Better motivation	6	–	1	1
15. Better employer-employee relations	2	–	1	–
16. Able to own shares	2	–	1	1
17. Profit as main motive	3	–	3	1
18. Better promotion prospects	1	–	–	–
TOTAL	268	6	215	94

[a]Only a proportion of the employees responded satisfactorily to the questions posed for this table. However, it must be emphasized here that there were only a handful of executives in PLUS, of which only a few responded to this survey.
Source: Survey data.

PLUS executives' responses corresponded very well with the responses of PLUS non-executives. In general, executives felt that employees receive better equipment and facilities, allowing them to perform their duties more satisfactorily. They also felt that with privatization, services have become more efficient and professional. Moreover, they felt that privatization would benefit the country through speedier development, which is expected to benefit the government further. It was also mentioned that privatizing public enterprises will reduce government expenditure due to the reduced size of their workforces, and thus reduce financial requirements as well as enable the organizations to become self-reliant.

Non-executives of PLUS had similar views to those of the executives, but their responses were more varied. Quite a number mentioned that employees re-

ceive better facilities at work, enabling them to work more satisfactorily, resulting in better quality service, greater efficiency and professionalism, and increased
productivity. In other words, PLUS employees were somewhat positive, being
more than happy to use improved technologies through better management, and
motivated to increase productivity, to provide better quality service, and to be
more professional.

TNB executives also felt that privatization was good for the firm and would
ensure better work facilities. This would enhance their own as well as their
organization's ability to be more efficient and professional after being privatized.
Non-executives, on the other hand, emphasized better work, better quality services to the public, and more dedicated workers with higher productivity. Non-
executives also felt that privatization would benefit the company and also reduce
government expenditure.

Overall, TNB respondents felt that with privatization, the employees concerned enjoy better work facilities. Generally, they felt that the quality of service
will be much better due to greater employee dedication. Privatization would also
benefit the government through reducing the fiscal burden on government expenditure, which in turn might lower foreign borrowing.

Objections

On the other hand, of those sampled, only five non-executives in PLUS, and
a small number of non-executives and executives in TNB, objected to privatization. While the sample shows that most PLUS employees were satisfied with
privatization, the few who expressed concerns were non-executives (Table 8.13).
Their grouses were mainly focused on the following concerns: privatization would
increase the costs of services and thus burden the public; the new privatized organization might not adhere to stipulations affecting workers, etc.; the future of
privatization was unknown; and privatization would benefit only a select group
of people.

In contrast, a few felt that "the government does not need to privatize, and if
productivity was the problem, then it could be cultivated in the workers concerned." TNB non-executives suggested that the move to privatize would benefit
only certain quarters, or more specifically, certain elite groups. Privatization would
eventually increase the cost of services to consumers, in contrast to the subsi-
dized levies for some government-provided services.

Some employees were still unsure about the effects of privatization. They
felt it was too early to judge the outcome of the privatization of TNB, and hence
could not decide whether or not more public enterprises should be privatized. Most
dissenting TNB executives who were sampled strongly felt that the move to
privatize would benefit only certain groups of people, and therefore, would further
widen the gap between the poor and the rich in the country.

The responses from PLUS were more uniform. The majority felt that a public enterprise can/should be privatized only if the department is suitable for com-

TABLE 8.13 Main Reasons Against Privatization[a]

Reason	PLUS		TNB	
	Non-executives	Executives	Non-executives	Executives
1. Privatization places importance on profits, while the government places importance on service to the people at reasonable rates	2	–	5	2
2. Productivity can be increased without privatizing services	2	–	2	1
3. Some employers violate rules and regulations	1	–	1	–
4. The future of privatization is still unknown/too early to judge its effects	1	–	3	1
5. Only benefits certain people and not the general public	1	–	6	7

[a]The figures represent only the responses received, indicating their objections to privatization.
Source: Survey data.

mercialization and is potentially revenue-oriented. They also said that certain services affecting national security (such as the police, navy, air force, army) cannot and should never be privatized as these services should always be the responsibility of the government.

Conditional Agreement

A PLUS executive said that a department should only be privatized if the newly privatized body is still under government control. He felt that the government should have a say in the administration of the company. Ironically, this view contradicts the rationale that privatization should encourage independence as well as reduced political influence. This view may have come about as a result of PLUS being controlled by the ruling party.

One non-executive respondent from PLUS commented that a department should only be privatized if workers are assured of job and income security. It is interesting to note that there is always a fear among workers that their livelihood or earnings may be affected by privatization.

Therefore, it can be concluded from the foregoing section that:

(a) more executives than non-executives feel that privatization will improve facilities and encourage better technology transfer;

TABLE 8.14 Conditional Approval for Privatization[a]

Condition	PLUS		TNB	
	Non-executives	Exe-cutives	Non-executives	Exe-cutives
1. Higher productivity if good workers are paid better	1	–	–	–
2. Only revenue–oriented departments should be privatized	1	1	–	2
3. Only commercial ones should be privatized, not services related to national security	–	–	1	1
4. Union should be recognized and the relationship between management and union strengthened	1	–	–	–
5. Privatization can be carried out if the poor can be assured that they will not be victims	–	1	–	1
6. For the benefit of the country, only profitable agencies should be privatized	–	1	–	1
7. Privatized entities should be controlled by government	–	1	–	–
8. Only if privatization can promise secure jobs and incomes	1	–	1	–
9. Too early to say anything	–	–	3	2
10. In–depth study first before privatizing	–	–	1	2
11. Monitoring body to ensure no abuses	–	–	–	1
12. Only if it benefits the staff, people and country	–	–	3	5
13. Depends on the economic situation of the country	–	–	–	1

[a]The figures represent only the responses received indicating conditional approval.

(b) privatization generates better quality services for the benefit of the public;

(c) employees were happy over their wage increments and bonus issues;

(d) the main ill-effect of privatization has been the price increases for services rendered, which have adversely affected the poor.

Does Privatization Benefit Employees?

How did privatization benefit the respondents, and in what ways did they benefit?

Table 8.15 describes the benefits enjoyed by employees of PLUS and TNB, indicating that PLUS employees have benefited from better bonuses, salaries, allowances and/or promotions. This appears to be true for both non-executives as well as executives. Nevertheless, it is not clear whether the PLUS workers sampled had received better increments. While non-executives regarded bonuses as the most important benefit to employees, these were insignificant to executives. The company also appears to have changed the employees' attitudes to their work. A large number of the non-executives admitted that they were currently more dedicated and disciplined at work than before.

However, where technology was concerned, there was a significant difference in perception between the executives and non-executives. Few non-executives felt that they enjoyed better facilities at work. This can be attributed to the nature of their work, where a manual worker may be left to work in the sun or in a toll booth, and there is no significant difference in the tools used in their work. Meanwhile, the executives may see their new appliances facilitating and speeding up their office work.

Apparently, executives' and non-executives' work facilities vary dramatically. It is also very clear that more non-executives—rather than executives—enjoy better facilities and exposure to the latest technology. It is also interesting to note that non-executives claim that their welfare is often taken care of by the company and that the company provides for better personal and career development.

As in PLUS, 50.9 percent of the TNB employees mentioned that upon privatization, employees received better remuneration through salaries, allowances and/or promotions. Ability to own company shares allocated by the company appears to be one fringe benefit given to TNB employees. This, in turn, has apparently made a substantial number of non-executives and executives more dedicated and disciplined. On the other hand, many non-executives—compared to only a few executives—described the provision of bonuses as the main benefit to them. Only a small proportion of executives and non-executives indicated that privatization had motivated them to work harder. Corporatization could mean that the role of key officers has changed very little, though the impact is much greater on non-executives.

On the other hand, there were negative responses about privatization such as: (a) "privatization only benefits certain people"; (b) "the benefits were better before privatization"; (c) "it depends on the type of service privatized"; (d) "there's

TABLE 8.15 Why Privatization Pleases Employees[a]

Reason	PLUS		TNB	
	Non-executives	Exe-cutives	Non-executives	Exe-cutives
1. Better perks (shares, pay, promotions, allowances)	75	5	102	79
2. More dedicated and disciplined employees	33	2	16	28
3. Bonuses	22	1	30	8
4. Produce quality work	20	–	16	3
5. Better for self and career development	19	–	2	–
6. Better exposure to latest technologies	11	1	4	1
7. Cultivates encouraging employee attitudes	11	–	12	7
8. Welfare of employees is satisfactorily taken care of	11	–	3	–
9. Increases productivity	9	6	4	4
10. Better salary increments	8	–	–	–
11. Better motivation to work harder	7	–	11	4
12. Better work facilities	6	1	14	2
13. Better job creation and opportunities	6	–	–	4
14. More professional at work	4	1	1	1

[a]The figures represent only responses received.

heavier workload and dissatisfied with pay" and (e) "reduced staff after privatization".

Table 8.16 indicates the costs of privatization to employees. Some members from PLUS stressed that the workload was heavier after privatization, and that they were dissatisfied with their salaries. This appeared to affect them more than their counterparts in TNB. Some also claimed that their benefits were better before privatization than after. It is also interesting to note that there were 3 non-executives from PLUS who were dissatisfied because there were fewer staff in their respective departments after privatization. (However, the size of PLUS workforce has grown since privatization while TNB has announced its intention to reduce its workforce from 23,000 in 1994 to 15,000 by the year 2000.)

TABLE 8.16 Costs of Privatization to Employees[a]

Reason	PLUS		TNB	
	Non-executives	Exe-cutives	Non-executives	Exe-cutives
1. Heavier workload and pay dissatisfaction	3	1	8	2
2. Only benefits certain quarters	3	–	10	3
3. Reduced staff after privatization	3	–	–	–
4. Better benefits prior to privatization	1	–	3	3
5. Depends on service to be privatized	–	1	–	2

[a]The figures represent only responses received.

Generally, non-executives were much happier than executives after privatization. Table 8.15 provides evidence that in most areas, non-executives were more satisfied, e.g. their pay increases were significantly more than for executives except when linked to productivity, where executives did better. For TNB, the situation was similar except that more executives claimed to be more dedicated and disciplined than non-executives in their organization. Respondents in both organizations indicated that monetary remuneration (salaries, allowances, and promotions) was the primary factor determining job satisfaction.

Conclusion

The foregoing discussion has provided a detailed review of employee perceptions of various issues pertaining to the impact of privatization on them. Privatization has increased the workload on employees, partly due to reduced manpower to carry out similar, if not more work, requiring workers to work harder than before. Although most MHA employees were "transferred" to PLUS, some, especially older staff members, remained with MHA. PLUS sources have indicated that there have been very few fresh recruits. This suggests an increased workload due to the reduced workforce size and the high expectations of the organization in meeting targets more quickly. Respondents also felt that after privatization, there were increased efforts to raise standards in both PLUS and TNB. As a result, there are now greater demands for teamwork and increased pressure on individuals to improve their personal and group performance. Privatization has also increased the desire to acquire further education, training or retraining to cope with increased workloads among its employees. There is also evidence of an increasing need for greater technical expertise after privatization.

Another significant finding is that privatization has reduced red-tape in both organizations, apparently to garner public support and increase productivity. Employees of both organizations have also indicated increased public expectations, which also adds to the work pressure on them. Due to the increased pressures and higher expectations within the privatized entities, superiors have exerted greater pressure on subordinates to work harder, adding to work pressure on these workers. However, the gap between expectations and realities as far as privatization is concerned has been small in most areas, except for workloads, which have generally increased after privatization.

The final part of this chapter highlights the reasons why more public enterprises should or should not be privatized as well as the effects of privatization on the labor force, as seen by the employees themselves—which supports earlier findings. However, one should take these findings with great caution as employees' perceptions of these issues cannot be easily quantified or measured.

Briefly, privatization seems to bring about: (i) more dedicated employees; (ii) increased productivity; (iii) better quality of services; (iv) increased opportunities to have better facilities and technology; (v) increased earnings (inclusive of bonuses), at least in the short term; (vi) enhanced interpersonal relations between superiors and subordinates, and (vii) opportunities to own company shares. Most privatized companies issue shares under their employees' share option scheme (ESOS). Unlike the case of Telekom Malaysia, where only the executives were given an ESOS when it was privatized, TNB has accommodated both categories, executives and non-executives. However, the quantum of shares depends on seniority and rank (*The Star*, 16 February, 1994). In addition, respondents were also aware that privatization will reduce government expenditure and accelerate growth.

In view of the above, it can be concluded that generally, there have been more advantages than disadvantages from privatization for the primary labor force. As long as there is no withdrawal or cancellation of pecuniary benefits or retrenchment in the process of privatizing, the privatization policy will be supported by the majority of employees in Malaysia. However, one cannot generalize about the impact of privatization in Malaysia from the above findings as they are partial in many ways. Such studies need to be extended to include a greater number of privatized enterprises in the country to verify the impact on various categories of labor of different types of privatization. Further analysis should also involve various occupational categories to determine the extent of the impact of privatization on various jobs. However, privatization in Malaysia appears to be focussed primarily on profit-making government-owned companies. Hence, the benefits enjoyed by employees in a privatized company will depend on a company's profits before it is privatized.

PART THREE

Sectors

9

Infrastructure

G. NAIDU

In nearly all countries, and until not too long ago, the public sector has dominated all aspects of infrastructure. The reason for public provision of infrastructure services was only partly because these services were considered far too important to be left to the private sector to supply. More importantly, it was assumed that the technology and economics of infrastructure supply precluded any substantial role for the market. From a technological perspective, infrastructure facilities are not only large and tied to a specific location, they also have economic payoffs over a very long period. The really important characteristic of infrastructure, however, is that they supply their services through a dedicated, networked delivery system to a very large number of users. These features have an important economic implication. Specifically, with natural monopoly situations, decreasing unit costs and externalities in the production and distribution of infrastructure services, and since infrastructure services often resembled pure public goods and merit goods, they were regarded as more suitable for provision by public agencies than private firms (Roth 1987). In short, it was presumed that the private sector would simply fail to provide infrastructure services efficiently, equitably and adequately. For well over a decade now, however, the true extent of "market failure" in the supply of infrastructure services has been under scrutiny. Furthermore, the many examples of "government failure", particularly the indifferent performance of SOEs and government departments in the infrastructure sector, have also contributed to a reappraisal of the appropriate roles for the public and private sectors in infrastructure provision (Berg 1989).

Up to a decade or so ago, the provision of infrastructure in Malaysia, as in many other countries, was also almost entirely undertaken by the public sector. In the mid-1980s, however, the Malaysian Government initiated its privatization policy and thus made known its intention to move away from the conventional public sector dominance in infrastructure. The policy has, among others, allowed the private sector to not only complement the public sector, but also to supplant it in many areas of infrastructure. Private sector resources now play a fairly important role both in the development as well as in the operation of infrastructure in Malaysia. And all indications are that the private sector's presence in the country's infrastructure system can only grow.

On account of the growing presence of the private sector in infrastructure, an assessment of the Government's privatization policy, as it applies to the infrastructure sector, is clearly in order. This chapter provides an evaluation of the privatization of infrastructure facilities in Malaysia. After a brief historical survey of infrastructure development by the public sector in the pre-privatization period, the discussion goes on to assess the extent of private sector involvement in Malaysian infrastructure. The different means by which the private sector has been allowed to participate in the development of infrastructure are also indicated. Privatization was aimed at achieving a number of objectives. The extent to which these aims have been achieved or, for that matter, even pursued, and whether the long-term development prospects of the country are being nurtured by the Malaysian Government's policy of privatizing infrastructure are also considered in some detail.

Background

During the period when the government was responsible for providing nearly all the infrastructure services in the country, i.e. up to about 1985, three broad considerations had a bearing on the scale and nature of infrastructure development. First was the economic objective. Investment by the government in infrastructure facilities was aimed at meeting the growing demands of the various sectors of the economy for infrastructure services and at avoiding infrastructure bottlenecks from emerging. Second, during the era of the NEP (1971–1990), infrastructure development also came to be seen in a much wider socio-economic perspective. Under the broad ambit of the redistributive objective of the NEP, the development of infrastructure in the less developed regions and states was seen as necessary to uplift the socio-economic conditions of the indigenous Bumiputera community. Finally, the need to promote national security was also a factor that influenced infrastructure development in Malaysia, particularly the construction of roads. In short, the need to meet economic demands for infrastructure facilities was not the only factor that influenced government policy towards the development of infrastructure. The alleviation of poverty, the elimination of racial and regional economic disparities and the promotion of national security have also impacted the sequencing, distribution and even pricing of infrastructure in Malaysia.

The allocation of development expenditure to the various sectors, in constant 1978 prices, is shown in Table 9.1. (The trends in the table up to 1985 coincide with the period before the implementation of the privatization policy.) That the government accorded a very high priority to infrastructure development is evident from the fact that the infrastructure sector has been the largest recipient of

TABLE 9.1 Malaysia: Allocations for Development Expenditure, 1966–1995

	1MP (1966–70)	2MP (1971–75)	3MP (1976-80)	4MP (1981–85)	5MP (1986–90)	6MP[a] (1991-95)
Economic Sector	4,291	7,121	13,261	43,567	28,725	39,977
Agriculture	1,809	2,573	4,558	6,828		
Federal				6,806	5,278	5,074
NFPEs				22		
Infrastructure	2,253	2,493	5,547	20,952	20,391	31,350
Federal				11,064	8,266	9,179
NFPEs				9,888	12,125	22,171
Industry	229	2,055	3,156	15,787		
Federal				4,928	3,056	3,553
NFPEs				10,859		
Social Sector	1,289	1,833	3,467	7,795	6,279	6,972
Education	534	998	1,505	3,661	4,084	4,754
Health	239	262	298	575	667	1,260
Housing	336	238	1,255	3,074	1,040	449
Other Services	180	335	409	485	488	509
General Admin.	224	215	452	633	805	1,056
Security	1,083	1,466	3,432	5,853	1,810	4,702
State Government		1,892	2,035	4,895	6,341	6,711
Statutory Bodies & Local Governments		1,519	1,596		0	1,119
TOTAL	6,887	14,046	24,243	62,743	43,960	60,537

[a]Proposed Expenditure.

Sources: First Malaysia Plan (pp. 69–70), Second Malaysia Plan (pp. 68–71), Third Malaysia Plan (pp. 240–241), Fourth Malaysia Plan (pp. 118–125, 240–241), Fifth Malaysia Plan (pp. 226–227, 449, 466, 478), Sixth Malaysia Plan (pp. 301, 321, 343).

development funds in three of the four plans, the exception being the Second Malaysia Plan (1971–75) when the sector's share was less than a fifth of total development expenditure. In all the other plans, investment in infrastructure consumed very much in excess of this proportion, with a third of total development expenditure spent on infrastructure during the first and fourth Malaysia plans. Investment in infrastructure during the Fourth Plan (1981–85) was so large that it came close to eight percent of GDP, a ratio not only twice as big as that achieved during the Third Plan (1976–80) but also very large, it would seem, by international norms.

The vast amount of resources devoted to the development of infrastructure facilities up to 1985—RM31 billion during the 20 years of the first four Malaysia Plans—certainly contributed to the growth of infrastructure stock and, undoubtedly, to its modernization as well. Information on the physical growth of infrastructure is not readily available but Table 9.2 provides some figures on the expansion of infrastructure facilities between 1965 and 1985. The statistics do show that during the period when the public sector was solely responsible for infrastructure development nearly all sub-sectors of infrastructure were expanded quite significantly This is not to deny that there were no instances of serious misinvestments leading to significant excess capacity. Any list of wasteful or untimely investments by the government would include the Penang Bridge, the Kuantan Port as well as the East-West and Kuantan-Segamat highways. Conversely, there were also cases where infrastructure facilities were not expanded quickly enough to keep pace with the growth in demand, resulting in severe shortages and deterioration in service levels. For example, congestion emerged in many parts of the country's road network, such as along Federal Route I and along the Kelang-Kuala Lumpur stretch of Federal Route II. Malaysian ports were not spared from capacity shortages either. Port Klang, for instance, was occasionally faced with inadequate berth facilities to cope with the growth in cargo traffic. The capacity constraints in the infrastructure sector were, however, not frequent and rarely of a magnitude to jeopardize the overall economic performance of the country. Taking a total view of the development of infrastructure up to the time of the government's privatization drive, there can be no denying that considerable progress was actually achieved. By way of illustration, road mileage in the country more than doubled between 1970 and 1985; similarly the national telephone penetration rate rose from one per 100 persons in 1970 to 2.9 in 1980 and to 6.1 in 1985; and electricity generating capacity in 1985 was twelve times higher than the level in 1965. An important feature of infrastructure development in Malaysia was that the facilities were not only concentrated in the well developed parts of the country. On the contrary, the facilities in 1985 were distributed much more evenly and equitably—between the better-off states and the poorer ones and between the urban centers and the rural areas—than was the case, for instance, at the time of independence in 1957. In short, the public sector had, by and large, succeeded in providing the requisite amounts of infrastructure for the economic and social development of Malaysia.

Privatization

As the government had been reasonably successful in making available the required amount of infrastructure in terms of both economic and social considerations why was it necessary to cut back on the role of the state, in favor of the private sector, in the provision of infrastructure services? Furthermore, were the arguments that, in the first instance, underpinned state intervention in the infra-

TABLE 9.2 Malaysia: Growth of Infrastructure, 1965–85

	1965	1970	1975	1980	1985
1. Length of Roads (Km)	15,356	21,995	24,037	26,219	38,973
Paved	12,464	15,566	16,951	18,910	25,125
Gravel	2,107	5,090	5,604	6,059	12,411
Earth	785	1,339	1,482	1,250	1,437
2. Length of Railway Track (Km)	2,115	2,115	2,115	2,218	2,222
3. Number of Major Ports	2	2	2	6	9
4. Telecommunications					
No. of Telephone Subscribers	n.a.	107,000	169,539	395,640	958,598
Telephone-Population Ratio (per 100)	n.a.	1	1.4	2.9	6.1
Number of ATUR Subscribers	nil	nil	nil	nil	4,630
Number of Telex Subscribers	n.a.	183	1,062	3,898	10,881
Number of Telefax Subscribers	nil	nil	nil	nil	559
Number of Rural Payphones	nil	nil	nil	nil	250
Percentage on waiting list (%)	n.a.	11.6	n.a.	23	n.a.
Telephone Exchange Line Capacity (no.)	n.a.	n.a.	n.a.	660,500	1,800,000
5. Electricity					
Generation Capacity (MW)	336	836	1,022	2,385	4197
Transmission Lines (Km)	n.a.	1,400	1,806	2,823	4,439
Distribution Lines (Km)	n.a.	2,085	4,402	11,513	17,840
6. Water Supply					
Production Capacity (million litres/day)	591	1,118	1,672	2,642	4,162
Urban Coverage (%)	n.a.	n.a.	n.a.	89	93
Rural Coverage (%)	n.a.	n.a.	n.a.	43	57

The figures for electricity generation capacity in 1985 were estimated based on the the capacity in 1980 and that of projects undertaken during the 4MP as documented in the 5MP (pp. 457–459). The figures for water production capacity in 1975 were estimated based on the capacity in 1970 and that of projects undertaken during the 2MP as documented in the 3MP (p. 377).

Sources: Data on roads, railways, and the number of major ports are from the Ministry of Transport, Malaysia, *Transport Statistics* (various issues). Data on telecommunications are from the Department of Statistics, *Yearbook of Statistics and the Sixth Malaysia Plan* (p. 284). Data on electricity and water supply are from the various five-year plans.

structure sector no longer valid? Or did the government embark on privatization because private firms were now considered more efficient than SOEs and government departments in the supply of infrastructure? These are pertinent questions, and answers are intimated in a later section. For now, the extent of privatization in the infrastructure sector needs to be first ascertained.

The one general observation that cannot be disputed is that the government's privatization policy—defined very broadly—has been very prominent in the infrastructure sector. Just about every component of the sector has either seen private sector participation or is being exposed to some measure of market discipline. (Table 9.3 contains a list of privatized projects in the infrastructure sector.) As a result of the policy, the public sector's relative role in the financing and supply of infrastructure in the country is slowly being reduced. A brief description of private sector involvement in the various segments of the infrastructure sector would help give an overall idea of the extent to which the private sector has been allowed to supplement and replace the government in the provision of infrastructure services.

Roads

The road network of Malaysia comprises 50 thousand kilometers of roads. The financing of road construction and their maintenance has traditionally been a public sector responsibility in Malaysia. With the commencement of privatization, however, a policy of awarding concessions to private companies for the construction and operation of tolled roads was introduced in the mid-1980s. The first privatized road project was the North-Kelang Straits Bypass, for which a concession was signed in 1984. Since then, six more concessions have been awarded, of which the most important has been the North-South Expressway project awarded to UEM in 1988 (Table 9.3). The 869 kilometer Expressway was completed in early 1994 and spans the entire west coast of Peninsular Malaysia from the Thai border in the north to Johor Bharu in the south. The Expressway, originally expected to require an estimated investment of RM3.2 billion from the private sector, in the event, cost more than RM6 billion. After an inexplicable five-year break in the award of concessions in the roads sector, three more highway projects have recently been privatized, these being the Shah Alam Expressway, the Seremban-Port Dickson Highway and the Second Link to Singapore. In addition to the total of seven concession agreements already signed, the government is also proposing to privatize a number of other road projects, including the new KL-Karak Highway.

Railways

After a failed attempt at outright sale, the Keretapi Tanah Melayu Berhad (KTMB) was incorporated under the Companies Act (1965), and in August 1992,

TABLE 9.3 Malaysia: Privatization of Major Infrastructure Projects

Sector	Status	Method
Roads		
North Klang Straits Bypass	Privatized (1984)	B-O-T
Jln. Kuching/Kepong Interchange	Privatized (1985)	B-O-T
K.L. Interchange	Privatized (1987)	B-O-T
North-South Expressway	Privatized (1988)	B-O-T
Seremban-Port Dickson Highway	Privatized (1993)	B-O-T
Shah Alam Highway	Privatized (1993)	B-O-T
Second Link to Singapore	Privatized (1994)	B-O-T
Ports		
Klang Container Terminal	Privatized (1986)	Divestiture
Rest of Port Klang	Privatized (1992)	Divestiture
Johor Port	Privatized (1993)	Corporatization
Bintulu Port	Privatized (1993)	Corporatization
Penang Port	Privatized (1994)	Corporatization
West Port, Port Klang	Privatized (1994)	Divestiture
Water Supply		
Labuan Water Supply	Privatized (1987)	B-O-T
Ipoh Water Supply	Privatized (1989)	B-O-T
Larut Matang Water Supply	Privatized (1989)	B-O-T
Semenyih Dam	Privatized (1987)	Management Contract
Maintenance of Tube Wells, Labuan	Privatized (1988)	Management Contract
Johor Water Authority	Privatized (1994)	Corporatization
Pulau Pinang Water Authority	Privatized (1994)	Corporatization
Utilities and Others		
Syarikat Telekom Malaysia Berhad	Privatized (1990)	Divestiture
Tenaga Nasional Berhad	Privatized (1992)	Divestiture
KTM Berhad (Malayan Railway)	Privatized (1992)	Corporatization
Malaysian Airports Berhad	Privatized (1992)	Corporatization
Light Rail Transit	Privatized (1992)	B-O-O
National Sewerage System	Privatized (1993)	B-O-T

Source: G. Naidu (1992), updated by author.

it officially took over the operations of the former Malayan Railway. At the same time, a sister company, the Railway Assets Corporation (RAC) was established to hold in trust all landed assets of the former Malayan Railway. The entire equity of both companies, however, is owned by the Government through the Ministry of Finance. The privatization of the Malayan Railway has stopped at the corporatization stage and there no plans as yet to divest the equity of KTMB and the RAC to private investors. The Malayan Railway was a loss-making SOE and, at this juncture, the financial prospects for KTMB have not been sufficiently attractive to elicit a positive response from private interests.

Ports

The 1985 *Guidelines on Privatization* identified the provision of port services as an important area of private sector participation. The first case of privatization in the ports sector was that of the container terminal at Port Klang, also discussed elsewhere in this volume. The privatization exercise was initiated by the formation of a company, Kelang Container Terminal (KCT), by the Klang Port Authority (KPA). The majority of shares of KCT—51 percent—was subsequently sold to a private company, Konnas Terminal Kelang Sdn Bhd. The movable assets of the terminal were sold to KCT, while the immovable assets, including the three container berths and land, were leased to it. KCT operates the container terminal under a 21-year licence granted by the KPA. It has since been listed on the Kuala Lumpur Stock Exchange. The remainder of the facilities at Port Klang, consisting of 22 berths, were subsequently privatized to Klang Port Management (KPM) in December 1992 (Rajasingam (1993)). By converting a few of its break-bulk berths, KPM has developed its own container terminal. There are thus two container terminals at Port Klang now.

The Government has also taken the first step towards privatizing three other Federal ports: Johor Port and Bintulu Port were corporatized in January 1993, while the Penang Port Commission was corporatized a year later. Although the three corporatized ports are still wholly-owned by the Government, plans are underway to divest their equity to the private sector. The only Federal ports which are yet to be privatized are Kuantan Port and the relatively new Kemaman Port.

Utilities

Before 1987, telecommunications services in the country were provided by the Government through its Telecommunications Department (JTM). The privatization of JTM took place in two stages. First, the JTM was corporatized in January 1987, when Syarikat Telekom Malaysia Berhad (now known as Telekom Malaysia) was established to take over the provision of telecommunications services and network from the JTM. Telekom Malaysia operates under a 20-year licence granted by the Minister responsible for telecommunications. The second stage in the privatization of the telecommunications sector occurred in 1990. In that year, a portion of the government's equity in the company was divested to the public through a public flotation. However, the Government, through the Ministry of Finance, however, is still the majority shareholder. The Government also continues to hold the "golden share"—one solitary special rights redeemable preference share—which makes government sanction necessary on all major policy decisions of Telekom Malaysia.

The process by which the electricity utility was privatized was identical to the way in which the JTM was privatized. The privatization of the National Electricity Board (NEB) in Malaysia began in September 1990, when the assets of the NEB were transferred to the newly corporatized Tenaga Nasional Berhad (TNB). On 28 May 1992, the Government divested 30 percent of its share in TNB to the public by way of a public flotation.

Other Infrastructure

A number of other infrastructure projects have also been privatized. The light rail transit system for the federal capital of Kuala Lumpur is one such project. A franchise agreement was signed between the Malaysian Government and Sistem Transit Aliran Ringan (STAR) in December 1992 for Phase One of the project. The concession period is 60 years, but renewable for an equivalent period on a commercial basis.

The construction and operation of a national sewerage system is one of the latest privatization exercises in the infrastructure sector. In December 1993, a RM6.2 billion concession agreement to privatize the development of the national sewerage system was signed between the government and Indah Water Konsortium. The project involves the upgrading and refurbishing of the existing sewerage systems as well as the construction of new multi-point sewerage systems. Upon completion of the project in 143 local authorities, the nationwide sewerage coverage is expected to reach 100 percent.

Water supply is another area of infrastructure where there has been some private sector entry. Thus far, however, the privatization of water supply services has mainly involved water treatment plants. Recently, however, the Works Ministry has expressed its dissatisfaction with past exercises in the privatization of water supply and has voiced its desire to see more comprehensive privatization programs, encompassing all the components of water supply (*Business Times*, 10 August, 1993). Lastly, the country's airports, which were previously operated by the Department of Civil Aviation, have been corporatized into Malaysian Airports Berhad and, as in the case of the corporatized ports, is awaiting divestiture of shares to the private sector.

The conditions under which infrastructure services are provided in Malaysia are clearly very different now from what they were before. The entry of the private sector into infrastructure and the exposure of some of the SOEs involved in the provision of infrastructure services, at least partially, to market conditions and even discipline suggest that there have been important changes in the way infrastructure services in Malaysia are being financed, produced and delivered.

Mechanisms

Privatization can take numerous forms (Vuylsteke (1988), Ng and Toh (1992) and Reddy in Gouri (ed.) (1991)). Among the possibilities is denationalization which involves the full or partial sale of shares of government-owned companies to the private sector. Leasing of government-owned assets (to the private sector) is also seen as a form of privatization. Another mode of privatization is deregulation. It involves allowing the private sector to provide a service traditionally supplied by the state. The "Build, Operate and Transfer" (B-O-T) approach where, under a concession agreement, a private company undertakes the financing and construction of a "green field" infrastructure project, operates it for a designated period, during which it collects user fees, and transfers the infrastructure facility to the government upon expiry of the concession, is an example of deregulation (Augenblick and Custer (1990)). The Build, Operate and Own (B-O-O) method is a variation of the B-O-T approach. Another form of privatization is licensing or contracting out. In this type of privatization, the government continues to finance the service such as a municipal service but invites private firms to bid for the right to provide the service under contract. In such instances, unlike the B-O-T or B-O-O approaches, the government only privatizes the production and sale of the service, but not the financing of the project. Finally, corporatization is also classified as a form of privatization in Malaysia. The corporatization of a SOE frees it from stifling bureaucratic interference and constraints and, it is argued, provides it with greater flexibility than a government enterprise to respond to market forces.

In the privatization of its infrastructure, the Malaysian Government has resorted to a range of techniques that encompass both the divestiture and non-divestiture options. Corporatization, an example of the latter approach, is one method that has been very frequently employed in the privatization of SOEs in Malaysian infrastructure. Of the public enterprises in the sector that have been corporatized, the prominent ones would include Malaysian Airports Berhad, KTMB (the Malayan Railway) and the Bintulu, Johor and Penang ports. In all these corporatization exercises, the legal status of the SOEs has been changed to that of a limited company, but their shares are still fully owned by the Government. Corporatization, in many respects the most rudimentary form of privatization, is often the precursor to the eventual divestment, partial or complete, of the shares in the SOE by the Government. For example, the privatization of the JTM and the NEB was brought about by the Government incorporating, in each case, a wholly government-owned company in the first instance, and thereafter divesting its equity in the company to the private sector by way of a public flotation of shares. From past practice, the equity of the three ports that have recently been corporatized and of the Malaysian Airports Berhad would eventually be divested (partially or completely), either by way of a negotiated sale to private sector companies, as has happened in the cases of KCT and KPM, or by a public flotation exercise which was the path adopted in the privatization of the telecommunications and electricity utilities.

The privatization of roads in Malaysia is being done through the B-O-T method. (In this chapter the term B-O-T has been used interchangeably with "concession"; see Berg (1989) and Augenblick and Custer (1990).) Each of the B-O-T road projects in Malaysia has involved a concession agreement between the government and a private company, under which the latter would finance the construction of the road and operate it for a specified period. The private company is allowed to collect tolls over the entire concession period. At the end of the concession period, the road would revert to public sector ownership. B-O-T arrangements tend to be highly deal specific and the concession agreements in Malaysia have been no exception (Naidu (1992)). Roads have not been the only segments of the infrastructure sector where the B-O-T method has been employed. The national sewerage project and a number of water supply agreements are also B-O-T arrangements. The Light Rail Transit project is the only B-O-O infrastructure project in Malaysia.

Notwithstanding the popularity of corporatization and of B-O-T projects in Malaysia, the most authentic form of privatization is, of course, denationalization or divestment. In the privatization of the infrastructure sector in Malaysia, however, instances of total divestiture are very rare, but partial divestiture is more common. A point to be borne in mind is that divestiture, at least in Malaysia, does not mean the sale in perpetuity of shares in government enterprises: in all cases, the privatized companies operate under a licence from the Government for a specified period, and strictly speaking, the infrastructure services will therefore be provided by private sector firms only for the duration of the concession agreements.

Assessment

The discussion in the previous sections has intimated that some, perhaps even considerable, progress has been achieved in the privatization of infrastructure in Malaysia. The question at this juncture is, how important is private provision of infrastructure services in Malaysia? A decade ago the infrastructure sector of the Malaysian economy was completely dominated by the public sector. There was simply no private sector involvement in the financing and production of infrastructure services. Within ten years, the situation has changed quite considerably. In each and every component of the infrastructure sector, the involvement of private capital and enterprise is clearly evident.

In the case of roads, the length of the privatized highways may be just over a thousand km., but the significance of private sector involvement in the roads sector goes well beyond the minuscule two percent share of the country's road network that privatized roads currently command. This is because the privatized roads constitute the critical portions of the Malaysian road system. Moreover, the role of the private sector in the provision of roads will undoubtedly grow as the more heavily used portions of Malaysia's road network, including urban roads, are privatized. It is thus possible that in the future, the public sector's role in the provision of road services will be confined to the construction of development and rural roads (Naidu, 1992).

Until a couple of years ago, the Malaysian Government's track record with regard to the privatization of ports appeared unimpressive, with only the container facilities at Port Klang having been privatized. But the priority accorded to the privatization of ports (in the *Guidelines on Privatization*) is now being borne out. By early 1994, Port Klang, Malaysia's largest port, had been completely privatized as KCT and the KPM terminal. (The new multi-purpose terminal being developed by the KPA on Pulau Indah as the West Port was also privatized in early 1994, well before its completion.) Three other large Federal ports in the country—Bintulu, Johor and Penang—have been corporatized and the divestiture of government equity in them is imminent. Port Klang and the three corporatized ports account for as much as three-quarters of the total throughput of the major ports in Malaysia. (A total of 11 ports were designated as major ports in Malaysia in the *Mid-Term Review of the Sixth Malaysia Plan*.) Private sector involvement in the ports sector, already significant with the privatization of the country's largest port, Port Klang, would become very large indeed when the Government sells its shares in the three corporatized ports.

Privatization elsewhere in the infrastructure sector is also extensive. At one extreme, the monopolistic electricity and telecommunications utilities have been privatized. Private capital is also involved in a number of water supply projects. In the transport sector, not only have roads and ports been privatized, the Malayan Railway and the country's airports have not been spared either. Both of these are now corporatized bodies and should the Malaysia Airports Berhad and KTMB prove to be financially attractive to private investors, the Government would almost certainly divest its interest in them. Urban transport has also not escaped the Government's privatization policy. Urban roads have been privatized since the very beginning of the policy. The privatization of Kuala Lumpur's Light Rail Transit extends the privatization policy in the urban transport sector further, and signifies an important change in the relative roles to be played by the public and private sectors in the future supply of urban transport infrastructure. The latest infrastructure facilities to be privatized are the national sewerage system and the Second Link to Singapore.

Every segment of the infrastructure sector has clearly been affected by the Government's privatization policy. Private firms and private sector funds are present, not only in transport infrastructure, but also in utilities. At the extreme, privatized firms are already monopolistic suppliers in some segments of the infrastructure sector. It may even be the case that the government's privatization policy has been most evident in the infrastructure sector of the Malaysian economy.

Appraisal

Notwithstanding the observation that private sector involvement in Malaysia's infrastructure is extensive, it is still true that many privatization exercises in Malaysia do not actually involve private capital in the development or delivery of infrastructure services. Given the very broad definition of privatization by the Malaysian Government, adopted uncritically up to now in this chapter, much of what goes on as privatization in the country is actually only commercialization. But as privatization gains momentum, and as privatization exercises move up from being mere exercises in commercialization and corporatization to involve actual divestment of equity, the role of private capital in the development of infrastructure and in the provision of infrastructure services can only increase. An appraisal of the privatization of infrastructure in Malaysia at this juncture is, therefore, neither inconsequential nor premature.

Privatization was intended to achieve a number of objectives. To recapitulate, the *Guidelines on Privatization* identified these to be as follows:

i)   to relieve the financial and administrative burden of the government,
ii) to promote competition, improve efficiency and increase productivity,
iii) to stimulate private entrepreneurship and investment and accelerate the rate of growth of the economy,
iv) to reduce the size and presence of the public sector in the economy, and
v)   to achieve the objectives of the NEP.

For obvious reasons, it is simply not feasible to exhaustively assess the privatization of the infrastructure sector against each of the stated objectives of the policy. Neither, for that matter, is it possible to ascertain the costs and benefits of each privatization exercise in the sector. (Some tentative examples of evaluating the effect of the policy include Ismail (1991), Levy, Hernan and Menendoz (1989) and Jones and Fadil (1992).) What is attempted in this chapter is somewhat more modest and even tentative. The aim is to see if there are *a priori* reasons to believe that the privatization of infrastructure has been, on the whole, beneficial to the Malaysian economy and to answer the not unrelated question of whether the privatization of infrastructure could not have been better planned and implemented.

That the privatization of infrastructure has somewhat reduced the size of the government bureaucracy is not in doubt. But in a public sector, with a total labor force of well over 800,000, the impact of the privatization of infrastructure services on total public sector employment cannot be very substantial. Privatization and the consequential rollback of the public sector could also be credited with having reduced the Government's financial burden. The one-off incomes, from the sale of infrastructure facilities, the savings on expenditure on infrastructure development (such as on roads), revenues from lease payments from KCT and the like, and the transfer of the Government's outstanding debt to private operators must have reduced the financial burden on the Government. But against these largely short-term positive effects, there have also been some negative impacts. The first matter relates to the validity of the assertion that privatization of infrastructure has contributed towards a reduction in the financial burden of the Government for infrastructure development. Not surprisingly, the Government has only been able to privatize the profitable segments of the infrastructure sector, leaving behind the unprofitable enterprises and facilities firmly within the realm of the public sector. For example, in the ports sector, the highly profitable ones— such as Klang, Bintulu, Penang and Johor—have either already been taken over by private investors or will soon be sold. Similarly, only the highly profitable segments of the road network have been privatized leaving the public sector responsible for, among others, the rural road network. Consequently, saddled with this unprofitable infrastructure, the financial position of the Government could actually worsen in the longer term. But this is not the only cause for concern. The deliberate undervaluation of Government assets in nearly every privatization exercise is also inconsistent with the claims that privatization of infrastructure facilities has contributed to the diminution of the financial burden on the Government. As a result of the heavy discounting in asset prices, the revenues from the sale of Government assets as well as the annual payments for the lease of Government assets have been less than they would otherwise have been. (It has, however, been claimed that offer prices were set low to achieve a wider spread of ownership. See Nankani (1988).) Finally, at the broader macro level, even if it has succeeded in reducing the financial and administrative burden on the Government, the reduction in the size of the public sector has also reduced the scope for short to medium term interventions to achieve desirable national goals of an economic or socio-economic nature.

A benefit of privatization, not entirely distinct from the reduction of the financial burden of the Government discussed above, is the reduced risk to the Government from project failure. But in the privatization of infrastructure in Malaysia, the question of a reduction in financial risk to the Government actually does not arise at all. Because of the assurances of profitability that have been extended to the private sector in many of the privatization exercises, which have included soft loans, traffic volume guarantees (for B-O-T road projects) and exchange rate guarantees, the probability of failure of the privatized projects is virtually non-existent. In any event, most of the B-O-T arrangements have been for near-certain profitable ventures. Equally important is the fact that divestitures in the infrastructure sector have largely meant the sale of SOEs with considerable market power such as KCT, Telekom Malaysia and TNB, which were highly profitable anyway. This conclusion that privatized projects are unlikely to fail is reinforced by the fact that the Government appears to have sanctioned substantial increases in user fees in many of the privatized infrastructure projects, for whose services there are really no substitutes.

Increased efficiency is often claimed to be the most important of the benefits of privatization and, in Malaysia, it constitutes an explicit justification for the policy. The case for efficiency improvements from privatization is predicated on the proposition that a transfer of ownership and control of an enterprise from the public sector to the private sector would alter the firm's behavior and compel it to pursue efficiency as its main goal. But the pursuit of efficiency would only occur when all or at least the majority of the shares of a public enterprise or its assets are sold to private shareholders and there is minimal government control over the privatized company. In the privatization of infrastructure facilities in Malaysia, instances of full or complete divestiture are not the norm. In actual fact, the only case of a complete transfer of ownership and control of a government enterprise in the infrastructure sector was the privatization of the non-container facilities at Port Klang to KPM. And there has also been only a single instance of the sale of a majority of the shares of a SOE in the infrastructure sector, this being the divestiture exercise in the KCT. The privatization of the telecommunications and electricity utilities (Telekom Malaysia and TNB, respectively) only involved partial divestiture and less than a third of their shares have been sold to private shareholders. Strictly speaking, partial divestment cannot be considered as privatization because the government's power to determine firm behavior is virtually unaffected. Even where the Government has relinquished all its shares in a SOE or only owns a minority of shares in the enterprise, the mechanism of the golden share has allowed the Malaysian Government to retain effective control and influence over firm behavior, and thus prevent efficiency-inducing changes in the behavior of the firm. Ownership divestment in Malaysia, therefore, has not necessarily resulted in a significant change in firm behavior. In short, since there has been no substantive change in ownership and also control in the privatization exercises in the infrastructure sector, either because only a minority of shares was sold to private investors or because of the golden share owned by the Government, firm behavior cannot have changed very substantially because of privatization. The partial nature of the divestitures is not the only reason for scepticism over the alleged efficiency-inducing effects of the privatization of infrastructure. An even more compelling reason why the pursuit of efficiency could not have been an outcome of the Government's privatization policy is that the privatization of infrastructure in Malaysia has not been accompanied by a competitive restructuring of the product or services market. Efficiency gains result from the interaction between private ownership and a competitive environment (Baumol and Kyu Sik Lee (1991) and Kay and Thompson (1986)). It could even be argued that it is competition, rather than private ownership *per se* that encourages more efficient firm behavior, and it is firms in a competitive market that have the incentives to achieve both productive and allocative efficiencies. In all the cases of privatization in the infrastructure sector of Malaysia, the enterprises have retained their monopoly power. Public monopolies in the infrastructure sector have been simply converted to private monopolies. In this regard, the privatization of monopolistic infrastructure facilities has ignored the fact that different production stages in the infrastructure sector have different characteristics. Unbundling of the services according to the technical characteristics of each discrete function such as generation, transmission and delivery would have allowed the services to be differentiated into different products and this could have revealed the possibilities for a competitive restructuring of the infrastructure industries. But the fact is infra-structure services have not been unbundled and because of this the opportunities for market restructuring have been lost. Furthermore, and even in the unlikely event that the privatized firm pursues efficiency, greater enterprise efficiency may only result in higher monopoly profits for the private shareholders rather than benefiting consumers. The efficiency and welfare gains could thus have been attained without divestiture. The gains could have been achieved by, for example, providing greater autonomy and flexibility to the SOEs through their corporati-zation and commercialization. These measures, when combined with marketization or competition, make up a tenable policy alternative to partial divestiture, but the corporatization of SOEs has not been seriously pursued as a way of improving their performance. Instead, in Malaysia corporatization of a SOE is a first step in its eventual sale. The manner in which the SOEs in infrastructure have been privatized—divestiture, usually partial, and unaccompanied by measures to enhance competition in the respective service markets, including the abolition of statutory monopoly powers—is, on the whole, a poor policy response to the inefficiency of the public sector in infrastructure. On the question of efficiency in the B-O-T projects, such as the roads, water and sewerage projects, it is true that the financing is wholly borne by the private sector and, for this reason, could be regarded as being analogous to complete divestiture that incorporates a change in ownership. But the monopolistic power of the private companies licensed to provide the infrastructure services is substantial. In the case of the privatized roads, for instance, the monopoly power of the private companies is already considerable and would increase even further if, for example, the Government fails to maintain the competing public sector roads at a level where they constitute an effective alternative to the privatized roads. Likewise, the company licensed to provide sewerage services, Indah Water Konsortium, would also be a monopolist. In view of their market power, the infrastructure services provided by the private companies need to be regulated if consumer welfare is not to be adversely affected. But as the discussion on this issue would reveal, the regulatory mechanisms that have been instituted are simply inadequate to protect consumers' or users' welfare.

It is often asserted that privatization can bring forth additional resources or "additionality" for investment. Foreign equity and foreign debt funding are addi-tionals, but both these sources of funds have not been very significant in the privatization of infrastructure in Malaysia. Private sector purchase of SOEs and investment in privatized infrastructure projects have been largely financed by private domestic equity and domestic debt. These are largely non-additional and do not represent a net increase in investment resources. In other words, there is little to suggest that privatization has significantly contributed to increased investment and thus to the growth of the Malaysian economy. On the contrary, private acquisition of public assets has probably diverted investment funds from other productive investment options. Resources that might have been used to increase the productive capacity of the economy could well have been diverted into acquiring existing public sector assets.

In the privatization of infrastructure in Malaysia, the achievement of the narrowly-defined inter-ethnic equity goal of the NEP has been a major influence (Puthucheary (1987)). In fact, from the pattern of divestiture of shares of the SOEs and the choice of private firms in the B-O-T projects, there can scarcely be any doubt that among all the objectives, the privatization of infrastructure has been most successful in contributing to the Government's NEP objective. The sale of shares of KCT, the parties selected to take over KPM, the distribution of shares in the privatization of Telekom Malaysia and TNB and the choice of private firms in the road and water projects all point towards an ethnic bias in the selection of beneficiaries in the privatization exercises. There is no denying that there are conflicts among the objectives contained in the *Guidelines on Privatization*, but what is also clear is that the trade-offs appear to have compromised the efficiency objective in favor of the NEP goal. The prioritization of the NEP objective has been a major factor undermining the achievement of the other aims of the privatization policy, including relegating the pursuit of efficiency to something less than an overriding objective of the privatization policy in the infrastructure sector.

If there is considerable scepticism about the benefits of the privatization of infrastructure, the way in which the policy has been implemented has also cast doubts about the real effect of the policy (Bennett (1991), Ismail (1991) and Puthucheary (1987)). The privatization procedures have even brought into question the true intent of the policy. The main criticism about the manner in which the policy has been implemented is that the procedures lack transparency. There are two reasons for this absence of transparency. First, the private sector is free to identify projects for privatization and the application of the "first-come, first-served" rule places a virtually exclusive premium on the company that submits the privatization proposal first. Second, even privatization projects initiated by the Government have not been awarded in accordance with an open tender system. On the contrary, the projects have been awarded via a closed tendering system. This is true of all the divestiture exercises in the ports sector, of the privatized road projects as well as the other infrastructure projects, such as the sewerage project and the LRT project. Even though it might be claimed that the pre-selection of the parties for the privatization exercises has helped to minimize the transaction costs involved in implementing the policy, both these practices encourage rent-seeking activities by individuals and firms. In addition, and though the evidence on the matter is sketchy, there are signs to suggest that many beneficiaries from the privatization of infrastructure have been chosen on the basis of political and personal connections. The legal battle over the award of the North South Highway project to UEM, a company controlled by UMNO, the dominant party in the ruling coalition, and the protests over the imposition of tolls along a section of the KL Roads and Interchanges B-O-T project were both, in their own ways, efforts at forcing greater governmental transparency and public accountability in the implementation of the privatization policy. Unfortunately, however, it is not only unproductive rent seeking that is encouraged. Because the privatized operators in the infrastructure sector possess considerable market power, they are also in a strong position to appropriate considerable amounts of rent.

An aspect of privatization that has received scant attention up to now is the role of the government in the post-privatization era. Privatization on a large scale will certainly result in a fundamental change in the distribution of power between the private and public sectors in the Malaysian economy. For this reason, and contrary to popular perception, the government's role in the post-privatization era will still be significant. Basically, the government has an important supervisory or regulatory role to play (Teplitz-Sembitzky (1990)). There are a number of fairly obvious reasons why the private operators of infrastructure would have to be regulated. The first reason is that the privatized infrastructure facilities will continue to occupy a strategic or pivotal role in the economy, not only because of strong linkages with the other sectors, but also because infrastructure facilities have strong links to growth, poverty and the environment. Second, many of the privatized infrastructure facilities possess considerable market power and provide their services in non-contestable markets. What this implies is that users are locked into a delivery system and cannot express dissatisfaction through choice. These two reasons simply mean that private providers of infrastructure must be subjected to some form of supervision. Yet another reason is that firms in the infrastructure sector, including privatized ones, can have social obligations imposed on them and some regulatory mechanism is needed to ensure the performance of such social functions. Finally, a regulatory mechanism is needed to ensure strict compliance with the conditions of the concession agreements and operating licences. In short, regulatory institutions should be created to perform supervisory and regulatory functions, not only to serve as a buffer between the private suppliers and users, but also to give effect to government policies.

In Malaysia, the regulatory system is *ad hoc* and still evolving although the privatization of infrastructure began about a decade ago. As matters now stand, in all the cases where infrastructure has been privatized, it is the Government department or statutory body that was previously supplying the services that has assumed the regulatory role. For example, the KPA is now the regulatory agency over the two (soon three) private companies at the port. Likewise, the Telecommunications Department is now the regulator of the telecommunications sector. The scope of regulatory action in Malaysia, however, is fairly rudimentary: no clear link, for example, exists between the functions of the regulatory agencies and the creation of incentives to achieve efficiency on the part of the privatized suppliers of infrastructure services. Another feature of regulation in Malaysia is that although regulatory agencies exist, the respective ministers still appear to have considerable influence over the policies of the privatized suppliers. Rate revisions, for example, are not completely a matter for the relevant regulatory agency to decide and almost always appear to require ministerial sanction. If this is already a source of considerable ambiguity about the independence of the regulatory agencies from ministerial or political interference, there is also a distinct possibility, in some cases, of capture of the regulatory agency by industry. The need for a tenable regulatory framework is a matter of some urgency in Malaysia not only because of the extent of privatization in the country but also because as time goes by privatized suppliers of infrastructure services are likely to feel less restrained to exploit their market power.

In spite of the criticisms of the manner in which infrastructure has been privatized in Malaysia, in the longer term, the policy can result in important externalities for the economy. And these might yet turn out to be the most important benefits from privatization. The externalities associated with privatization include such long-term effects as the enhanced dynamism of the economy as a result of a larger private sector and the benefits from an international perception of an improved investment climate in the country. Another possible externality is a strengthening of the local capital market. Privatization has undoubtedly contributed to a broadening and deepening of the KLSE. There are now seventeen privatization issues listed on the Exchange. And the two largest companies listed on the KLSE are privatized infrastructure companies, namely, Telekom Malaysia and the TNB. The externalities associated with privatization are difficult to measure, but they are important considerations in any comprehensive assessment of the Government's privatization policy.

Conclusion

This chapter has shown that since the policy was initiated, a fairly significant segment of the infrastructure sector of Malaysia has been privatized, in one form or another. In fact, the infrastructure sector would appear to the principal target of the Government's privatization program. If the program proposed by the PMP is adhered to, then private provision of infrastructure could well become extensive. It must, however, be pointed out that for a long while yet, the public sector will remain the major supplier of infrastructure (Table 9.1).

Privatization in Malaysia has been intended to serve a number of objectives, including, *inter alia*, equity as well as efficiency goals. Not surprisingly, in the implementation of the policy, trade-offs have had to be made, largely between equity and efficiency goals. The manner in which the policy has been implemented, however, would appear to suggest that the pursuit of efficiency has not been the dominant objective of the Government. In almost all the privatization exercises, the inter-ethnic redistribution objective, as defined by the NEP, would appear to have taken precedence over all other aims of the policy. Whether or not the trade-off in favor of equity actually improved income distribution is, however, quite another matter.

The manner in which infrastructure has been privatized in Malaysia has not been sufficiently transparent. Nearly all the infrastructure projects that have been privatized were offered to the private sector without going through a transparent tender and selection process. Ports, road projects, water supply as well as sewerage projects and the LRT facility were all privatized via privately negotiated deals between pre-selected private firms and the Government. If accusations of favoritism have occasionally surfaced, the secrecy surrounding the selection process has not helped to dispel them nor has it improved the image of the policy.

Technological developments in infrastructure industries, such as in the telecommunications and electricity sectors, have made it possible to unbundle infrastructure services and, possibly, to even supply them competitively. These opportunities have been largely unexplored in Malaysia, with the result that in the infrastructure sector, public monopolies have been converted, as a result of their privatization, to private monopolies. For this and other reasons, the absence of a proper regulatory regime—with adequate powers to protect consumers' interests—is a major flaw in the Malaysian Government's privatization of infrastructure.

Under the present modalities of privatization in Malaysia, not only is there no tenable system to protect users' welfare, there are also no mechanisms through which consumers' needs and preferences can be discovered. In other words, there appears to be no place for "voice."

This chapter has not questioned the theoretical premises upon which privatization stands. That the policy offers a way of reforming the public sector is not in doubt. Moreover, and in spite of all the flaws in the way in which the policy has been implemented, in the final analysis, the policy has been beneficial to the Malaysian economy on the whole. In the longer run, when the externalities associated with the policy begin to materialize, the Government's decision to privatize infrastructure may yet turn out to be a good initiative towards resolving the problems of public dominance in infrastructure. But this should not be allowed to detract from the fact that the way in which the policy is being implemented can be considerably improved. With a decade long experience of privatization, there is no excuse not to address the question of how to go about making the infrastructure sector an attractive area for private investment without, at the same time, compromising the public interest. More transparency in the privatization of infrastructure facilities, a greater effort at improving the performance of privatized infrastructure facilities and, at the same time, affording effective protection to consumers and a place for "voice" might not only eliminate much of the scepticism associated with the policy, but may also enhance the positive impact of the policy. Notwithstanding the issues related to privatization of infrastructure, the fundamental questions surrounding public provision of infrastructure services, long ignored because of the enthusiasm over privatization, also need to be carefully studied. After all, for the foreseeable future, the public sector will continue to bear the major responsibility for infrastructure development in Malaysia.

10

Telecommunications*

LAUREL KENNEDY

In the early 1980s, Malaysia embarked on a program of privatization that has affected a broad span of government activities, ranging from road construction to the operation of a major port and to the establishment of a private national television channel. As a result of these actions, Malaysia has received international attention and not a little praise, particularly from the US and Great Britain, where expansion of the private sector has been viewed over the last decade as the panacea for the ills besetting the developing world. Anxious to see doors opened to private foreign investment and trade, the Western industrialized nations have looked favorably upon Malaysia's privatization initiative as a positive indication that the country permits and even encourages the invisible hand of the market to guide the growth of its economy.

Is this an accurate appraisal of Malaysia's privatization program? A close examination of the telecommunications sector, which since 1982 has undergone liberalization and, since 1987, the privatization of its state-run telecommunications system, suggests that Malaysia is enjoying praises for accomplishments it may not, in fact, have achieved. Malaysia's program of privatization has been rather more ambitious than its efforts towards liberalization. Rather than rationalizing decision-making, under the auspices of liberalization and privatization, Malaysia has created a state regulatory bureaucracy whose actions are closely controlled by politicians at the level of the Ministry or the Cabinet. This bureaucracy then functions to award contracts and licenses on terms which apparently have little to do with market competitiveness or with the economics and functioning of telecommunications markets, and much to do with the size and political ties of the firms involved.

*The research reported here was undertaken through the assistance of a Fulbright Scholarship and owes much to the institutional support of the Institute of Strategic and International Studies (ISIS) Malaysia. This paper is a revised draft of earlier papers presented at the International Communications Association Annual Meeting in 1991 and the Association for Asian Studies in 1992. The author is solely responsible for the content and conclusions of the paper.

This chapter will trace the policies of liberalization and privatization in Malaysian telecommunications and will show that the early beneficiaries of these policies have been a handful of well-connected firms which, since the 1970s, have been accruing increasing power within the young Malaysian telecommunications market and influence within the government which regulates it. To the extent that the objectives of these firms have coincided with those of the Malaysian state and of international and bilateral financial institutions, Malaysia has effected a policy winning it both domestic and international support. Matters of increased competition within the industry are quite another issue, however.

Malaysia's policies of liberalization and privatization are best understood in a historical and political-economic context. For this reason, the chapter begins with a brief review of changes that occurred during the 1970s in Malaysia, to set the stage for the implementation of these policies in the 1980s. Liberalization and privatization are then discussed in turn, followed by a discussion of the significance of their implementation for their ultimate outcome.

Malaysian Telecommunications in the 1970s

The implementation of the New Economic Policy (NEP) from 1971 had profound effects on the nature and size of the Malaysian state, and these were felt in the telecommunications sector. The NEP reaffirmed the role of the state as "protector" of the Malay people, thereby creating a rationale for a burgeoning government bureaucracy to oversee and promote the process of restructuring. One very visible product of the policy was a nearly fourfold increase in the federal public service which, while it expanded its provision of services and took on the new responsibilities of carrying out the NEP, at the same time provided job opportunities to the underemployed Malay population.

Jabatan Telekom Malaysia (JTM, Malaysian Telecoms Department)[1] was immediately affected by the NEP. On the premise that economic growth required rapid improvements in infrastructure and services, the JTM workforce ballooned. While the number of employees had been just under 7,000 in the late 1950s and had increased by the end of the 1960s only to about 8,000, during the 1970s, the staff increased to over 21,000—a 211 percent increase for the decade. Problematically, these increases had little to do with improving the operations of the Department and much to do with providing jobs. JTM's consistent complaint throughout the period was that it was not permitted to hire the trained engineers it needed. Rather, as the ranks of the unskilled swelled and training programs remained underfunded, JTM rapidly became a behemoth, impaired by its size from anything approximating operational efficiency.

At the same time, the NEP was promoting urbanization and a restructuring of Malaysia's industrial sector, which jointly drove up demand for telecommunications services. Unable to cope with the management problems associated with its rapid staff growth and stymied by the persistent refusal of the government to allocate funds for technology development, JTM's service record plummeted. While the World Bank had pointed to JTM in the 1960s as a model worthy of emulation by other developing countries, and still gave the Department its highest rating in the early 1980s (Crawford, 1984), within Malaysia, JTM became a public symbol of slothful inefficiency and corruption.

If NEP implementation helped JTM to go into a tailspin, its effects on the private telecommunications sector were quite the reverse. In particular, the NEP produced very positive outcomes for the private Malay firms which sprang up to take advantage of preferences awarded to Bumiputera companies. Among the first of these were three firms that, because they would come to dominate the industry, deserve special attention. Uniphone was among the earliest to be established. Originally a subsidiary of UMW, a large automotives concern then owned by a Chinese Malaysian, Uniphone was managed by Shamsuddin Kadir, a former Telecoms Department employee. Shamsuddin had been brought to UMW by its Executive Director, Eric Chia, who wanted to recruit bright and energetic Malays to management posts at UMW.[2] Shamsuddin had left the post of Acting Director of Telecommunications at JTM, a position equal in rank to that of Buyong Abdullah, JTM's next Director-General. Shamsuddin might, in other words, have shortly ascended to the highest rank within JTM, but saw greater promise in the private sector than in the civil service.

In his new post, Shamsuddin approached his former colleagues at Telecoms about relieving them of the burden of installing and maintaining public pay telephones. He quickly received a franchise to service all urban pay phones. Making an early success of the venture, Shamsuddin in 1975 bought out the young firm from UMW, and shortly thereafter established a new parent company, Sapura Holdings, to oversee Uniphone and a growing number of other telecommunications concerns he established in the late 1970s.

Other Malays, who shared Shamsuddin's background with the Telecoms Department and his sense that the private sector held out vast opportunities, also set up new firms. Among these were Karim Ikram, who established Zal Enterprises and later Binafon to manufacture cable connectors, distribution boxes, and other telecommunications equipment, and Mohktar Mohiddin, who provided services on contract to the Telecoms Department.

After 1975, a series of policies went into place which signaled tremendous growth for these young firms. In 1975, the Telecoms Department abandoned the use of competitive bidding for so-called "civil service" jobs, such as digging trenches for cables. Under a new policy, these contracts would instead be issued on a "round-robin basis" to contractors registered expressly for this purpose. In 1979, the system was further modified to permit contracting out not just of "civil service" jobs, but of the actual laying and hanging of cables as well. Further, contractors seeking registration would be reviewed in terms of Bumiputera equity and staffing in addition to technical expertise, and then placed in classes ranked by the complexity of the jobs they could take on.

These policies had far-reaching implications. First, this system of contract allocations effectively eliminated competition in bidding for contracts and placed in the hands of government bureaucrats the role of distributing contracts, sometimes valued as high as RM5 million. Second, it permitted the rapid development of a domestic telecommunications industry; the contracts let under this system, which were monetarily quite substantial, permitted the firms to build up a workforce, a vehicle fleet, a core of trained technicians, and a recognizable name in the telecommunications sector. Third, the policies permitted the increasing localization of what had formerly been an industry dominated by foreign telecommunications giants. Several of the firms, including Sapura Holdings/Uniphone and Binafon, invested in manufacturing capability and began producing equipment such as telephone handsets. The more sophisticated manufactures were typically foreign-trademarked goods produced through licensing agreements with foreign firms such as Siemens and Philips, but others were entirely domestically produced, such as telephone poles and manhole covers. By the end of the decade, there were enough private firms doing business in telecommunications to constitute a significant, young domestic telecoms industry.

By the late 1970s, JTM had slumped to all-time lows in terms of operational efficiency.[3] The larger of the private domestic firms accurately perceived this as a situation in which the government's liability was their own route to success. Increasingly influential in the Ministry and above, these firms saw the solutions to JTM's problems within their own business activities. In a surprise turn of events, after decades of rejection of its budget requests, in 1980, JTM was provided the full budget allocation it had sought, and the government announced plans to modernize and upgrade the national telecommunications system. It soon became clear, however, that the Department would not be trusted with either the work to be done nor with decision-making about key aspects of the project. On the contrary, the Ministry assumed responsibility for designating private contractors, who would then hold very broad authority for design of network expansion. Four Bumiputera firms, whose principals were described by a Telekom official as having "close rapport" with the government, were each awarded RM636 million turnkey contracts to upgrade and extend segments of the national telecommunications network. Among these firms were Sapura Holdings' Uniphone, Binafon, Mohktar Mohiddin's Electroscon, and a fourth firm, Sri Communication, established by two other former JTM employees. The same firms won additional contracts to modernize other elements of the system and, in some instances, became sole providers of JTM equipment. Although smaller Bumiputera firms fought the contracts, the political influence of the larger firms was sufficient to overcome any wavering—or to eliminate dissenting voices.

At the start of the 1970s, the primary players in the telecommunications industry had been the Telecoms Department and a variety of international telecommunications suppliers. By the end of the decade, a domestic industry had arisen, taken on a clear internal hierarchy of size and influence, and displaced or, at the least, become an essential partner for foreign firms wishing to do business in the Malaysian market. Further, the willingness of the government to encourage and itself invest in the industry's growth was clear. However, the domestic firms were blocked from achieving their aspirations for continued growth: law rendered to JTM a monopoly in the operation of the network, supply of terminal equipment to customers, and provision of Value Added Network Services. It was against this historical backdrop that liberalization and privatization were placed on Malaysia's telecommunications policy agenda.

Liberalization of Malaysian Telecommunications Markets

Throughout the 1970s, the policies described in the previous section encouraged private Bumiputera firms to enter the telecommunications sector. None of these policies, however, caused the Telecommunications Department to compete with private operators or suppliers. Between 1983 and 1985, several new measures were instituted which placed JTM in competition with private suppliers of goods and services, suggesting a significant step towards liberalization.

The first of these measures was prompted by terminal equipment supply problems which JTM had begun to suffer in the late 1970s. The 1978 *Annual Report* of the Department noted that for a number of important items, severe shortages existed. Among the most acute of these was the shortage of telex machines, for which demand in the business community was high and growing.

According to a Ministry official, a number of dissatisfied business users approached the Ministry in 1982 to argue that existing local private firms could provide telex machines, and that if JTM's monopoly was ended, demand could be met. A former middle-level Ministry official indicated that such proposals for liberalization found a positive response within the Ministry, since they represented new opportunities for the expansion of Bumiputera businesses, which officials had been directed to encourage.

JTM, according to these officials, was amenable to the change. In the first place, liberalization provided a relief from JTM's budgetary pressures and permitted it to conserve funds for other uses. Second, because telecommunications operates on the principle of derived demand—the network receives only as much use as there are terminal facilities to connect to—liberalization offered a means of increasing consumption without imposing upon the Department additional demand for facilities. JTM would continue to establish the technical standards, and all equipment connected to the network would be JTM-approved. With this broad support for the policy, in June 1983, the Ministry announced that telephones and teleprinters would henceforth be provided by both JTM and the private sector (*Business Times*, 10 June 1983).

Almost immediately, there was a rush among telecommunications firms to enter the market. Shamsuddin Kadir's Sapura Holdings—whose subsidiaries now held manufacturing licenses and import agreements from ITT, Northern Telecom,

Siemens, NEC, and others—began to market US-manufactured "Mickey Mouse" telephones and other special feature and novelty equipment (Goh, 1987). Electcoms, a firm related to one of the largest Bumiputera contractors, entered the terminal equipment market. Major Malaysian conglomerates not previously operating in the telecommunications sector, such as Sime Darby, also established subsidiaries to market terminal equipment.

Foreign firms from Australia, the US, the Netherlands, Sweden, Germany, Italy, France, and Denmark also moved quickly to enter or expand their presence in the Malaysian market. Many of these sought partnerships with Malaysian firms in order to facilitate access to the market. Noteworthy among these was Electronic Systems Malaysia (ESM), established by Philips in 1983 to market high technology. Within a year of its registration, ESM announced that 45 percent of its equity had been purchased by the Fleet Group, then the main investment holding company of the ruling party, the United Malays National Organization (UMNO). This was the first indication that Fleet, whose presence in the commercial world was growing rapidly, intended to become an active player in the telecommunications sector.

Gaining momentum, within two years, liberalization was extended to some value-added services markets as well. Although it is difficult to trace the origins of the VANS liberalization policy, it is clear that Shamsuddin Kadir took the opportunity to lobby the Cabinet on the issue through the circuitous route of a privatization feasibility study which he commissioned. This study, authored by the American consulting firm Arthur D. Little (ADL), was ostensibly to address two questions: whether a privatized JTM would be more responsive to the nation's telecommunications needs, and whether privatization was feasible. The report, however, made a tactical diversion from the subject of privatization to raise the possibility of liberalizing the VANS market.

The study raised the issue of liberalization in the context of JTM's inability "to devote sufficient physical or management resources to the development of value-added services" (ADL, 1983: 50). The report provided a lengthy discussion of the benefits VANS would provide the Malaysian economy, and ideas for how the market might be developed, the latter based on a fibre-optic network, the technology for which Sapura Holdings subsidiaries were adapting. A description of services which might be liberalized, and of how the sector should be regulated, was also provided. Finally, the report cautioned that while VANS would best be provided in a competitive environment, certain VANS "need to be protected against too much competitors [*sic*]. Indeed, it is possible that where markets are too small to support more than one entrant, certain services are best provided in a regulated monopoly" (ADL, 1983: 53). Within just over a year, the decision to liberalize the VANS market was announced and implemented by the Ministry. With this, the business opportunities available to the ADL study's sponsor, Sapura Holdings, expanded dramatically.

The first service in which liberalization was evident was radio paging, a service described in the Malaysian newspaper, *Business Times*, as a "cash cow" because it yielded quick returns on nominal investment (Devi, 1989e: 2). In October 1985, the press reported that a new firm called Komtel had received a license to provide radio paging (Halim, 1985). Komtel was 60 percent owned by Sapura Holdings.[4] Four months later, the Ministry announced that additional licenses had been granted to three other firms, of which two had been recipients of the RM636 million turnkey contracts and the third was owned by yet another former Telecoms Department Director-General. These licenses were all for service to the lucrative Klang Valley, which includes the Federal Territory of Kuala Lumpur, the neighboring suburbs of Petaling Jaya and Shah Alam, and Port Kelang. Sapura Holdings later gained an additional license for another subsidiary, Sija Sendirian, to operate in Johor Bahru. Sri Communication, the fourth winner of a network expansion contract, gained two licenses through subsidiaries.

In all, by 1992, 38 licenses had been issued for radio paging. Despite the large number of licensees, the benefits accruing to each varied widely, as certain service areas were more lucrative than others. These licenses went to the largest and most politically influential firms.[5] Dissatisfaction with the licensing process was suggested when the government prepared its first draft policy on national paging systems, the creation of which would effectively eliminate all smaller players. *Business Times* reported broad support among paging operators for the establishment of national systems "provided each company is given a 'fair' chance to compete" (*Business Times*, 26 January 1990: 2); nonetheless, the strongest support for the idea came from large companies already operating in lucrative areas, while small firms in low-revenue areas were more generally opposed to the plan.

The granting of licenses by the Ministry is not a matter of public record, and Ministry officials are reluctant to provide information, either about the criteria used in the evaluation of license applications or even about which firms have been granted licenses. Despite the mystery, the entry of private firms into a number of other VANS markets is known, and suggest that the evaluation process employs political considerations. This is particularly evident in the two markets, mobile and data communications, which the executive chairman of Telekom identified as the major growth areas for the 1990s. For example, the press reported in 1985 that a new firm had been established to provide private satellite transmission of voice and data messages. A joint venture of politically well-situated Malaysians and Indonesians, the firm was reported to have received Prime Minister Mahathir's personal approval as well as exclusive rights to provide this service (Clad, 1985; see also Sussman, 1988: 290).

The liberalization of mobile communications has very clearly been influenced by political considerations. Cellular telephones had provided JTM with a surprise success when its 450 Mhz ATUR system was introduced in 1985, and by 1989, mobile phones were growing at a rate of over 30 percent per annum (Devi, 1989a). When the press announced in mid-1988 that this market would be opened to a new entrant, both the pre-selection and the source of competition were a surprise to many: the Fleet Group, the ruling party's investment arm, had received a license and immediately formed Celcom, a joint venture with the now-privatized Telekom, and was accepting proposals for a 900 Mhz cellular radio network that would compete with the existing system offered by Telekom. The widely-held retrospective view that Telekom had been pressured into joining the partnership was supported by the incongruence of Telekom taking a partner with no telecommunications expertise or experience, to provide a service which would compete with its own established and successful offering.

If the birth of Celcom was a surprise to Telekom watchers, its early development was no less a puzzle. Just one year into the venture, Telekom announced that it was selling its 49 percent share in Celcom to an industry unknown, Alpine Resources. Not only was the price-tag a shock—a mere RM4 million, as compared to the RM81.5 million, for which Fleet sold its share a year later—but Alpine was described in the press at the time as a little-known "low profile investment holding company" making its "maiden foray" into telecommunications (*Business Times*, 4 January 1990: 1). Nonetheless, a *Business Times* editorial praised the decision as a signal that Telekom would now set up a third competitive mobile phone service (*Business Times*, 5 January 1990). Indeed, press reports indicated that Telekom had received written confirmation from the Ministry of Energy, Telecommunications and Posts that it would be permitted to establish the third service. Within weeks, however, a Cabinet-level decision prohibited Telekom from establishing the third service for an undisclosed period, in order to protect Celcom's new owners from competition.[6] The purchaser, Alpine Resources, was indeed a "low-profile" firm—determinedly so, for its principal, Tajudin Ramli, a former Fleet board member and close associate of Tun Daim Zainuddin, Finance Minister at the time of the sale, avoids public attention. Tajudin found his 49 percent ownership sufficiently profitable that within two years of his RM4 million purchase, he was able to buy the remaining 51 percent of the business for RM271 million.[7]

Divergences from transparent licensing practices also occurred in the case of CT2 service, the second-generation cordless telephones said to be "reshaping" the telecommunications market throughout Asia (see Johnstone, 1990a, 1990b). In 1990, newspapers reported that three licenses had been granted for the development of the CT2 service in Malaysia. If this service is as important as prognosticators of telecommunications anticipate, the holders of these licenses will stand in good stead to enjoy huge rewards for their early entry. The licenses, granted to Sapura Holdings, Telekom, and Serting Communications (a firm which also holds a radio paging license), were said to have been awarded to these firms because they were the first to apply (*Business Times*, 18 January 1990). This was consistent with the "first-come-first-served" policy of privatization which the government announced in 1988 (*New Straits Times*, 16 June 1988). What was curious, however, was that the Ministry, having granted the licenses on this basis, then announced that the three firms could delay introduction of the service for a year while studying the technology, without the threat of outside competitors who might be able to offer the service earlier, but for the lack of a license.

Liberalization, then, has opened vast new opportunities for expansion, both for domestic firms and for international firms willing to enter markets through local partners. Whether liberalization gave free play to competitive forces is another question, however. Certainly anyone could apply to the Ministry for a license to enter the telecommunications market. But the process and criteria by which applications are evaluated is unclear. The assertion by a middle-ranking Ministry official, during a 1988 interview, that applications from non-Bumiputera firms were not given consideration is borne out by the exclusively Bumiputera ethnic composition of the firms which have received licenses in all liberalized markets. However, other factors appear to be involved as well, for even among Bumiputera firms, there are distinctions. The licenses for the technological markets with the greatest growth potential, as well as for the geographical markets which are most attractive, have gone to a handful of by now familiar Bumiputera telecommunications firms—Sapura Holdings/Uniphone, Binafon, Electcoms, Sri Communications, and a few others—and to politically influential holdings such as Fleet/Renong companies and Sime Darby. Smaller firms may also have received licenses, but these have been for less lucrative markets. Thus, while "liberalization" has allowed many firms to enter markets from which they were previously barred by law, it has neither provided all bidders with equal opportunities nor subjected all firms equally to the vagaries of a competitive marketplace.

Privatization of Jabatan Telekom Malaysia

Privatization appeared on the Malaysian policy agenda at a time when the country was experiencing internal domestic and economic problems and was coming under increasing pressure from multilateral and bilateral institutions to carry out economic reforms. In many ways, privatization was an unusually attractive solution to many of the ills besetting Malaysia at the time: Malaysia's flagging economy would benefit by the reduction in state expenditures and by the injection of capital which the sale of public enterprises could administer, and Malaysia would win favor with those governments and institutions for which privatization had become a *cause celebre*. But in addition, following a series of political crises that had shaken popular support of the government, privatization offered a means of expanding the business opportunities available, so that a broader constituency could be addressed—the rewards of patronage could be extended more widely. Thus, privatization, like liberalization, although usually understood primarily in economic terms, had an explicitly political dimension. The particular nature of that political dimension was suggested by aspects of the policy's implementation and by its early beneficiaries.

According to a Ministry official, interest in privatizing the Telecommunications Department began in 1981, shortly after Mahathir assumed the post of Prime

Minister, and the decision to go ahead had already been made within the top levels of government by 1983, when the first ruminations of the policy appeared in the press. Although operational control would not be turned over for nearly three years, by mid-1984, the successor firm, Syarikat Telekom Malaysia (STM, later TM), was registered with paid-up capital of RM1 million. How actually to implement the policy was a daunting problem, however. With about 30,000 employees, JTM represented the largest workforce in the country, and its far-flung assets and liabilities would be difficult to compile for review, let alone assessment, in determining the Department's net worth. In August 1984, the government commissioned a study which was called a privatization feasibility study, but, since the successor firm already existed, was in fact more an analysis of JTM's current position and a series of recommendations regarding implementation of privatization.[8]

Envisioning privatization to occur by mid-1985, the study predicted that the private successor to JTM would encounter severe financial strains during its first years of operation as a result of its bloated staff and high interest payments on its loans, including the Treasury loans which had paid for the turnkey network expansion contracts. In order to facilitate the process of privatization, the report recommended a number of measures, including a detailed assessment of JTM's assets and liabilities, and the introduction of systematic corporate planning and review. The study urged a rapid increase in line connections in order to increase revenues, as well as the restructuring of JTM's tariffs. With regard to the newly privatized firm, the report recommended that the government ease taxes and duties in order to boost the firm's financial position in its early years and that it guarantee Telekom Malaysia's fresh borrowings. Finally, the report advised the government to assist TM in resolving thorny issues relating to ownership of land used for telecommunications facilities.

By 1985, the government's enthusiasm for privatization had become well known. At a conference on privatization early in 1985, representatives of the Economic Planning Unit of the Prime Minister's Department indicated that privatization was under consideration or already being implemented in a number of settings, and they articulated the objectives of the privatization policy, namely: (1) relief of the financial burden borne by the state, (2) reduction of the size and presence of government, (3) promotion of economic growth, (4) increased competition, efficiency and productivity, and (5) redistribution of wealth along the lines set in the NEP (Radin & Zainal, 1985: 225–228). Although hindrances were to be anticipated, these were viewed as minor matters which could be dealt with administratively.

The implementation of the privatization policy was, at least in the case of JTM, more difficult and more time-consuming than these official remarks suggested. In particular, issues relating to land were more sensitive, and the resistance of JTM's labor union more unified, than the government had anticipated. The initial and then the revised target dates for corporatization—1 January 1985,

1 April, 1 October—passed without execution of the policy. Instead, 1985 and 1986 were occupied with laying the groundwork for privatization and with seeking accord on major issues so as to avoid further political dissension.

Late in 1985, the government appointed members of Telekom Malaysia's Board of Directors and made its initial moves to restructure JTM; these decisions, of course, were also sensitive. In November, the selection of Tan Sri Dr. Mohd. Rashdan Baba as chairman of TM was announced. He was joined on the board by the Secretary-General of the Ministry of Energy, Telecommunications, and Posts and by the Secretary-General of the Treasury. Daud Ishak, the director-general of JTM, became Telekom Malaysia's Managing Director. The following year, Daud's successor as director-general, Mohd. Radzi Mansor, became Operations Manager.

The recruitment of outsiders for the successor firm's Board of Directors touched off much unhappiness among both the management and the rank and file of JTM. It also underscored much about the decision-making process surrounding JTM's privatization, which involved JTM staff only minimally, and about the low esteem which the government accorded to the civil servants who ran JTM. While the government created opportunities for input by JTM authorities, some of those who participated later indicated in interviews that, despite their training in and knowledge of telecommunications markets and networks, they had had little substantive input, and that authority was really held by a committee formed by the Economic Planning Unit, an office within the Prime Minister's Department. The appointment of former Directors-General Daud and Radzi as Managing Director and Operations Director, respectively, did little to dispel dissatisfaction. On the contrary, the selections perhaps deepened discontent: The postings actually placed the two in positions lower in the management hierarchy than they had held in JTM, since they now had a new layer of management to whom they must report. Resentment ran high; indeed, the recruitment of outsiders to top management posts ultimately prompted Daud Ishak to resign, giving only 24 hours notice, when Dr. Syed Hussein Mohamed, the director of corporate planning with Sime Darby, was selected as executive director and chief operations officer of Telekom Malaysia (*New Straits Times*, 16 December 1987).

Despite the lingering problems of land ownership and the apparent malaise within JTM, by late 1986, the government announced that it was prepared to carry out the next stage of privatization, the relinquishment of operational responsibility to Telekom Malaysia. On 1 December 1986, a license was granted to TM to provide telecommunications services. On 1 January 1987 some 98 percent of JTM's employees officially joined the staff of Telekom Malaysia, while 102 employees were transferred to the new regulatory authority, which retained the JTM name (Daud, 1989: 119).

With the corporatization of the Telecoms Department, sights were set on creating the conditions necessary to list the successor firm on the Kuala Lumpur Stock Exchange. A record of three profitable years of operations was the most significant hurdle, and an initial hope was that the company would be able to achieve and maintain profitability from the very start in order to list by 1991. Within eight months of corporatization, the Minister of Energy, Telecommunications, and Posts already found Telekom Malaysia's record wanting, and he urged the company to review its operations and increase efficiency and productivity in order to expedite plans for a public listing.

There were a number of challenges associated with the goal of an early listing. The necessity of overcoming the "civil service mentality" of former JTM employees was perhaps the best publicized of these. This referred to the staff's lack of both experience in a profit-oriented environment and of a sense of competitiveness, a desire to prove oneself invaluable, within the workplace. The company took a number of actions both to modify the staff's behavior and to improve its public image, such as "courtesy campaigns" to teach Telekom Malaysia workers new methods of interaction with the public (*New Straits Times*, 6 November 1987) and the appearance of TM booths at night markets to register applicants for telephone service. Finally, in December 1988, the company underwent a reorganization exercise intended to underscore TM's commitment to customer service, particularly within the business community. A new division, Customer Services and Marketing, featured some 1000 retrained TM staff members now working as marketing teams to assist large corporate customers.

In addition to concerns over the customer-orientation of TM, a second set of issues preoccupying the company concerned the delineation of its business domain. Corporate strategy hinged on receiving licenses, and decisions regarding the services to be licensed to TM, made at the level of the Ministry and above, did not always favor the company. An issue which particularly provoked dissent concerned the license to provide public telephone services. While Uniphone held a license, expiring in 1988, to provide urban services, Telekom Malaysia was required by its own license to provide pay telephones to non-economical rural areas. As a private, competitive firm, TM now sought to regain the urban segment of this market as well, and tried to convince the Ministry that this business was important for the company's profitability, particularly in light of the prior liberalization of other "bread-and-butter" markets. The Ministry did not oblige. On the contrary, a non-competitively awarded, 15-year monopoly license was granted to Uniphone, Shamsuddin Kadir's Sapura Holdings' subsidiary, to supply, install, and maintain public payphones, at a license fee of RM5,000 per year (Yap, 1988). While TM registered no official protest to the action, the National Union of Telecommunications Employees claimed that Telekom Malaysia would forgo revenues of RM45 million per year as a result of the Uniphone licensing, and claimed that the move was unfair, defeated the purpose of privatization, and perhaps violated extant law and regulation (*The Star*, 19 July 1988). Tensions over the issue escalated a year later, when Uniphone's remittance to TM was significantly less than TM was given to expect under the terms of the license. According to press accounts, the government did little to clarify the terms of the license it had awarded to Uniphone, TM wrote off losses of RM792,431, and the struggle between the two companies continued unresolved. Telekom Malaysia was initially also prohibited from the telephone-calling-card market, which Uniphone was permitted to monopolize. The revenues from these two services were estimated at RM30–36 million annually for Uniphone (Phoon, 1992).

Concerns about Telekom Malaysia's autonomy were also evident. Through three mechanisms, the Ministry of Energy, Telecommunications, and Posts maintained a tight grip over the company, prompting observers within the firm, in the telecommunications industry, and among corporate users to question whether the privatization exercise had been anything more than nominal. First, the Minister was authorized to change, at will, the terms of the operating license. Second, the Minister was provided ultimate rate-making power. In the absence of any formula for rate revisions, as had been provided in British Telecom's license, the Minister was guided by other, unspecified, standards.[9] Third, the Minister was authorized to decide who would serve on the successor firm's Board of Directors, rendering to the Ministry significant influence over decisions on personnel selection for top management posts and over business decisions made by the new firm.

The authority of the Ministry to select Board members caused concern that selections would be made on the basis of candidates' political affiliations rather than their qualifications and abilities. Observers both within Telekom Malaysia's middle management and in private industry questioned the basis for selection of some of TM's top personnel, arguing that directors were being chosen despite limited background in telecommunications or poor performance in other enterprises. Clearly, the government was faced with a dilemma: how to gain the experience of individuals working within the industry without placing those individuals in a conflict of interest between their primary employment and their board membership. In confronting this paradox, the government appeared to prefer risking the conflict of interest. Thus, for example, it courted a member of the board of Malayan Cables, a subsidiary of Sapura Holdings—a development that Sapura's management indicated, in an interview, it had hopefully anticipated in supporting JTM's privatization. Given the Board's authority to determine Telekom Malaysia's business course, such conflicts of interests could have severe ramifications.

Additionally, Telekom Malaysia's autonomy from the government is circumscribed by the ultimate financial control held by the Finance Ministry by virtue of its 76 percent share and the "Golden Share" provision in TM. Here too, there have been indications of politicization of decision-making. Early in 1992, for example, controversy erupted over a Finance Ministry decision on the award of contracts for the supply of digital equipment to TM. The Ministry overruled the recommendation of TM, casting aside lower bids in order to award contracts to firms with connections to UMNO, to the Finance Minister himself, and to Sapura Holdings (Tsuruoka, 1992). The decision had not only financial implications for Telekom Malaysia, but was also seen as tainting Malaysia's image among international investors.

Despite the difficulties of carving out an independent presence, Telekom Malaysia has been strikingly successful. The firm's first year financial reports were dismal: although the company had a pre-tax profit of RM4.91 million, unexpected paper liabilities produced a net loss of RM96.63 million, which would have precluded a listing before 1991.[10] By contrast, the following year's financial reports from TM were astounding: Pre-tax profits (and TM would pay no taxes under its government-approved tax holiday) were reported at RM180.41 million, a 36-fold increase over 1987 profits of RM4.91 million. The rather astonishing increase was attributed to cost-cutting by Telekom Malaysia's management, as operating expenditure increased by only 3.7 percent over 1988, while non-operating expenditure fell by 52 percent (Loganathan, 1989a).[11] Pre-tax profits continued to climb to RM366 million and RM564 million in 1989 and 1990 respectively. In 1991, with pre-tax profits of RM1,079 million, Telekom Malaysia registered the highest pre-tax profits of any firm in Malaysia (*Malaysian Business*, 15 August 1992: 23).

How can such success be evaluated? Clearly, corporatization has been financially very effective for Telekom Malaysia. By focusing its energies on improving customer services, particularly among business users, expanding value-added services of interest to corporate users, and rationalizing its accounting practices, TM has become highly profitable.

In spite of Telekom Malaysia's remarkable performance after its first year, Ministry officials have continued to hint that an action to open TM's basic services monopoly to competition is under consideration. According to the Deputy Minister, speaking in 1989, "If competition can help boost the use of telecoms services, why not create such competition?" (Rodhiah, 1989). According to the Deputy Minister, TM was failing to meet two objectives set by the government: increasing the local telephone penetration rate and improving the utilization of value-added services. While he acknowledged the quality of the services TM offered, he said the company needed to establish a more active promotion strategy to increase utilization. It appeared from these statements that the government was backing away from assumptions that basic telephone services were a natural monopoly, but it was not clear that this move was grounded in any reconsideration of the industry's structure. Rather, it appeared that a key objective of the government was to spread the gains available in the industry to a larger number of players.

Not surprisingly, many representatives of the telecommunications industry were initially quite pleased with the announcement. Press reports suggested that Shamsuddin Kadir had been pressing the government to open the market to competition for some time. Others were more cautious. One of the major firms holding a network expansion contract, for example, expressed concerns that the move was premature, claiming that it would be "an expensive exercise in duplication" until telephone penetration was higher (Devi, Rodiah, & Vong, 1989: 1). A second industry spokesperson argued that eliminating TM's monopoly would be wise, he claimed, only if the second operator relied on local expertise rather than "front men for foreign players" (Devi, Rodiah, and Vong, 1989: 17).

The strong financial reports did make Telekom Malaysia attractive to foreign investors. Late in 1989, the Minister of Energy, Telecommunications and Posts, Samy Vellu, was reported to have said that Bell Telephone, Motorola and British Telecoms all sought equity participation in Telekom Malaysia (Devi, 1989d). At that point, TM had not received its equity guidelines from the government, but the experience of other privatized enterprises seemed to suggest that substantial foreign ownership was likely.[12]

More recently, however, it has appeared that the Malaysian government will take a more time-honored approach: Time Engineering, a subsidiary of UMNO-linked Renong, has already received a license to operate data, voice, video and audio-transmission services along the North–South Highway—the first competition to Telekom Malaysia of this kind—and has been mentioned by name by the Minister of Energy, Telecommunications and Posts as a likely candidate to participate in a second national network (Lim, 1993).

Discussion

Privatization and liberalization are policies which are ostensibly used to improve efficiency and promote competition. In their application to the Malaysian telecommunications industry, those benefits have been partially precluded by the nature of implementation. In the awarding of licenses for liberalized services, for example, it is not clear that applicants have been evaluated strictly on the merits of their business performance. Little about the process is known at all, in fact. Further, licenses have frequently been awarded on a non-competitive basis. Indeed, the "first-come, first-served" policy of privatization embodies a most extreme form of non-competitive awards.

On what basis have awards of licenses been made? In September 1989, the Director-General of the Economic Planning Unit in the Prime Minister's Department described the role and nature of regulation: "Where monopolies remain, effective regulation will be essential to protect consumer interests. The guiding principles for regulatory framework are that discretionary powers to intervene in the commercial decisions of the privatized entity should be avoided. This is to minimize uncertainty and preserve the scope for commercial initiative." (Tan Chew Mau, 1990: 13.)

This study of the government's implementation of liberalization and privatization suggests that, on the contrary, full use of discretionary powers has been made. The telecommunications industry has been fundamentally restructured through the power to license, which the government achieved through the policies of liberalization and privatization. The criteria used in licensing are suggested by the awards that have been made. Virtually all the licenses have gone to Bumiputera firms, indicating that non-Bumiputera firms are not admitted to the competition and that ethnicity is thus a key determinant of success in applications. Among Bumiputera contenders, differences also appear, however: clear distinctions can be made between licenses on the basis of their potential economic value. Those firms which have received the most lucrative licenses are those which arose as the elite of the telecommunications industry—largely through previous, also non-competitive, policies—and who enjoy close affiliations with the ruling party, UMNO. This very clearly was the case with Sapura Holdings, which by the late 1980s held large blocks of stock in Fleet Group properties and received substantial government grants for its research and development efforts (Devi, 1989c). The relationships of firms to the ruling party were in other cases more direct, as in links between both Alcatel and Philips with the Fleet Group, and the relationship between Time Engineering and Renong.

Privatization has thus been used by the UMNO-led government to channel resources to its supporters or to its own subsidiary firms. This predilection of the government has been documented elsewhere for other industries (see, for example, Pura, 1988; and Tsuruoka, 1990). In telecommunications, representatives of the firms favored in license awards under liberalization pressed the government to accelerate, through the mechanism of privatization, the flow of economic benefits. The influence of these firms in the privatization of JTM was manifested in the form of studies written on the government's behalf. Interlocking directorships and informal affiliations may have provided other means of influence although these, particularly the latter, are difficult to gauge. The rewards of such influence—licenses to operate lucrative services—are of tremendous value and have been generously distributed to members of the elite.

Telekom Malaysia, on the other hand, faces uncertainty over how the government views it in license awards, and even whether the government will allow it to maintain its existing, limited monopoly. Further, it suffers from a lack of autonomy in many areas of its enterprise which its competitors do not face, including external authority over the composition of its Board and management, over its rates and its ability to enter or remain in markets, and over the disposition of its equity.

Liberalization and privatization have apparently contributed to the development of a national telecommunications industry: A new generation of telecommunications firms have been established and have grown to such size that they now compete for contracts in foreign markets. More broadly, the policies have assisted in the stabilization of the Malaysian economy since the mid-1980s. In the case of the Telecommunications Department, the government estimated a savings of RM2.1 billion in expenditures, and will eventually earn considerable income on taxes. However, at the same time, the government has forgone tremendous revenues. Further, while the service record of Telekom Malaysia is much improved over its days as a government department, in fact, many of those improvements had begun well before privatization, as the government sought to improve the image and operational efficiency of the department to enhance its eventual marketability. Finally, the government has opened the door to heavy foreign equity participation and control, such that not only will operating profits leave Malaysia, but issues of national sovereignty—which European PTTs have held out as reason not to privatize—are raised. These are risks and costs which the government of Malaysia, the World Bank, and others have neglected in reviewing the successes of Malaysia's privatization program. A complete account of Malaysia's experience must consider whether the implementation of the policies of liberalization and privatization have produced the gains anticipated, and at what cost.

Notes

1. Because the names used to refer to the telecommunications monopoly and its regulator are confusing, the following conventions are employed. "JTM" and "Telecoms" are used to refer to the pre-privatization Telecommunications Department. In the post-privatization period, "JTM" refers to the regulatory body. Syarikat Telekom Malaysia, the initial name for the successor firm, was changed in common usage to Telekom Malaysia (TM) about four years after privatization occurred. "Telekom Malaysia" or "TM" refers to the successor company.

2. The author acknowledges Kit Machado for drawing to her attention this information about Eric Chia.

3. Two measures of efficiency suggest the extent of JTM's difficulties. The ability of a service provider to coordinate the level of supply to meet demand is calculated as the proportion of total demand which remains unmet. In 1970, unmet demand stood at about 10 percent, but by 1977, had more than doubled. In a second measure, JTM's exchange capacity utilization declined throughout the 1970s, from 79.3 percent in 1970 to a decade low of 56.0 percent in 1978 (Kennedy, 1990: 101–6).

4. The remaining 40 percent of equity was held by an undisclosed investment company. Repeated efforts to obtain the company's public record of this information through the Registrar of Companies were unsuccessful as the files were persistently off the shelf.

5. It is worth noting here that although smaller firms seemed able to win licenses only for potentially less profitable markets, simply by holding radio paging licenses, these firms enhanced their appeal to foreign telecommunications firms wishing to invest in the Malaysian market. Several of these firms were reported to have been approached by foreign companies seeking equity participation (Devi, 1989e).

6. Not until 1993 was a third license granted, and then only to a consortium in which Telekom Malaysia was a member. The other members included, among others, Sapura Holdings and Permodalan Nasional Berhad (PNB). Industry observers claimed that by the start-up date for this third system, Celcom would have "cornered the market". In any case, by early 1993, Celcom was sufficiently successful to have entered markets throughout Asia, Africa and the Middle East (Wong, 1993: 24).

7. This hefty sum was paid to Time Engineering, a Renong company that had bought out the Fleet Group share for RM81.5 million just a year earlier. Tajudin described his own windfall in almost patriotic terms: having "made some money... I then thought the best thing to do would be to give something back to this country. When the Celcom license was issued, I realized trust had been placed in us" ("Keeping Faith", 1992: 51).

8. The report was written by the British Kleinwort, Benson Limited and the Malaysian firm, Hanafiah, Raslan & Mohamed, under the coordination of the Arab-Malaysian Merchant Bank. Because the report is a confidential document, it cannot be quoted.

9. The departure from the British model was notable because in other aspects, the Telekom Malaysia license was nearly identical to and had clearly been modelled on the British Telecoms license.

10. In fact, in October 1990, the government floated 25 percent of its Telekom Malaysia equity to Bumiputera institutions and investors and to TM employees (Westlake, 1991).

11. One possible source of savings was the renegotiation of foreign debt held by JTM/TM. During interviews in 1988, TM officials indicated that they were seeking to improve their interest payments through such renegotiation.

12. The Malaysian Airlines System (MAS), for example, was approximately 22 percent foreign owned, and some 17 percent of the Malaysian International Shipping Corporation (MISC) was foreign owned (Nankani, 1988: 74, 80).

11

Television Programming*

RAHMAH HASHIM

Unlike the privatization of most other services such as telecommunications, air and land transportation, hospitals, and electricity, which have been planned, supervised, co-ordinated, and evaluated by the Economic Planning Unit (EPU) in the Prime Minister's Department, the privatization of television broadcasting in Malaysia was initiated by the Ministry of Information which coordinates the Departments of Broadcasting, Information and Film. However, according to Hanafiah Omar, then head of the EPU's Privatization Unit, Ministry officials, including members of the Technical Committee in which Radio Television Malaysia is represented, attend sub-committee meetings of the Privatization Task Force "whenever they are affected."

Privatization of Television Broadcasting

In Malaysian broadcasting, there are three forms of privatization, namely, the privatization of local programming as well as airtime in the government-owned Radio Television Malaysia (RTM), and the licensing of a private television network (TV3) alongside RTM's two channels. TV3's establishment in 1984 occurred at a time when the government had decided to reduce the size of official debt. TV3 was also formed to counteract the growing video cassette recorder (VCR) phenomenon, and to provide an alternative to the two Government channels. Moreover, it was also intended to provide competition to RTM, which had been highly criticized for allegedly showing low quality, uninteresting, and outdated programs.

The inception of TV3 has not reduced the role of the public sector in the area of television broadcasting, but has certainly broken the monopoly enjoyed

*An earlier version of this paper was presented at the seminar on "Television Violence and Family Health," organized by the Malaysian Mental Health Association in Kuala Lumpur on 25 May 1991.

by RTM in the previous twenty years. Within the first few months of TV3's presence, RTM not only had to compete with TV3 for viewers, but also for advertising revenue. As a result of the competition, RTM has given more attention to viewer preferences, and is now considered more profit-oriented, especially in dealing with advertisers.

RTM launched its own internal privatization exercises about three years after the birth of TV3 to help deal with budgetary pressures, viewer dissatisfaction, the advent of new communication technologies, and competition from other television stations (TV3 and those in neighboring countries). TV3 thus provided the impetus for change in RTM. Indeed, the competition induced by TV3 was taken seriously by RTM, judging by the changes in programming and transmission hours as well as the new RTM policies involving airtime and programming.

Malaysian Television Stakeholders

RTM (comprising TV1 and TV2) and TV3 are interlinked with other stakeholders, including advertisers, advertising agencies, policy makers, regulators, program suppliers and producers, as well as viewers. Figure 11.1 identifies the various stakeholders or players in the broadcasting industry.

Television Networks

Malaysian television was a government monopoly from its inception in December 1963 until mid-1984, when TV3 began transmission after the government changed its broadcasting policy. Motivated by various considerations—including the lucrative revenue potential of a private television for the politically influential, especially with the ascendancy of television at the expense of the print media—the government licensed the privately-owned, profit-oriented Sistem Television Malaysia Berhad (STMB), popularly known as TV3. The presence of this new channel injected a competitive spirit into the government network, which visibly changed its programming policy.

In 1987, Dato' Jaafar Kamin, then Deputy Director-General of the Department of Broadcasting, regarded the privatization policy as a revolutionary and positive innovation for the film/television industry, especially for RTM, which welcomed the government's new attitude. Speaking as a government servant, however, Jaafar reiterated that RTM existed to achieve certain national goals, but emphasized that the duty of instilling national consciousness should not fall on the medium of television alone since television broadcasters have their own personal, financial, and technological constraints.

With a rival network in existence, the RTM staff found it easier to convince the powers-that-be that RTM required additional financing for new equipment to replace obsolete hardware and to reduce bureaucracy in order to function more

FIGURE 11.1 Inter-organizational Relations of the Television Industry in Malaysia

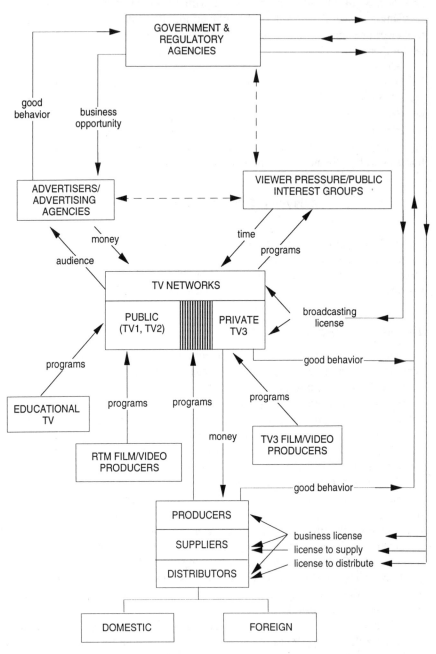

Source: Rahmah Hashim, 1989.

effectively. With privatization, RTM's management believes that the government network now gets more attention from the bureaucracy. Previously, for example, RTM had to go through the Information Ministry and the Federal Treasury in order to purchase even petty items such as new wardrobes for its newsreaders. Evidently, such procedures took time, and newsreaders are known to have worn the same clothes for a whole year, adversely affecting RTM's image.

Although privatization promises a more liberalized broadcasting environment, TV3 is not as independent as it may appear to be, and the private network remains just as vulnerable to government pressures on media policy. Being the only television networks in Malaysia, RTM and TV3 have been targets of public criticisms over choice of programs. An ongoing controversy is the issue of violent programs, which the two television stations are accused of broadcasting excessively. The criticism is not new, but the hue and cry has been highlighted by the Prime Minister himself, who voiced concern over excessive violence and sex on Malaysian TV in January 1991. Accusing fingers have been pointed at the television networks for "promoting" violence and sex, instead of culturally refined, family, and development-oriented programs for the current and future well-being of society.

Although Bahasa Malaysia is the official language of the country, increasingly spoken by all ethnic groups, the majority of Malaysian Chinese and Indians still seem to prefer entertainment programs imported from Hong Kong and Taiwan, and from India respectively, because of the common languages used. Despite continuing efforts to encourage Malaysian-made Chinese and Tamil language productions, and to project Malaysian culture on television, the pull of such foreign programs remains strong, particularly because of their ready supply, relatively low cost, and easy access. To ignore the viewing needs of ethnic minorities could spell trouble for the government, as suggested by the growth of the VCR phenomenon in the 1980s and the preference for programs from television stations in neighboring countries, especially Singapore. To draw the predominantly Chinese VCR viewers back to television programming, RTM and TV3 allowed the importation of programs that portrayed foreign customs and cultures previously prohibited on national television.

In terms of television programming, the networks now seem willing to sacrifice certain national goals embodied in the National Cultural Policy and the National Language Policy. With regard to the National Language Policy, RTM has come to a broadly accepted compromise by designating TV1 as an essentially Bahasa Malaysia channel and TV2 as mainly for other language programming. Cultural policy is more difficult, however, reflecting the continuing ambiguity of and controversy over national culture in multi-cultural Malaysia. The TV stations have compromised some of these official goals to increase advertising revenue by appealing to the cultural preferences of minority groups using low-cost options (imported programs) and the lowest common cultural denominators of the mass audience, vulgar and morally undesirable though these might be.

Advertisers and Advertising Agencies

Advertisement is one of RTM's main financial sources apart from federal government funds and receiver license fees costing RM24 per year. In 1983, 54 percent (RM100 million) of the budget allocation came from the government, 34 percent (RM58 million) from advertisements and 15 percent (RM27 million) from receiver licenses. Although RTM has never depended entirely upon advertising revenues, it has needed an audience in order to ensure the effectiveness of its message dissemination and to justify·its existence. This dilemma is reflected in a statement by Jaafar Kamin (1985: 6), who contended that "for RTM to be effective, it must be viewed. What are viewed are only the popular programs. Popular programs are expensive. Money can only be generated from advertisements. The advertisers only sponsor popular programs."

For over twenty years, commercials broadcast over RTM were managed by the Commercial Division of the Ministry of Information, but in 1986, Netcom Sdn Bhd was commissioned to sell the hour-long privatized airtime between 6 p.m. and 7 p.m. daily on behalf of RTM. In 1988, the contract was awarded to GT Consultant Sdn Bhd, and since 1991, all advertising airtime for RTM has been handled by GT Consultant (Ramli, 1991).

Thus far, TV3's presence in broadcasting has not reduced the television industry's share of the cake. Instead, it has helped increase television's share of (mainly advertising) revenue at the expense of other media. In 1983, TV advertising expenditure was 18.8 percent (RM66.912 million) of the total advertising expenditure of RM355.218 million. With TV3's formation in 1984, total TV advertising expenditure increased to 28.3 percent (RM114.030 million) of RM403.663 million in 1985. In 1986, television's share of advertising was 37 percent, second only to the newspapers in terms of its share of media advertising expenditure. Despite budget cuts to media advertising generally in 1988, television secured about 45 percent of the total. By 1990, the medium had increased its slice of the cake to 48 percent.

In the first ten months of its existence from mid-1984, TV3 gained 53 percent of total television advertising revenue. As a result, RTM revised its programming schedules and reduced its advertising rates. Since the Chinese belt was introduced by TV3, however, its revenues for the 6 p.m. to 7 p.m. airtime slot has increased to about 60 percent of total advertising revenue. This induced some changes in RTM, which also introduced a Chinese belt on TV2 every day from Monday to Friday at 7 p.m. As a result, RTM's share rose to 55 percent of total TV advertising revenue in 1987. With its improved relationship with advertisers, and "more entertaining" programs transmitted over government-owned channels, RTM regained the lead in the advertisement stakes in 1987. In late May 1991, the Minister announced a long-overdue increase in RTM advertising rates.

An estimated 95 percent of Malaysian advertising revenue is channeled through a small number of transnational advertising agencies (TNAAs) or joint-venture firms in Malaysia with larger budgets to spend. With powerful intracompany global communication networks, they are able to produce, invest, and transfer data, funds, and other related information on a global scale. In fact, as Garnham (1985: 68) has observed, there is increasingly intense competition among advertisers and providers of information and entertainment services, as well as among those marketing a growing range of financial and retail services, for access to the domestic TV screen. In comparison, local advertising agencies, which are generally smaller in terms of budget and size, are easily dominated by the TNAAs because of the latter's superior technical, financial, and managerial resources, and because of the stiff advertising requirements of media owners (Anderson, 1984: 205).

Although the television networks deny accusations that they are bending rules to accommodate advertisers, it seems likely that they are influenced by the prospects of handsome advertising revenues. There have been cases where programs have been initially rejected by the Censorship Board, but appeals have been successfully made (by the TV networks) because of the potentially high incomes to be generated from advertisers. Programs earning good revenue for the networks have also been reluctantly withdrawn because of public criticisms.

Program Producers, Suppliers and Distributors

Most station owners, especially in developing countries, cannot produce all the programs they broadcast (Head, 1990; Goonasekera, 1985). Television networks the world over rarely rely completely on their own in-house productions, but use extra "feeds" from independent production houses. RTM cannot rely on Filem Negara, FINAS, or its own production team to fulfill all the network's needs, especially to provide all of TV1's programs in Bahasa Malaysia.

Although RTM network producers work in concert to produce programs over TV1 and TV2, programs are also supplied by licensed producers, suppliers, and distributors registered in Malaysia. Between 1984 and 1987, RTM imported between 30 and 45 percent of its programs from the West (largely from the USA), about 10 percent from Asia (particularly Hong Kong, Taiwan, and India), and about 5 percent from Egypt. In 1984, TV3 imported almost 80 percent of its programs from the West (also largely from the USA), and over 12 percent from other parts of Asia (mainly Hong Kong and Taiwan); by 1987, though, TV3 had reduced overall foreign imports to about 70 percent. RTM and TV3 also send representatives to the Cannes Festival in Monte Carlo, where they select programs believed to be suitable for Malaysian viewers.

Imported programs broadcast during television prime hours are often sponsored by transnational cigarette companies advertising brands such as Dunhill, Benson & Hedges, and Salem. Although RTM and TV3 have been criticized for this heavily foreign visual diet, both networks agree that these usually action-packed programs attract viewers and generate much revenue for the stations.

When the Ministry of Information privatized local program production and airtime on RTM, it also wanted, among other things, to help revive the dying Malaysian film industry. The new policy triggered the mushrooming of over 200 independent production houses vying for the limited opportunities to air their productions. Private companies approved by the Ministry of Information are also responsible for the purchase and importation of programs. Since in-house production of Chinese (Mandarin and Cantonese), Indian (Tamil and Hindi) and English programs is almost non-existent, programs for the Chinese belt have to be imported from Hong Kong and Taiwan, while those for the Indian belt are imported from India. The introduction of the belts was an attempt to meet the entertainment needs of minority groups, and to win back an audience from among those who had turned to video cassettes for their entertainment.

Jaafar Kamin expressed hopes that contributions from local production companies would reduce the importation of foreign programs, increase Malaysian-made programs, develop the Malaysian video and film industries, and tap the nation's rich cultures. Meanwhile, RTM is supposed to concentrate on development programs that are not financially lucrative, but considered necessary for nation-building. However, in its effort to win audiences, RTM has been criticized for broadcasting violent programs, sacrificing its own principles and not reflecting the "credibility, intelligence, and dignity expected of a government network" (Mohd. Nor Salleh, 1987).

Viewers and Public Interest Groups

According to the Research Division, Ministry of Information (Kementerian Penerangan Malaysia, 1984), 49 percent (9,908,000) of the total number of adults (aged 15 and above) surveyed in Peninsular Malaysia in mid-1984 were television viewers. Of these, 52 percent were women while 51 percent were of the 15–29 age group, and 59 percent were rural. The data are based on Survey Research Malaysia's (SRM) Media Index Reports which are commonly used by the networks to make programming decisions and to attract advertisers. Programs are also scheduled according to the perceived needs of target audiences, generally based on the following time allocations:

Mondays, Tuesdays and Wednesdays

5.00 p.m.–6.30 p.m.	...	children
6.30 p.m.– 8.00 p.m.	...	youth/general
8.00 p.m.–10.00 p.m.	...	general
10.00 p.m. and after	...	adults

Other Days

8.00 a.m.–10.00 a.m.	...	women/general
10.00 a.m.–3.00 p.m.	...	children/general
3.00 p.m.–5.30 p.m.	...	youth/general

5.30 p.m.–6.30 p.m.	...	children
6.30 p.m.–8.00 p.m.	...	children/general
8.00 p.m.–10.00 p.m.	...	general
10.00 p.m. and after	...	adults

Television networks are expected to be morally obliged to take into account the value systems and way of life of the major ethnic groups in Malaysia, to balance the viewing needs and wants of the main age groups (children, youth, adults), gender, and geographical location (rural/urban). TV networks that are not sensitive to these diverse needs and preferences, are more likely to encounter criticisms from the public. As one newspaper columnist commented:

"(There are) the moghuls who frown on the immodest dressers and too explicit scenes; the Tamil lobby who want proportional representation on the airwaves; the Chinese sector who ask why Chinese characters are conspicuously absent in Chinese-language advertisements and news programs; ruffled Catholic feathers over the Thorn Birds controversy...." (*The Star*, 22 February 1985).

When TV3 was launched on 1 June 1984, there were criticisms from the Muslim audience because it was during Ramadan, the Muslim fasting month, when abstinence from worldly pleasures is encouraged. Some claimed that TV3 was openly challenging the government's policy of assimilation of Islamic values.

Apart from the general public, the Federation of Consumers Association in Malaysia (FOMCA), Consumers Association of Penang (CAP), and Angkatan Belia Islam Malaysia (ABIM) (Malaysian Muslim Youth Organization) are among the more active public-interest groups expressing concern regarding television programming, and thus influencing network decisions. CAP has voiced dismay over RTM's reaction to the presence of TV3. CAP's criticisms include the following (*Utusan Konsumer*, 1987: 18, 22):

i)   RTM is subjecting itself to the dictates of Western television markets even more than before. Its emphasis on imported programs has upset a hard-won ratio of 60 percent local programs to 40 percent imported programs. This ratio has now been reversed.

ii) RTM has demonstrated a marked relaxation of moral standards in controlling elements of sex, violence and other undesirable mind contaminators in imported programs in order to spice up its entertainment. While in the past, such excessive sexual and violent elements had come from Hollywood TV packages, now these elements come from Chinese programs produced in Hong Kong and Taiwan, and, to a lesser extent, from Indonesian and Indian films.

If before this, RTM had rejected gang warfare and associated violence in Chinese kung-fu and the customs and culture of pre-colonial China, all these are now allowed in order to capture the Chinese audience. Kissing and explicit bedroom scenes frequently escaped the censor's scissors. It was so bad that even the General Manager of the rival TV3 described it as "shocking."

RTM and TV3 are competing for the best Chinese programs and the latest Hollywood soap operas. As such, local artistes now dress, sing, sway and rock to the Hollywood model, and drama writers incorporate a certain amount of violence and sex in order to catch the attention of audience "trained in the Hollywood model."

CAP has also voiced concern over the effects of TV violence on the "young and impressionable minds dazed in the glamour of urbanization and consumerism." Although these criticisms were raised in 1987, the issues remain just as relevant today.

Regulators and Policy-makers

There are various ministries and agencies that regulate and control the media environment. While policies relating to broadcasting are formulated at Cabinet level, the electronic and print media are also subject to other rules and regulations, both implicit and explicit (see Figure 11.2).

The Ministry of Information

The Ministry functions as the main government agency that monitors and controls advertising in Malaysia to ensure that advertisers project the national culture (as officially defined), reflect the multi-ethnic composition of the country and advocate the spirit of the official National Ideology, or Rukunegara. In addition, RTM and TV3 also have to abide by the Ministry's advertising code.

With the enactment of the Broadcasting Act 1988, the Minister of Information is now empowered to issue, revoke or impose conditions for licenses to operate radio and television broadcasting stations, a task previously undertaken by the Jabatan Telekom Malaysia. The Broadcasting Act also secures a more distinct and effective role for the Information Ministry in matters pertaining to broadcasting. However, in order to give greater clout to the Information Minister to control the contents of programs aired on TV and radio, amendments will have to be made to the Telecommunications Act (see *New Straits Times*, 11 February 1991).

The National Film Development Corporation (FINAS)

FINAS, which is under the Ministry of Information, awards licenses to private film distributors, production companies and exhibitors. Under FINAS's 1983 (Licensing) Regulations (p. 2540), separate annual licenses have to be obtained for production, distribution and exhibition of films. A license holder has to be duly registered under the Companies Act, 1965. Under the FINAS's (Film Charges) Regulations, 1988, licensed distributors are required to submit a declaration of film importation and to pay appropriate film charges (p. 910).

FIGURE 11.2 Regulatory Environment for Broadcasting in Malaysia

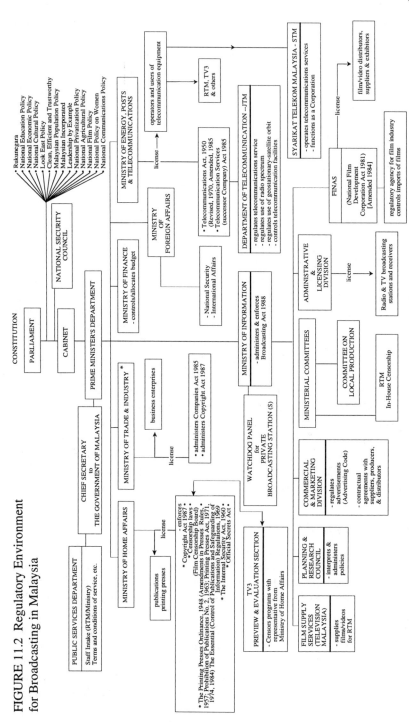

FINAS is also responsible, among other things, "to regulate and coordinate the activities of persons and bodies relating to matters pertaining to the film industry" [Act 244, Section 6 (1)(c)]; "to regulate and control the production, distribution and exhibition of films in Malaysia, and to provide for the issue of licenses" [Section 6 (1)(e)]. Any license holder who fails to fulfill the conditions stipulated stands to lose the permit.

The importation of films or videotapes by TV3 and other private companies has to be declared, and film charges paid to the National Film Development Corporation (FINAS) which regulates and controls such activities. Only RTM is exempt from paying import duties.

Ministry of Home Affairs and Ministry of Foreign Affairs

Both ministries and the National Security Council are responsible for policy matters regarding national security and international relations.

The Ministry of Home Affairs enforces laws, such as the Copyright Act and the Film Censorship Act, to ensure that foreign and domestic aspects of broadcasting by any operators are not prejudicial to the national interest or security, and do not infringe on the rights of others. The government exerts its authority ostensibly to safeguard the country's multi-ethnic population, religious sensitivities, and political stability. The Ministry, through the Film Censorship Board, is also responsible for television content, and has the power to permit, censor, or discontinue transmission of programs on privately-owned television networks.

A representative of the Ministry of Home Affairs meets on a daily basis with members of TV3's Preview and Evaluation Section prior to program transmission to assess and censor about eight hours of daily program contents according to certain guidelines. RTM's programs used to be subject to in-house censorship, but are now back under the scrutiny of the Film Censorship Board. However, the guidelines are subject to various interpretations, resulting in inconsistencies in the interpretation of these guidelines.

Ministry of Energy, Posts and Telecommunications

This Ministry is responsible for the hardware aspects of broadcasting. Even the extension of viewing hours must have the Minister's permission. Until 1988, the license to operate a radio or television station—private or government-owned—was issued by the Ministry based on the Telecommunications Act, 1950 (Revised 1970) (Amended 1972, 1977, 1984, 1985). Jabatan Telekom Malaysia (JTM)—in the Ministry of Energy, Posts and Telecommunications—allocates the broadcast spectrum, considered a scarce natural resource.

Allocations of radio frequencies to all privately-owned and government-owned radio and television stations, including those run by the Defense Ministry, have been made by JTM, under the direct supervision of the Ministry of Energy,

Posts and Telecommunication. Network planning to allocate scarce frequencies is worked out by JTM, which has to take into account the frequency allocations of neighboring countries. For instance, when TV3 expanded its services from the Klang Valley to the state of Johor, JTM had to assure the neighboring Republic of Singapore that the new frequency would not interfere with Singapore's. Similarly, JTM has to consider Thailand to the north of Peninsular Malaysia. According to Haji Ali Yusof, then (1987) Director of JTM, Malaysia meets on a monthly basis with the Frequency Allocation Committee (FACSMAB) comprising Singapore, Brunei, Malaysia and the Malaysian Armed Forces. Monitoring stations—such as those in Klang, Kota Kinabalu, and Kuching—also detect interferences and/or transmissions by illegal broadcasting stations.

Malaysia has a total of 60 television channels including 12 Very High Frequency (VHF) channels. Since RTM has used many of the VHF channels, which range from 30 MHz to 300 MHz, TV3 has to accept the allocation of UHF channels in certain transmission areas due to the scarcity of VHF TV channels. This has also meant that TV3 has to purchase more expensive equipment and to pay higher operational costs for Ultra High Frequency (UHF) channels. Reception of VHF/UHF signals poses no problems since viewer television sets are VHF/UHF compatible.[1]

Syarikat Telekom Malaysia

Syarikat Telekom Malaysia, now referred to as Telekom Malaysia (TM), is the privatized arm of the Jabatan Telekom Malaysia, which is responsible for the technical maintenance and manning of transmitters, earth stations, and microwave stations throughout the country. In return, RTM and TV3 pay a stipulated leasing fee to TM for such services rendered. Except for TV3 studios, the purchase of all other broadcasting equipment, including the purchase, instalment and operation of transmitters, has been handled by Telekom Malaysia. Although TV3 purchased all its transmitting equipment, these had to be handed over to TM "by virtue of Syarikat Telekom Malaysia's monopoly to operate the microwave stations" (Daud Isahak, 1987). However, since the purchasing and building costs had been borne by TV3, according to Jaafar Daud, TV3's Chief Engineer, in 1987, rentals were waived "for a number of years" after which TV3 would have to pay rental on transmission facilities.

With TM's establishment in 1987, policies regarding the use of transmitters on TM sites (previously JTM sites) have been adjusted. Where TV3 and RTM use the same video path, circuits have been upgraded by TM to allow three-operating circuits (for TV1, TV2, and TV3) plus a standby circuit. According to Jaafar Daud, should any of the operating circuits fail, TV3 would automatically switch to the standby circuit. However, should both RTM and TV3's operating circuits fail, priority would be given to RTM to use the standby circuit. RTM and TV3 also share the same aerial and/or mast where all three networks use the same band. TV3 has also been required to have its transmitting towers and buildings sited with RTM's.

The concept of sharing has not been as time saving and cost effective as it appears to be. In places where the size of an existing building is small, it has been impossible for TV3 to share the site. RTM's towers have also been described as being of old designs without planning for future expansion or additional facilities. Daud Isahak explained that some old RTM towers had to be demolished or modified. In certain circumstances, TV3 has been given new locations to build bigger and more massive structures to cater for its needs, as well as those of RTM and TM, but all costs of the required renovations, expansions, and modifications have been borne by TV3. Since the license to operate the private network is the government's prerogative, TV3 remains susceptible to government influence.

Conclusion

Television broadcasting is a very fast-changing and very expensive industry in terms of operations and programming. Broadcasting considerations are linked to audience demands, program ratings, consumer interests, advertising interests, national interests, corporate image as well as network financial investments.

The complex and financially burdensome nature of the Department of Broadcasting justifies the case for RTM being run as a corporation. As a government network, RTM has previously not been able to react quickly to changes in broadcasting technology because of financial and administrative constraints. Broadcasting content has also triggered debates in Parliament. As such, the existing environment in RTM may not be conducive for creative producers. RTM staff hence tend to be government officials first and broadcasters second. RTM has been constrained by its administrative structure and by too many non-professionals making policy decisions. Frequent changes in leadership as well as the constant involvement of politicians, civil service officers, and other non-professionals in matters pertaining to broadcasting and production have been among the factors said to have impeded RTM's development.

The announcement, in February 1989, by Information Minister, Dato' Mohamed Rahmat, that the government intended to corporatize the Department of Broadcasting reflected the Ministry's growing empathy with RTM, which has long needed greater autonomy to be more receptive to rapid advancements in broadcasting technology. A corporatized RTM could remain answerable to Parliament, but its new status would enable it to operate more effectively without having to depend on financial allocations from the Government, or being slowed down by government bureaucracies. However, developments in early 1993 suggest that RTM may remain a government institution for the foreseeable future despite longstanding speculation about the imminence of a broadcasting corporation.

Since television is here to stay, it is up to the authorities to decide whether to allow television networks to have the final say on what viewers should watch, or to allow such decisions to be dictated by advertisers, or to be sensitive to the needs and interests of the people, especially the younger generation.

Note

1. Most radio and television applications are in the megahertz (MHz) range. A television station uses a great deal more bandwidth than a radio station. The bandwidth for a television station is 6000 KHz or 6 MHz, compared with 10 KHz for an AM radio station, and 200 KHz for a FM radio station. Ultra High Frequency (UHF), ranging from 300 MHz to 3000 MHz, is the weaker channel, because it is easily absorbed by the atmosphere and easily cut off by buildings and hills. Even by building higher towers, the low signal strength of the UHF transmission is not compensated for. The only available option for stronger transmission is to increase power, which requires higher expenses.

Bibliography

Abdul Hamid Sawal (1990) "The Malaysian Government's Privatization Programme," paper presented to the Institute of Directors, Malaysia, October 18.

Abdul Khalid Abdul Aziz (1992) "An Evaluation of Corporatisation and Privatization Strategy: Success Stories and Lessons to be Learnt," paper presented at the National Conference on Corporatisation and Privatization organized by EPU-INTAN-MSC, Kuala Lumpur, 29–30 June.

Abdul Khalid bin Ibrahim (1987) "Privatization and the New Economic Policy," paper presented at the National Conference on "Privatization: Towards the Formulation of a Masterplan", ISIS, Malaysia.

Abdullah Abdul Rahman (1992) "Malaysia Incorporated Revisited: Towards Greater Public-Private Sector Cooperation to Achieve Vision 2020," working paper presented at the National Conference on "Corporation and Privatisation" organized by EPU-INTAN-MSC, Kuala Lumpur, 29–30 June.

Adam, Christopher, William Cavendish and Percy S. Mistry (1991) *Adjusting Privatisation: Case Studies from Developing Countries*, James Currey, London.

——— (1985) *Privatization: Policies, Methods and Procedures*, Asian Development Bank, Manila.

——— (1989a) *Asian Development Outlook 1990*, Asian Development Bank, Manila.

——— (1989b) *Key Indicators of Developing Member Countries of ADB*, Vol. XX, Asian Development Bank, Manila.

Ahmad bin Mohd Idrus (1992) "Wage Fixation and Terms and Conditions of Service: the Effect of Privatisation," Third Lawasia Labour Law conference, Kuala Lumpur, 20–22 August.

Ali Abul Hassan Sulaiman (1992) "Overview of the Privatization Master Plan: Strategic Issues, Opportunities and Future Thrusts," paper presented at the National Conference on "Corporatisation and Privatization" organized by EPU-INTAN-MSC, Kuala Lumpur, 29–30 June.

Amsden, Alice (1989) *Asia's Next Giant: South Korea and Late Industrialization*, Oxford University Press, New York.

Anderson, M.H. (1984) *Madison Avenue in Asia: Politics and Transnational Advertising*, Associated University Press, New Jersey.

Anwar Ibrahim (1992) *The 1993 Budget Speech*, Government Printer, Kuala Lumpur, October.

Arcirio, R. (1988) "The Brazilian Public Enterprise Performance Evaluation System," *Public Enterprise*, vol. 8, no. 1.

Ariff, M. (1987) "Malaysia In a Recessionary Setting: An Overview," *Southeast Asian Affairs*, ISEAS, Singapore, pp. 197–216.

——— and H. Hill (1985) *Export-Oriented Industrialisation: The ASEAN Experience*, Allen and Unwin, Sydney.

——— and M. Semudram (1987) *Trade And Financing Strategies: A Case Study of Malaysia*, Working Paper No. 21, Overseas Development Institute, London.

Arthur D. Little Company (1983) *The Advantages and Feasibility of Privatising Jabatan Telekom Malaysia*, Report to Sapura Holdings Sdn. Bhd., November.

Asian Business, September 1991.

Asnan Pi'i (1987) "Privatisation—Its Impact on Labour Relations—The Malaysian Experience," paper on behalf of Ministry of Labour, in ILO, *Privatisation: Its Impact on Labour Relations in ASEAN*, ILO/UNDP/ASEAN Programme for Industrial Relations for Development, Geneva.

Augenblick, Mark and B. Scott Custer Jr. (1990) "The Build, Operate and Transfer (BOT) Approach to Infrastructure Projects in Developing Countries," WPS 498, World Bank, Washington D.C.

Bank Negara Malaysia (1989) *Annual Report, 1988*, BNM, Kuala Lumpur.

_____ (1990) *Annual Report, 1989*, BNM, Kuala Lumpur.

Baumol, W. (ed.) (1980) *Public and Private Enterprises in a Mixed Economy*, Macmillan, London.

_____ and Kyu Sik Lee (1991) "Contestable Markets, Trade and Development," *Research Observer*, The World Bank, Volume 6, No. 1.

Beesley, M. and S. Littlechild (1983) "Privatisation: Principles, Problems and Priorities," *Lloyd Bank Review*, 149: 1–20.

Bennett, Michael (1991) "Trade or Treasury: Who Benefits from Port Privatization?", The First Asian Port Management Conference, Kuala Lumpur, Malaysia.

Berg, Elliot and associates (1989) "Private Provision of Public Services, A Literature Review," a review prepared for the Public Sector Management and Private Sector Development Division, Country Economics Department of the World Bank, Washongton D.C.

Bienen, Henry and John Waterbury (1989) "The Political Economy of Privatization in Developing Countries," *World Development*, 17, 5: 617–32.

Bouin, Oliver (1992) *Privatisation in Developing Countries: Reflections on a Panacea*, Policy brief no. 3, OECD Development Centre, Paris.

Boukaraoun, Hacene (1991) "The Privatization Process in Algeria," *The Developing Economies*, 29, 2: 89–123.

Brand, S.S. (1988) "Privatization: An Economist's View," *The South African Journal of Economics*, 56, 4: 235–249.

Brittan, Samuel (1984) "The Politics and Economics of Privatisation," *Political Quarterly*, 55: 109–28.

Broadcasting Act 1988 (Act 338), Jabatan Percetakan Negara, Kuala Lumpur.

Bruce, Alistair (1986) "State-to-Private Sector Divestment: The Case of Sealink" in John Coyne and Mike Wright (eds) *Divestment and Strategic Change*, Philip Allan, Oxford and Barnes & Noble Books, New Jersey.

Buchanan, I. (1992) "Managing the Transition from Public to private Sector Organisation: Leading the Change," paper presented at the National Conference on Corporatisation and Privatization organized by EPU-INTAN-MSC, Kuala Lumpur, 29–30 June.

Burnham, John (1989) "Financial Services and Privatisation: Opportunities for Malaysia and the United Kingdom," HMY Brittania, Port Kelang, 5 October.

Business Times, "Private Phones," 10 June 1983.

_____, "STM Sells Stake in 900 MHz Network to Alpine," 4 January 1990: 1, 16.

_____, "Good News for Mobile Phone Users," 5 January 1990: 6.

_____, "3 firms to hold back CT2 phones," 18 January 1990.

_____, "Telecoms Submits Draft on Radio-paging Policy," 26 January 1990: 2.

_____, "Tapping Skills via MBO Mode of Privatization," 30 June 1992.

_____, "MAS Ready for Challenge: Better Current Year Performance Seen," 7 August 1992.

_____, "Tenaga Seen Flourishing in Rapidly Growing Area," 17 August 1992.

Butler, Stuart M. (1986) "Privatizing Government Services," *Economic Impact*, 55, 4: 21–25.

Central Electricity Board, *Annual Report*, various years.

Chang, Ha-Joon and Ajit Singh (1991) "Public Enterprises in Developing Countries and Economic Efficiency: a Critical Examination of Analytical, Empirical and Policy Issues" (mimeo).

Chee, Stephen (1990) "The Political Economy of Privatisation with Reference to Malaysia" in *Issues and Challenges for National Development*, Faculty of Economics and Administration, University of Malaya, Kuala Lumpur.

Cheong, Sally (1991) *Bumiputera Controlled Companies in the KLSE*, Modern Law Publishers & Distributors, Petaling Jaya.

Chua Lee Boon (1989) "Problems and Issues on Malaysian Expressways and Toll Highways," paper presented at the symposium on "Sistem Kawalan & Pengurusan Lalulintas & Lebuhraya di Malaysia," Kuala Lumpur, 11–13 December.

Clad, J. (1985) "Ringing in the Changes," *Far Eastern Economic Review*, 25 July: 47.

Commander, S. & T. Killick (1988) "Privatisation in Developing Countries: A Survey of the Issues" in P. Cook & C. Kirkpatrick (eds), *Privatisation in Less Developed Countries*, Harvester Wheatsheaf, New York.

Cook, P. & C. Kirkpatrick (1988) "Privatisation in Less Developed Countries: An Overview" in P. Cook & C. Kirkpatrick (eds), *Privatisation in Less Developed Countries*, Harvester Wheatsheaf, New York.

_____ and Martin Minogue (1990) "Waiting for Privatization in Developing Countries: Towards the Integration of Economic and Non-Economic Explanations," *Public Administration and Development*, 10: 389–403.

Copyright Act 1987 (Act 332), Jabatan Percetakan Negara, Kuala Lumpur.

Coyne, John (1986) "Divestment by Management Buy-Out: Variant and Variety" in John Coyne and Mike Wright (eds) *Divestment and Strategic Change*, Philip Allan, Oxford and Barnes & Noble Books, New Jersey.

_____ and Mike Wright (1985) *Management Buy-Outs*, Croom Helm, London.

_____ and Mike Wright (eds) (1986) *Divestment and Strategic Change*, Philip Allan, Oxford and Barnes & Noble Books, New Jersey.

Craig, J. (1988), "Privatization in Malaysia: Past Trends and Future Prospects," in P. Cook and C. Kirkpatrick (eds), *Privatization in Less Developed Countries*, Harvester Press, Brighton: 248-58.

Crawford, M.H. (1984) *Information Technology and Industrialization Policy in the Third World*, Center for Information Policy Research, Harvard University, Cambridge, Mass.

Daim Zainuddin (1990) "Penswastaan dan Pensyarikatan Malaysia: Pegawai Kerajaan Perlu Menjayakan," *Buletin Intan*, 14, 2: 4–6.

Daud Isahak (1989) "Meeting the Challenges of Privatization in Malaysia" in Bjorn Wellenius, Peter Stern, Timothy Nulty and Richard Stern (eds), *Restructuring and Managing the Telecommunications Sector*, The World Bank, Washington D.C.: 118–121.

_____ (1987) *Majalah Kawat*, Januari: 8–9.

Devi, R. (1989a) "STM Revenue Up," *Business Times*, 6 April: 16.

_____ (1989b) "STM Plans Exercise to Prepare for Flotation," *Business Times*, 13 April.

_____ (1989c) "Sapura R&D Efforts Pay Off," *Business Times*, 26 September.

_____ (1989d) "STM Yet to Receive Its Privatization Guidelines," *Business Times*, 29 November.

_____ (1989e) "World Leaders in Telecoms Make Beeline for Malaysia," *Business Times*, 27 November: 1–2.

_____, Rodiah I. & Vong, Y. (1989) "Industry Generally Excited With Move," *Business Times*, 12 December: 1, 17.

Economic Intelligence Unit (1991) "Country Report Analysis of Economic and Political Trends Every Quarter," No. 1.

Economic Planning Unit (1988) "National Ports Plan," PRC Engineering, Inc. in association with Sepakat Setia Perunding Sdn. Bhd. and Aseambankers Malaysia Berhad, Vol. 1: Overview.

Economist (1985) "Privatization: Everybody's Doing It, Differently," 21 December: 71–86.

Eddy Lee (1990) "The Path to Private Enterprise," *Malaysian Business*, May.

Engku Mohd. Anuar (1977) "Public Corporation in Malaysia: General Problems and Issues," Seminar for the Management Science Students of INTAN, Penang, April.

Fadil Azim Abbas (1985) "The Effectiveness of Public and Private Organisations: The Case of Malaysia's Stock Exchange Companies," Ph.D. thesis, American University, Washington D.C.

_____ (1992) "Privatization in Malaysia: A Case of Privatization in the Context of Achieving Growth and Equity" in World Bank conference on the "Welfare Consequences of Selling Public Enterprise: Case Studies from Chile, Malaysia, Mexico and the U.K.," Washington D.C, 11–12 June.

Faridatul Akmal Omar, Jamatul Shahidah Shaari, Roslizan Abd Rahman, Faridah Salehan (1991) "The Privatization of Tenaga Nasional Berhad: Process and Management Issues," (mimeo).

Fielding, G. L. (1992) "Wage Fixation and Conditions of Employment: the Effect of Privatisation," Third Lawasia Labour Law conference, Kuala Lumpur, 20–22 August.

Fisher, B. (1988) "Public Enterprises in Developing Countries: Market Structure, Competition,

Efficiency and the Scope for Privatization," *Malaysian Journal of Economic Studies*, 25, 2 December: 45–61.

Fong Chan Onn (1986) *Technological Leap: Malaysian Industry in Transition*, Oxford University Press, Singapore.

_____ (1989) *The Malaysian Economic Challenge in the 1990s: Transformation for Growth*, Longmans, Singapore.

_____ (1989) *The Malaysian Economic Challenges in 1990s*, Oxford University Press, Kuala Lumpur.

_____ (1991) "Opportunities for Privatisation in the 1990s," May (mimeo).

_____ and Lim Kok Cheong (1984) "Investment Incentives And Trends Of Manufacturing Investments In Malaysia," *The Developing Economies*, 22, 4: 396–418.

Galal, Abdul (1986) "A Theory of Capital Utilization in Public Enterprises with an Application to Egypt," Ph.D thesis, Boston University, Boston.

Gale, Bruce (1981) *Politics and Public Enterprise in Malaysia*, Eastern Universities Press, Petaling Jaya.

Garnham, N. (1985) "Communication Technology and Policy" in M. Gurevitch & M.R. Levy (eds), *Mass Communication Review Yearbook*, 5: 65–74.

Goh, L. (1987) "Fancy Hello," *The Star*, 29 March.

Gomez, E.T. (1990) *Politics in Business: UMNO's Corporate Investments*, Forum, Kuala Lumpur.

_____ (1991a) *Money Politics in the Barisan Nasional*, Forum, Kuala Lumpur.

_____ (1991b) "Malaysia's Phantom Privatization," *Asian Wall Street Journal*, 8 May.

_____ (1992) "Corporate Involvement of Political Parties in Malaysia," Ph.D. thesis, Institute for Advanced Studies, University of Malaya, Kuala Lumpur.

_____ (1993) "UMNO Factionalism and Control of Economic Sectors—Management Buy-out of New Straits Times Press and TV3," *Aliran Monthly*, 13, 2: 2–6.

Goodman, J.B. and G.W. Loveman (1991) "Does Privatization Serve the Public Interest?", *Harvard Business Review*, November.

Goonasekera, A. (1985) "Television and Culture," *The Third Channel*, 1: 103–124.

Gouri, Geeta (ed.) (1991) *Privatization and Public Enterprise—the Asian-Pacific Experience*, Institute of Public Enterprise, Hyderabad.

Haile-Mariam, Yacob and Berhana Mengistu (1988) "Public Enterprises and the Privatisation Thesis in the Third World," *Thirld World Quarterly*, 10, 4: 1565–87.

Halim A.W., A. (1985) "Komtel Takes Over Telecoms Paging Service," *Business Times*, 10 October.

Head, David (1990) "The Relevance of Privatization to Developing Economies," *Public Administration and Development*, 10: 3–18.

Head, S.W. (1985) *World Broadcasting Systems: A Comparative Analysis*, Wadsworth Publishing, Belmont, California.

Heller, Peter and Christian Schiller (1989) "The Fiscal Impact of Privatization, with some examples from Arab countries," *World Development*, 17, 5: 757–67.

Helmi Mohd Noor (1992) "Regulating Corporatised and Privatised Entities: Issues for Regulatory and Future Management Challenges," paper presented at the National Conference on Corporatisation and Privatization organised by EPU-INTAN-MSC, Kuala Lumpur, 29–30 June.

Henig, Jeffrey R. (1989) "Privatization in the United States: Theory and Practice," *Political Science Quarterly*, 104, 4: 649–670.

Hirschman, A. (1970) *Exit, Voice and Loyalty—Responses to Decline in Firms, Organisations, and States*, Harvard University Press, Cambridge, Massachusetts.

Ismail Muhd Salleh (1987) "Privatization: a New Direction in Development Strategy," paper presented at the ITM seminar on "Privatization in Malaysia: Perspective and Prospects," Kuala Lumpur, 26–27 January.

_____ (1990) "Port Klang: A Privatization Case Study," Institute of Strategic and International Studies, Kuala Lumpur.

_____ (1991) "Privatisation: The Malaysian Experience" in H. Yokoyama and Mokhtar Tamin (eds) *Malaysian Economy in Transition*, Institute of Developing Economies, Tokyo.

Ismail Muhd. Salleh and Lee Tin Hui (1990) "The Emerging Role of the Private Sector in Malaysia:

The Privatisation Process So Far," paper presented at the Pacific Outlook Conference, 11–12 October.

_____ and Abd. Wahid Ahmad Shuhaime (1991) "Implikasi Ekonomi Perusahaan Awam di Malaysia," *Negarawan*, 20: 20–23.

_____ and Abdul Rauf Salim (1987) "Privatization: Can It Contribute to a Sustainable Economic Recovery?", paper presented at the National Outlook Conference organized by MIER, Kuala Lumpur, 25–26 November.

_____ and H. Osman Rani (1991) *The Growth of the Public Sector in Malaysia*, Institute of Strategic and International Studies, Kuala Lumpur.

Jaafar Kamin (1985) "Tugas, Keberkesanan Serta Perspektif RTM Sebagai Sarana Penghubung Nilai Sosial dan Pembekal Maklumat Umum" (RTM's Functions, Effectiveness and Perspective as a Linkage for Social Values and Information Provider), paper presented at the Seminar on "Communication and Information Issues," UKM Bangi, 23 March.

Jayasankaran, S. (1987) "Conditions that Make Privatization Work," *New Straits Times*, 21 August: 8.

Johnstone, B. (1990a) "Cutting the Cord," *Far Eastern Economic Review*, 2 August: 38–41.

_____ (1990b) "Street-wise Callers," *Far Eastern Economic Review*, 2 August: 40.

Jomo K.S. (ed.) (1985) *The Sun Also Sets: Lessons in 'Looking East'*, 2nd. ed., INSAN, Kuala Lumpur.

_____ (1986) *A Question of Class: Capital, The State and Uneven Development in Malaya*, Oxford University Press, Singapore.

_____ (1987) "Privatisation: Lessons from the Developed and Developing Nations," paper presented to the ITM seminar on "Privatisation in Malaysia: Perspective and Prospects," Kuala Lumpur, 26–27 January.

_____ (1989) *Beyond 1990: Considerations For A New National Development Strategy*, Institute for Advanced Studies, University of Malaya, Kuala Lumpur.

_____ (1990) *Growth and Structural Change in the Malaysian Economy*, Macmillan, London.

_____ *et al.* (1989) *Mahathir's Economic Policies*, 2nd. ed., INSAN, Kuala Lumpur.

Jones, Leroy and Fadil Azim Abbas (1992a) "Kelang Container Terminal" in World Bank conference on the "Welfare Consequences of Selling Public Enterprise: Case Studies from Chile, Malaysia, Mexico and the U.K.," Washington D.C., 11–12 June.

_____ (1992b) "Sports Toto Malaysia Berhad" in World Bank conference on the Welfare Consequences of Selling Public Enterprise: Case Studies from Chile, Malaysia, Mexico and the U.K., Washington D.C., 11–12 June.

_____ (1992c) "Case Studies for Malaysia" in World Bank Conference on the Welfare Consequences of Selling Public Enterprises: Case Studies from Chile, Malaysia, Mexico and the U.K., Washington D.C., 11–12 June.

_____ with Yong-Min Chen (1992) "Malaysian Airline Systems Berhad" in World Bank conference on the Welfare Consequences of Selling Public Enterprise: Case Studies from Chile, Malaysia, Mexico and the U.K., Washington D.C, 11–12 June.

Jones, Susan K. (1991) "The Road to Privatization," *Finance & Development*, March: 39–41.

Kamal Salih and Zainal Aznam Yusoff (1989) "Overview of the NEP and Framework for a Post-1990 National Economic Policy: Options," *Malaysian Management Review*, 24, 2: 13–61.

Kamarazaman Yacob (1988) *Skandal Mahathir di Lebuhraya*, Media Jaya, Kuala Lumpur.

Kartini Abdul Kadir (1991) "New Chapter in History of Postal Services," *Business Times*, 31 December.

Kay, J.A. and D.J. Thompson (1986) "Privatization: A Policy in Search of a Rationale," *The Economic Journal*, 96 (381).

Kementerian Penerangan Malaysia (1984) "Purata Penonton Harian TV bagi Bulan Julai/Ogos 1984 Mengikut Negeri Selangor," (Average Daily TV Viewers in July/August 1984 for State of Selangor), published data.

Kementerian Penerangan Malaysia (1985) "Laporan Media Massa Semenanjung Malaysia" (Media Report for Peninsular Malaysia), published data, June.

Kennedy, L.B. (1990) "Privatization and Its Policy Antecedents in Malaysian Telecommunications," Ph.D. dissertation, Ohio University, Dissertation Abstracts International.

_____ (1991a) "Privatization as a Method of Wealth Redistribution: the Case of Malaysian Telecoms," paper presented at the Seventh International Conference on Culture and Communication, Temple University, Philadelphia, 5 October.

_____ (1991b) "Liberalization, Privatization and the Politics of Patronage in Malaysian Telecommunications," paper presented at 41st Annual Conference of the International Communications Association, Chicago, Illinois, 24 May.

Kent, Calvin A. (1987) "Privatization of Public Functions: Promises and Problems," *Entrepreneurship and the Privatizing of Government*, Quorum Books, Washington D.C.

Kharmazan Ahmad Meah (1992) "The Concept of Privatisation and Corporatisation," Third Lawasia Labour Law Conference, Kuala Lumpur.

Killick, Tony and Simon Commander (1988) "State Divestiture as a Policy Instrument in Developing Countries," *World Development*, 16, 12: 1465–79.

Kolderie, Ted (1986) "The Two Different Concepts of Privatization," *Public Administration Review*, 46, 4: 285–291.

Kuppusamy Singaravelloo (1992) "The Impact of Privatisation on Employees: A Sample of Opinions and Perceptions of Tenaga Nasional Berhad (TNB) and Projek Lebuhraya Utara-Selatan (PLUS)," MPA dissertation, Faculty of Economics and Administration, University Malaya.

Lee, K.E. (1989) "LLN: Prime Target," *Investors Digest*, August.

_____ (1990a) "NEB's Billion Ringgit Plan," *Investors Digest*, May.

_____ (1990b) "How Will NEB Diversify," *Investors Digest*, July.

Leeds, Roger (1989) "Malaysia: Genesis of a Privatisation Transaction," *World Development*, 17, 5.

Levy, Hernan and Aurelio Menendez (1989) *Privatization in Transport: The Case of Port Kelang (Malaysia) Container Terminal*, EDI Working Papers, Economic Development Institute, World Bank, Washington D.C.

Lim, C. (1993) "Only Time Will Tell," *Malaysian Business*, 1–15 March, pp. 30-33.

Lim, D. (1983) (ed.) *Further Readings on Malaysian Economic Development*, Oxford University Press, Kuala Lumpur.

Lim Kit Siang (1986) *BMF: Scandal of Scandals*, Democratic Action Party, Kuala Lumpur.

_____ (1987) *The RM62 Billion North-South Highway Scandal*, Democratic Action Party, Kuala Lumpur.

Lobo, B. (1992) "Privatisation and its Impact on Trade Union Membership in Malaysia," Third Lawasia Labour Law Conference, Kuala Lumpur.

Loganathan, S. (1989a) "Big STM Profit Augurs Well for Flotation," *Business Times*, 10 July.

_____ (1989b) "All Systems Go for STM," *Investors Digest*, August.

_____ (1989c) "Shades of Privacy," *Investors Digest*, August.

M. Zainuddin Salleh (1990) "Privatization of Electricity Supply in Malaysia: Issues and Problems," in Jacques Pelkmans and Norbert Wagner (eds) *Privatization and Deregulation in ASEAN and the EC: Making Markets More Effective*, ASEAN Economic Research Unit, Institute of South East Asian Studies, Singapore.

Mahathir Mohamad (1970) *The Malay Dilemma*, Donald Moore, Singapore.

_____ (1976) *Menghadapi Cabaran*, Penerbit Utusan Melayu, Kuala Lumpur.

_____ (1984) "Malaysia Incorporated and Privatization: Its Rationale and Purpose," in Mohd. Nor Abdul Ghani *et al.* (eds), *Malaysia Incorporated & Privatization: Towards National Unity*, Pelanduk Publications, Petaling Jaya: 1–8.

_____ (1989) "New Government Policies," in Jomo K.S. (ed.), *Mahathir's Economic Policies*, INSAN, Kuala Lumpur.

_____ (1991) *The Way Forward*, ISIS, Kuala Lumpur.

Malaysia (1965) *Official Year Book 1965*, Government Printer, Kuala Lumpur.

_____ (1971) *Second Malaysia Plan, 1971–1975*, Government Printer, Kuala Lumpur.

_____ (1972) *Organisation of the Government of Malaysia*, Government Printer, Kuala Lumpur.

_____ (1976) *Third Malaysia Plan, 1976–1980*, Government Printer, Kuala Lumpur.

_____ (1985) *Guidelines on Privatization*, Economic Planning Unit, Kuala Lumpur.

_____ (1989) "Privatization Masterplan," prepared by Schroders in association with Arab-Malaysian Merchant Bank Berhad, Arthur D. Little, Inc. and Hanafiah, Raslan and Mohamad.

_____ (1991a) *Privatization Masterplan*, Economic Planning Unit, Kuala Lumpur.

_____ (1991b) *The Second Outline Perspective Plan, 1991–2000*, Economic Planning Unit, Kuala Lumpur.

_____ (1991c) *Sixth Malaysia Plan, 1991–1995*, Economic Planning Unit, Kuala Lumpur.

Malaysia, Ministry of Public Enterprises (1988) "Country Paper: Privatisation—Malaysia", Inter-Regional Workshop on Privatisation, Document No. 23, 1–58, 23–27 May.

Malaysia, National Electricity Board, *Annual Report*, various years.

Malaysian Business, "KTM Privatization: Which Track?", May 1989.

_____, "Leaders and Laggards," 1–15 August 1992: 20–23.

_____, "Projek Lebuhraya Utara-Selatan: More Costs, More Returns," 1–15 August 1992.

_____, "Keeping Faith: Interview with Tajudin Ramli," 16–30 November 1992: 51.

Malaysian Economic Association (1991) "Bintulu Port Privatization Study," Vol. 1.

Mallon, R. (1982) "Public Enterprise Versus Other Methods of State Intervention as Instruments of Redistribution Policy: the Malaysian Experience" in L. Jones (ed.), *Public Enterprise in Less-developed Countries*, Cambridge University Press, Cambridge.

May, N.S. (1988) "Syarikat Telekom Malaysia: Living Up to Promise of Privatization," *Malaysian Business*, November.

May, T.C. (1990) "Dialling for Success," *Malaysian Business*, June.

Mazida Kamaruddin (1992) "KCT to Float," *Investors Digest*, October.

McDaniel, D. (1986) "Privatization of Television in Malaysia," paper presented to a conference on "Culture and Communications," Philadelphia.

McMaster, Jim (1987) "Arguments For and Against Privatisation," Course on Urban Finance and Management in East Asia, Kuala Lumpur, 7 September–2 October.

Md. Zabid Abdul Rashid and Zainal Abidin Mohamed (1990) "Divestment Strategies and Processes in Malaysia: The Case of MAS, MISC and STM," Universiti Pertanian Malaysia, Department of Management and Marketing Staff Papers, No. 5, November.

MIDA-UNIDO (1985) *Medium and Long Term Industrial Master Plan—Malaysia 1986–1995, Executive Highlights*, Malaysian Industrial Development Authority, Kuala Lumpur.

_____ (1986) *The Industrial Master Plan, 1986–1995*, Malaysian Industrial Development Authority, Kuala Lumpur.

Milne, R.S. (1986) "Privatization in Malaysia," *Euro-Asia Business Review*, 5, 1 (January): 21–24.

_____ (1991) "The Politics of Privatization in the ASEAN States," *ASEAN Economic Bulletin*, 7, 3: 322–333.

_____ (1992) "Privatization in the ASEAN States: Who Gets What, Why, and With What Effect?", *Pacific Affairs*, 65, 1: 7–29, Spring.

Ministry of Finance, *Economic Report* (various issues), Government Printer, Kuala Lumpur.

MMR (1989) *Malaysian Management Review*, 24, 2, Special issue on the New Economic Policy.

Mohd. Munir Abdul Majid (1992) "Structuring a Privatization Deal-minimising Risks, Maximising Returns," paper presented at the National Conference on "Corporatisation and Privatization" organized by EPU-INTAN-MSC, Kuala Lumpur, 29–30 June.

Mohd. Nor Abdul Ghani, Bernard T. H. Wang, Ian K. M. Chia and Bruce Gale (eds) (1984) *Malaysia Incorporated and Privatisation: Towards National Unity*, Pelanduk Publications, Petaling Jaya.

Moore, Chris (1990) "Displacement, Partnership and Privatization: Local Government and Urban Economic Regeneration in the 1980s" in Desmond S. King & Jon Pierre (eds), *Challenges to Local Government,* Sage Publications, London.

Morgan, David R. and Robert E. England (1988) "The Two Faces of Privatzation," *Public Administration Review* (November/December): 979–987.

MTUC (undated) "MTUC's Comments on the Paper on Guidelines on Privatization," MTUC, Petaling Jaya (mimeo).

Muhd. Ismail Salleh (1989) "The Role of Public Sector," in *Issues and Challenges for National Development*, Faculty of Economics and Administration, University of Malaya, Kuala Lumpur.

Mustapha Johan Abdullah & K.A. Shamsulbahriah (eds) (1987) *Penswastaan: Kebajikan Pekerja atau Untung Kapitalis*, MBPBK, Kuala Lumpur.

Naidu, G. (1992) *Private Provision of Physical Infrastructure: The Malaysian Experience*, EDI Working Paper, Economic Development Institute, World Bank, Washington D.C.

Nair, G. and A. Fillippides (1988) "How Much Do State-owned Enterprises Contribute to Public Sector Deficits in Developing Countries—and Why?", *World Development Report*, World Bank, Washington D.C., WPS 45.

Nair, K.P. Gengadharan (1992) "Wage Fixation and Terms and Conditions of Service—the Effect of Privatisation," Third Lawasia Labour Law conference, Kuala Lumpur.

Nair, Govind and Mark Frazier (1987) "Debt-Equity Conversion and Privatization," *Economic Impact*, 60, 4: 12–17.

Nankani, H. (1988) *Techniques of Privatization of State-owned Enterprises, Volume II: Selected Country Case Studies*, World Bank Technical Paper no. 89, Washington D.C.: 62–92.

_____ (1990) "Lessons in Privatization," *Malaysian Business*, May.

Nasir Zihni Yusoff (1992) "Legal Aspects of Corporatisation and Privatization: Key Issues and Pitfalls to Avoid," paper presented at the National Conference on "Corporatisation and Privatization" organized by EPU-INTAN-MSC, Kuala Lumpur, 29–30 June.

Nellis, John and Sunita Kikeri (1989) "Public Enterprise Reform: Privatization and the World Bank," *World Development*, 17, 5: 659–72.

New Straits Times, "STM Streamlining its Operations, Says MD," 6 November 1987.

_____, "Hussein of Sime to Head Syarikat Telekom," 16 December 1987.

_____, "First-come First-served," 16 June 1988: 1.

_____, "Tenaga Employees to Get Ex-gratia Payment Too" and "Samy Vellu Announces 25 to 100 per cent Increase: Postal Rates to go up in Early April," 24 January 1992.

_____, "Tenaga Nasional Workers to Picket," 31 January 1992.

_____, "Tenaga Men Cane Chief's Effigy," 1 February 1992.

_____, "D-G: Make It More Viable for Investors," 30 June 1992.

_____, "Keeping Tabs to Ensure Efficient Privatization," 1 July 1992.

_____, "The Many Benefits of Privatization," 31 August 1992.

_____, "Hopes to Corporatise DCA on Nov. 1: Ling," 4 September 1992.

_____, "Prospectus Telekom Malaysia," 26 September 1992.

_____, "KPA: Privatization To Go Ahead as Scheduled," 13 November 1992.

_____, "Agencies Identified for Privatization," 17 December 1992.

_____, "Plan to Corporatise LPN," 22 December 1992.

_____, "High Time Tenaga Told the Whole Truth to Consumers," 13 February 1993.

Ng Chee Yuen and N. Wagner (1989) "Privatization and Deregulation in Asean: An Overview," *Asean Economic Bulletin*, 5, 3 March: 209–223.

_____ and Toh Kin Woon (1992) "Privatization in the Asian-Pacific Region," *Asian Pacific Economic Literature*, November 6 (2).

Paul, Samuel (1985) "Privatization and the Public Sector," *Finance and Development*, December.

Peacock, A. (1984) "Privatisation in Perspective," *The Three Bank Review*, 144, December.

Perbadanan Kemajuan Filem Nasional Malaysia Act 1981 (Act 244), Jabatan Percetakan Negara, Kuala Lumpur.

Philip, Koshy (1992) "On Privatization Track," *Investors Digest*, October.

Phoon, Z. (1992) "The Cash Cow Connection," *Malaysian Business*, 1–15 April: 38–40.

Popenoe, O. (1970) "Malay Enterprises: An Analysis of the Social Backgrounds, Careers and Attitudes of the Leading Malay Businessmen in Western Malaysia," Ph.D thesis, London School of Economics.

Pura, R. (1988) "Malaysia's Daim Tied to Contract Award," *Asian Wall Street Journal*, 31 May: 1, 6.

Puthucheary, J. (1960) *Ownership and Control in the Malayan Economy*, Eastern Universities Press, Singapore.

Puthucheary, Mavis (1987) "An Assessment of the Privatisation Guidelines With Reference to Objective Setting," paper presented at the National Conference on "Privatization: Towards the Formulation of a Master Plan," Institute of Strategic and International Studies, Kuala Lumpur, 26–27 October.

Radin Soenarno and Zainal Aznam Yusof (1985) "The Experience of Malaysia" in Asian Development Bank, *Privatization: Policies, Methods and Procedures*, ADB, Manila: 215–36.

Rafidah Aziz (1990) "Pensyarikatan Malaysia," *Buletin Intan*, 14, 2: 7–9.

Ragunathan, A. (1987) "Participation in the Privatization Guidelines with Reference to Objective Setting," paper presented at the National Conference on "Privatization: Towards the Formulation of a Master Plan", ISIS, Kuala Lumpur, 26–27 October.

_____ (1990) "The Labour Perspective of Privatization in Malaysia," in Jacques Pelkmans and Norbert Wagner (eds), *Privatization and Deregulation in ASEAN and EC: Making Markets More Effective*, Institute of Southeast Asian Studies, Singapore.

Rahmah Hashim (1989) "Accomodating National Goals and Conflicting Societal Needs through Privatization of Television Broadcasting: The Malaysian case," Ph.D. thesis, Ohio State University, Columbus, Ohio.

Raja Mohd. Affandi Raja Halim (1975) *Coordination of Public Enterprises, Country Study: Malaysia*, Asian Centre for Development Administration Expert Group Meeting, Kuala Lumpur, September.

Rajasekaran, G. (1987) "Privatisation—Its Impact on Labour Relations," paper presented on behalf of Malaysian Trades Union Congress, in ILO, "Privatisation: Its Impact on Labour Relations in ASEAN," ILO/UNDP/ASEAN Programme for Industrial Relations for Development, Geneva.

Rajasingam, M. (1993) "Privatization of Ports in Malaysia," Inter-governmental Group of Exports on Ports, Geneva.

Ramanadham, V.V. (ed.) (1989) *Privatization in Developing Countries*, Routledge, London.

Rodan, Garry (1989) *The Political Economy of Singapore's Industrialization*, Macmillan, London.

Rodhiah Ismail (1989) "Competition for Telekom?", *Business Times*, 12 December: 1.

_____ (1991) "Vibrant Postals in the Making," *Business Times*, 18 December.

Roth, Gabriel (1987) *The Private Provision of Public Services in Developing Countries*, EDI Series in Economic Development, Oxford University Press, New York.

Rowthorn, R.E. (1990) "Privatisation in the UK," Faculty of Economics, Cambridge University (mimeo).

_____ (1991) "Notes on Competition and Public Ownership," Faculty of Economics, Cambridge University (mimeo).

Rugayah Mohamed (1991) "Comparative Performance of Public and Private Enterprises in Malaysia," Ph.D thesis, Development and Project Planning Centre, University of Bradford.

_____ (1992) *The Efficiency of Public Versus Private Enterprises*, Institute of Strategic and International Studies Malaysia—Harvard Institute for International Development (HIID) USA, Working Paper, September.

_____ (1993) "The Measurement of Market Concentration in Malaysian Manufacturing Industries," *Malaysian Management Review*, 28, 3.

Saiful Bahri Sufar (1989) "Performance of New Issues: the Malaysian Case," *Jurnal Pengurusan*, 8: 17–27.

Shahril Hj. Abdul Karim (1991a) "The Privatization of Public Enterprises in Malaysia," paper presented at the Pan-Pacific Conference organized jointly by University of Nebraska and Universiti Pertanian Malaysia, Kuala Lumpur, June.

_____ (1991b) "The Privatization of GOEs in the Agricultural Sector: Some Policy Implications," paper presented at the seminar on "National Agricultural Policy (NAP): An Agenda for Change" organized jointly by Centre for Agricultural Policy Studies (CAPS) and Malaysian Agricultural Economics Association, Serdang, 3–4 September.

Sheriff, Kassim, Mohd. (1989) "Privatization: Performance, Problems and Prospects," paper presented at the Tenth Economic Convention, 7–9 August.

_____ (1990) "The Privatization Masterplan and Capital Growth Opportunities," An address to the Kuala Lumpur Stock Exchange, October.

_____ (1991) "Privatization: Performance, Problems and Prospects" in Lee Kiong Hock & Shyamala Nagaraj (eds) *The Malaysian Economy Beyond 1990*, Malaysian Economic Association, Kuala Lumpur.

_____ (1992) "Economic Outlook and Privatization Trends Towards 2020," paper presented at the National Conference on "Corporatisation and Privatization" organized by EPU-INTAN-MSC, Kuala Lumpur, 29–30 June.

Siti Rohani Yahaya (1993) "Penggunaan dan Fleksibiliti Buruh: Teori dan Kajian Kes di Malaysia," Ph.D. thesis, Faculty of Economics and Administration, University of Malaya, Kuala Lumpur.

Soong Siew Hoong (1989) "Analysis and Assessment of the NEP and a Strategy for Post-1990 National Economic Policy," *Malaysian Management Review*, 24, 2: 89–91.

Supian Haji Ali (1988) "Malaysia," in G. Edgren (ed.), *The Growing Sector: Studies of Public Sector Employment in Asia*, ILO-ARTEP, New Delhi.

Sussman, G. (1988) "Information Technologies for the ASEAN Region: The Political Economy of Privatization," in Vincent Mosco and Janet Wasko (eds), *The Political Economy of Information*, University of Wisconsin Press, Madison, WI: 274–296.

Syed Husin Ali (1987) "Ke Arah Baru Pembangunan Malaysia," in S. Husin Ali *et al.* (ed.) *Pembangunan Di Malaysia: Perencanaan, Perlaksanaan dan Prestasi*, Persatuan Sains Sosial Malaysia, Kuala Lumpur.

Soong S.H. (1989) "Analysis and Assessment of the NEP and a Strategy for Post-1990 National Economic Policy," *Malaysian Management Review*, 24, 2: 89–91.

Supian, H.A. (1988) "Malaysia," in G. Edgren (ed.), *The Growing Sector: Studies of Public Sector Employment in Asia*, ILO-ARTEP, New Delhi.

Tan Boon Kean (1993) "The Role of the Construction Sector in National Development: Malaysia," Ph.D. thesis, Institute for Advanced Studies, University of Malaya, Kuala Lumpur.

Tan Chew May (1990) "A Long and Winding Road," *Malaysian Business*, 1–15 June: 13–14.

Tan Chwee Huat (1991) "Privatization in Malaysia and Singapore: a Comparison," *Journal of Southeast Asian Business*, 7, 4 (Fall): 12–25.

Telecommunications Act, 1950 (Revised 1970) (Act 20), Government Printing Department, Kuala Lumpur.

Telecommunications (Amendment) Act, 1972 (Act A115), Government Printing Department, Kuala Lumpur.

Telecommunications Amendment Act, 1977 (Act A373), Government Printing Department, Kuala Lumpur.

Telecommunications Amendment Act, 1980 (Act A593), Government Printing Department, Kuala Lumpur.

Telecommunications Amendment Act, 1985 (Act A628), Government Printing Department, Kuala Lumpur.

Tenaga Nasional Berhad (1992) *Prospectus*, February 29.

Teplitz-Sembitzky, W. (1990) "Regulation, Deregulation, or Reregulation—What is Needed in the LDCs Power Sector?", Energy Series Paper No. 30, World Bank, Washington D.C.

The Star, "Telecoms D-G," 19 July 1988: 4.

_____, "Telecommunications Poised for Growth," 6 February 1992.

_____, "Improve Your Productivity, Government Men Told," 10 February 1992.

_____, "More Heads Will Roll at British Telecoms," 8 April 1992.

The Straits Times, "Work on Second Link to Start Soon, Says MB," 9 March 1994, Singapore.

Thillainathan, R. (19??) "Privatisation in Malaysia: Guidelines for Action," paper presented to the Malaysian Economic Association seminar on "Privatisation and the Implementation of the Malaysia Incorporated Concept," Kuala Lumpur.

Tison, Gerardo S. (1987) *The Privatisation of Public Enterprises in the SEACEN Countries*, Staff Paper No. 20, SEACEN Research and Training Centre, Kuala Lumpur.

Toh Kin Woon (1989) "Privatization in Malaysia: Restructuring or Efficiency?", *Asean Economic Bulletin*, 5, 3 (March): 242–58.

_____ (1990a) "The Liberalization and Privatization of Telecommunications: the Malaysian Experience" in Jacques Pelkmans and Norbert Wagner (eds), *Privatization and Deregulation in ASEAN and the EC: Making Markets More Effective*, ASEAN Economic Research Unit, Institute of South East Asian Studies, Singapore.

_____ (1990b) "Privatization and the Role of Transnational Corporations in Malaysia," *Asia-Pacific TNC Review*, ESCAP/UNCTC Publication Series A, No. 7, United Nations ESCAP, Bangkok: 22–29.

Tong Veng Wye (1989) "Privatisation and the Public Good," *Aliran Monthly*, 9, 2: 16–20.

Truu, M.L. (1988) "Economics of Privatization," *The South African Journal of Economics*, 56, 4: 251–269.

Tsuruoka, D. (1990) "UMNO's Money Machine," *Far Eastern Economic Review*, 5 July: 48–52.

_____ (1992) "Five Party Line," *Far Eastern Economic Review*, 26 March: 50–51.

UNDP (1988) "Country Paper: Privatisation—Malaysia," United Nations Development Programme Inter-Regional Workshop on Privatisation, Document No. 23.

_____ (1991) "Guidelines on Privatisation: Inter-regional Network on Privatisation," Division for Global and Inter-regional Programmes, New York.

UNIDO, *Industry and Development, Global Report*, United Nations Industrial Development Organisation, Vienna (1984–1990, various years).

_____ (1985) *Malaysia*, Industrial Development Review Series, United Nations Industrial Development Organisation, Vienna.

United Engineers Malaysia, *Annual Report*, various issues.

Van De Walle, Nicolas (1989) "Privatization in Developing Countries: A Review of the Issues," *World Development*, 17, 5.

Veerasingam, V. (1983) "Privatising Health: the Long Road Ahead," *Malaysian Business*, August.

Veljanovski, Cento (ed.) *Privatisation and Competition: a Market Prospectus*, Institute of Economic Affairs, London.

Vernon-Wortzel, Heidi and Lawrence Wortzel (1989) "Privatization: Not the Only Answer," *World Development*, 17, 5: 633–41.

Vernon, Raymond (ed.) (1988) *The Promise of Privatization: a Challenge for US Policy*, Council on Foreign Relations, New York.

Vickers, J. and Yarrow, G. (1988) *Privatisation: An Economic Analysis*, The MIT Press, Cambridge, Massachusetts.

Vining, Aidan R. and Bryan J. Poulin (1989) "Will Corporatisation and Partial Privatisation Work," *Public Sector*, 12, 4.

von Thadden, Ernst-Ludwig (1990) "On the Efficiency of the Market for Corporate Control," *Kyklos*, 43, 4: 635–658.

Vuylsteke, Charles (1988) *Techniques of Privatization of State-Owned Enterprises, Volume I: Methods and Implementation*, World Bank Technical Paper No. 88, Washington D.C.

Wade, Robert (1990) *Governing The Market: Economic Theory and the Role of Government in East Asian Industrialization*, Princeton University Press, Princeton.

Webb, Ian (1985) *Management Buy-Out: A Guide for the Prospective Entrepreneur*, Gowe Publishing Co. Ltd., Aldershot.

Westlake, M. (1991) "The Big Switch," *Far Eastern Economic Review*, 7 March.

Wheelwright, E.L. (1965) *Industrialisation in Malaysia*, Melbourne University Press, Melbourne.

White, John (1988) "Privatization and the State-Owned Enterprises; Logic or Ideology?", *Public Sector*, 11, 1&2: 19–22.

Wong, R. (1993) "TRI Gets Focussed," *Malaysian Business*, 1–15 March: 20–24.

World Bank (1989), *Malaysia: Matching Risks and Rewards in a Mixed Economy*, The World Bank, Washington D.C.

World Bank, *World Debt Tables, 1988/89*, The World Bank, Washington D.C.

World Bank Policy Research (1992) "Privatization: Eight Lessons of Experience," Bulletin, 3, 4, August–October: 2–4.

World Development, 17, 5 (special issue on privatization).

Wright, Mike and Trevor Buck (1992) "Employee Buy-outs and Privatization: Issues and Implications for LDCs and Post-Communist Countries of UK Experience," *Public Administration and Development*, 12: 279–96.

Yap L.K. (1988) "Uniphone to Go Big on Telephones," *The Star*, 28 June, Business section: 1.

Zainal Rampak (1988) "Labour Issues in Privatisation," in Conference on "Privatization in Malaysia's Practical Aspects and Implications,", July Association of Merchant Bankers in Malaysia, Kuala Lumpur.

Zainuddin Saleh (1989) "Privatization of Electricity Supply in Malaysia: Issues and Problems," paper presented at the symposium on "Privatization: Lessons from Europe and ASEAN" jointly organised by EIPA and ISEAS, February 16–18, Singapore.

Newspapers and Magazines

Asian Business
Asian Wall Street Journal
Eksklusif
Investors Digest
Malaysian Business
New Straits Times
The Star
Utusan Konsumer

About the Book

In this first critical, multidisciplinary assessment of recent privatization in a developing country, the contributors offer valuable lessons for the comparative study of denationalization and related public policy options. After an introductory survey, the volume presents broad perspectives on the context, formulation, and adjustment of privatization policy in Malaysia. The contributors review the distributional implications of specific privatizations for the public interest as well as for consumer and employee welfare. The book concludes with an examination of the economic, political, and cultural impacts of the privatization of physical infrastructure, telecommunications, and television programming.

About the Contributors

Christopher Adam is at the Centre for the Study of African Economies, Institute of Economics and Statistics, University of Oxford, and was co-author of *Adjusting Privatisation* (James Currey, 1991).

William Cavendish is at the Centre for the Study of African Economies, Institute of Economics and Statistics, University of Oxford, and was co-author of *Adjusting Privatisation* (James Currey, 1991).

Edmund Terence Gomez is Lecturer at the Institute for Advanced Studies, University of Malaya. He is the author of *Politics in Business: UMNO's Corporate Investments* (Forum, 1990), *Money Politics in the Barisan Nasional* (Forum, 1991) and *Political Business: Corporate Involvement of Malaysian Political Parties* (James Cook University, Townsville, 1994).

Winnie Goh is an economics lecturer at Damansara Utama College in Malaysia.

Jomo Kwame Sundaram is Professor in the Faculty of Economics and Administration, University of Malaya, Kuala Lumpur, and was Visiting Professor at Cornell University during Fall 1993. He is author of *A Question of Class: Capital, the State and Uneven Development in Malaya* (Oxford University Press, 1986) and *Growth and Structural Change in the Malaysian Economy* (Macmillan, 1990), among others.

Laurel Kennedy is Assistant Professor and Head of the Department of Communications, Denison University, Granville, Ohio.

Kuppusamy S. is Lecturer in the Faculty of Economics and Administration, University of Malaya.

G. Naidu is Associate Professor in the Applied Economics Division, Faculty of Economics and Administration, University of Malaya.

Rahmah Hashim is Associate Professor in the Mass Communications Department, Faculty of Social Sciences and Humanities, National University of Malaysia, Bangi, Selangor, Malaysia.

Rugayah Mohamed is Associate Professor in the Faculty of Economics and Administration, University of Malaya.

Index

Practices, 14
Public sector, 14
Engineers, 220
English programs, 242
Enterprise efficiency, 55, 60, 154
    Management, 79
    Reorganization, 55
Entertainment, 242
Entrepreneurial, 143
Environment, 216
EON. *See* Edaran Otomobil Nâsional
EPF. *See* Employees Provident Fund
EPU. *See* Economic Planning Unit
Equal opportunities, 227
Equity
    Capital, 17
    Distribution, 14, 15, 211, 217
    Foreign, 214
    Government, 16, 17
    Ownership, 14, 107, 123
    Participation, 16
    Trading, 38
Eric Chia, Tan Sri, 221
ESM. *See* Electronic Systems Malaysia
ESOS. *See* Employees' Share Option Scheme
Ethnic bias, 56, 214
Ethnic composition, 227
Ethnic groups, 243
Ethnic redistribution, 6
Ethnically-biased privatization, 56
Ethnicity, 232
Euromoney, 98
European PTTs, 234
Excess capacity, 202
Exchange-rate guarantees, 212
Exchange-rate policy, 22, 26
Executive agency, 27
Executives, 189
Exhibitors, 244
Exogenous demand, 158
Expansion, 173, 228
Expansionary fiscal strategy, 65
Expediency, 142
Expenditures, 234
Export-led industrialization, 160
Exports, 158, 160
    Boom, 5
    Competitiveness, 22
    Earnings, 5, 13
    Manufacturing, 5
Expressways, 43, 177, 179
Extant law, 230
Extenuating circumstances, 154
External barriers, 112

External debt, 27, 67
Externalities, 74, 154, 199, 217, 218
Exxon, 26

Facilities, 223
FACSMAB. *See* Frequency Allocation
    Committee
Factories & Machinery Department, 174
Far East Holding, 73
Fares, 162, 165
Favoritism, 177, 218
Feasibility study, 224
Federal agencies, 70
Federal Government, 68
Federal Highway, 179, 180
    Routes I & II, 202
Federal Roads (Private Management) Act
    (1984), 113
Federal Territory, 225
Federal Treasury, 114, 239
    Reform Program, 115
Federation of Consumers Association in
    Malaysia (FOMCA), 243
Fibre-optic network, 224
FIC. *See* Foreign Investments Committee
Fifth Malaysia Plan (5MP, 1986–90), 81, 120,
    201
Filem Negara, 241
Film Censorship Act, 246
Film Censorship Board, 241, 246
Film importation, 244
Film industry, 237, 242
Film producers
    Foreign, 239
    Local, 242
Films, 246
FIMA. *See* Food Industries of Malaysia
Fima Fraser's Hill, 116
Fima Holdings Ltd, 72
Fima Mr. Juicy, 116
Fima Rantei, 117
Fima Timuran, 117
Fimajaya Foods, 116
Finance and property sector, 34
Finance Minister. *See* Anwar Ibrahim, Datuk
    Seri
Financial market, foreign, 22
Financial system, 13, 14, 37, 40
    Burden, 211, 212, 228
    Institutions, 220
    Performance, 26
FINAS. *See* National Film Development
    Corporation
FINAS (Film Charges) Regulations (1988), 244